Buffy the Vampire Slayer™

NIGHT OF A THOUSAND VAMPIRES

and

Ugly Little Monsters

publisher
MIKE RICHARDSON

editor
SCOTT ALLIE
with MICHAEL CARRIGLITTO

designer
LANI SCHREIBSTEIN

art director
MARK COX

special thanks to
DEBBIE OLSHAN AT FOX LICENSING
AND DAVID CAMPITI AT GLASS HOUSE GRAPHICS

Buffy the Vampire Slayer™: Ugly Little Monsters. Published by Titan Books, a division of Titan Publishing Group Ltd, 144 Southwark Street London SE1 0UP

A CIP catalogue record for this book is available from the British Library

PUBLISHED BY
TITAN BOOKS
144 SOUTHWARK STREET
LONDON SE1 0UP

FIRST EDITION
SEPTEMBER 2002
ISBN: 1-84023-514-4

1 3 5 7 9 10 8 6 4 2

printed in Italy

Buffy THE VAMPIRE SLAYER™

NIGHT OF A THOUSAND VAMPIRES

based on the television series created by
JOSS WHEDON

writers TOM FASSBENDER & JIM PASCOE

penciller CLIFF RICHARDS

inkers JOE PIMENTEL & WILL CONRAD

colorist DIGITAL CHAMELEON

letterer CLEM ROBINS

This story takes place during Buffy the Vampire Slayer's fifth season.

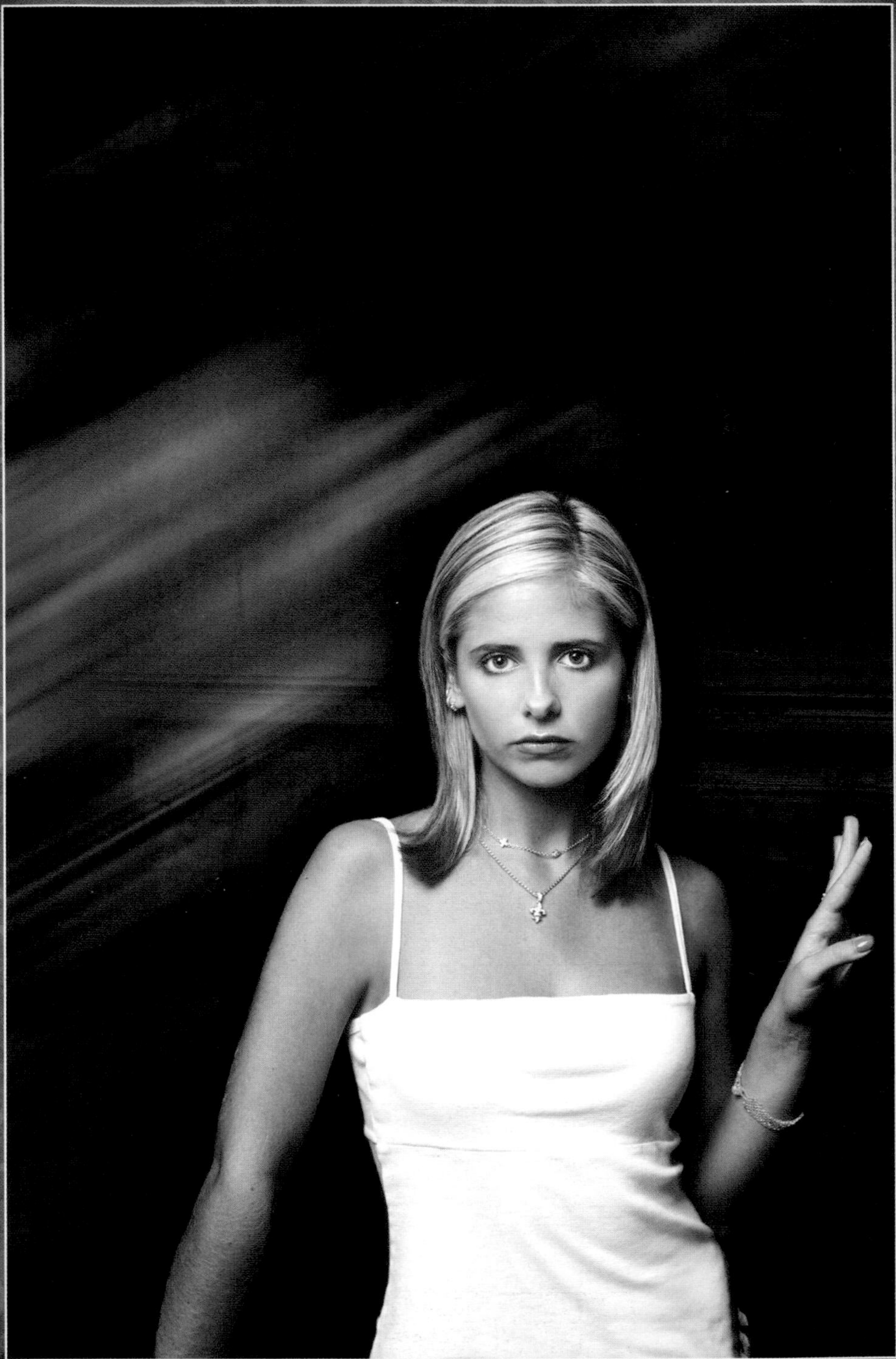

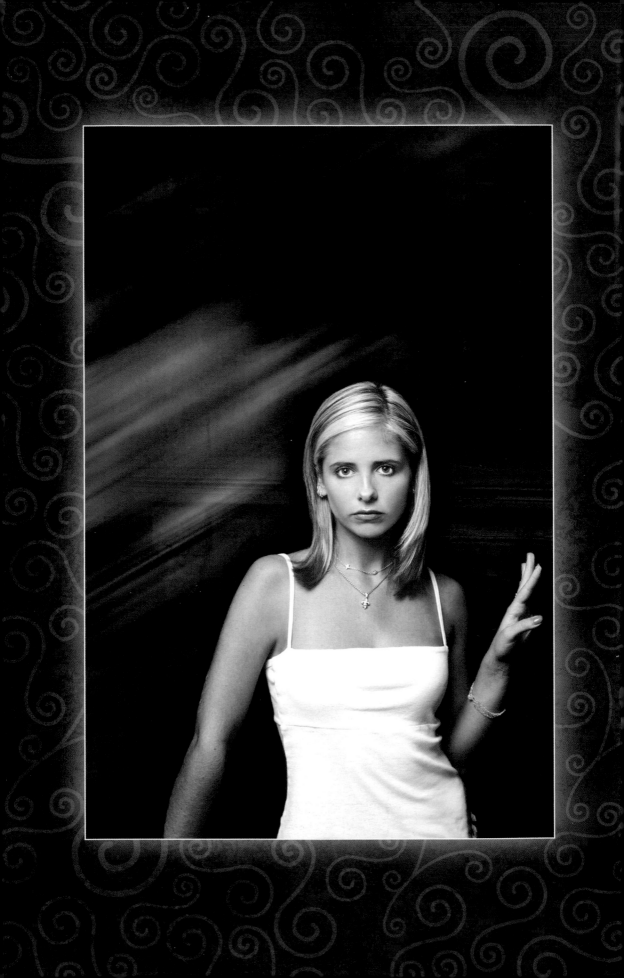

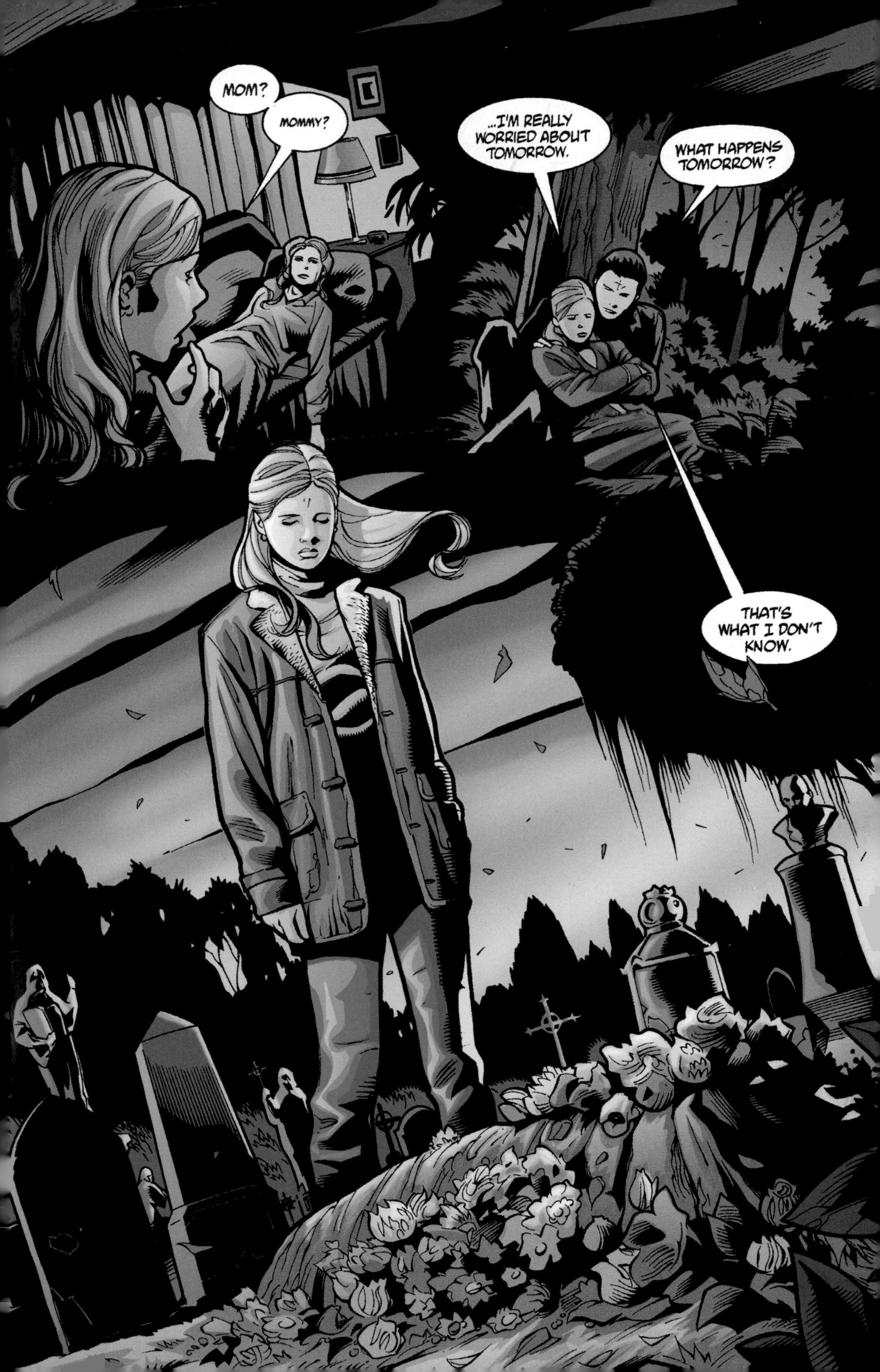
MOM?
MOMMY?
...I'M REALLY WORRIED ABOUT TOMORROW.
WHAT HAPPENS TOMORROW?
THAT'S WHAT I DON'T KNOW.

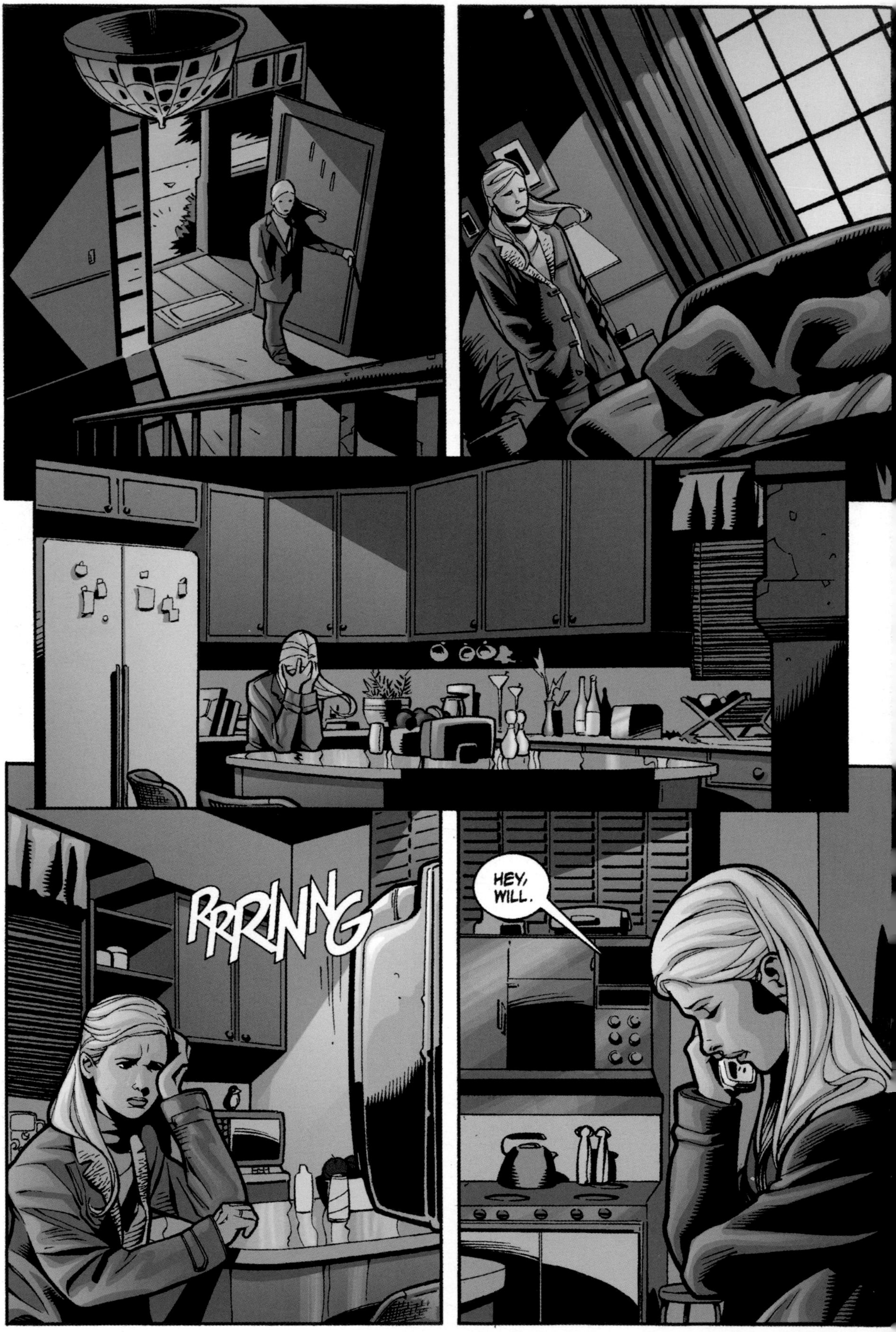
RRRINNG
HEY, WILL.

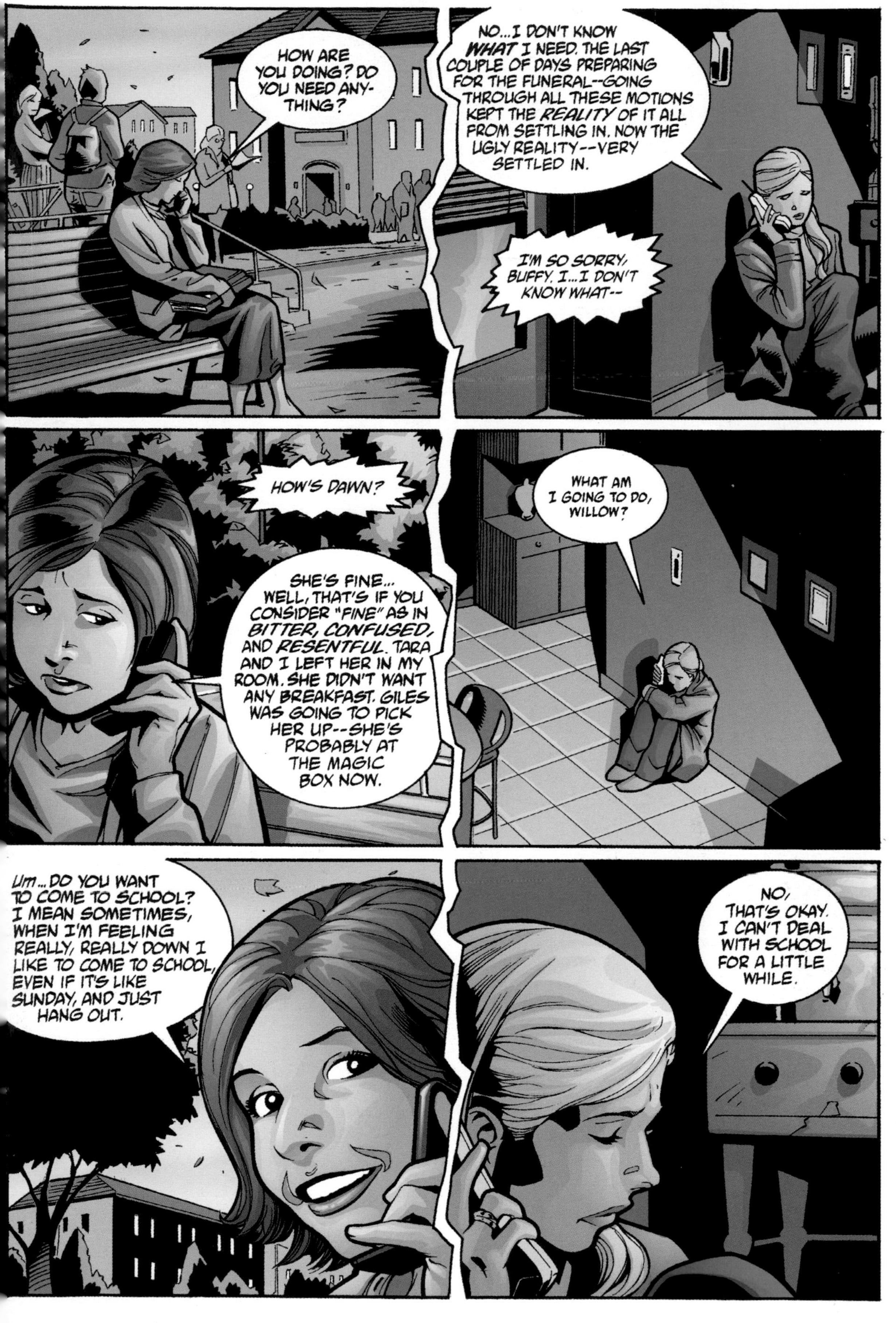
HOW ARE YOU DOING? DO YOU NEED ANY-THING?
NO...I DON'T KNOW WHAT I NEED. THE LAST COUPLE OF DAYS PREPARING FOR THE FUNERAL--GOING THROUGH ALL THESE MOTIONS KEPT THE REALITY OF IT ALL FROM SETTLING IN. NOW THE UGLY REALITY--VERY SETTLED IN.
I'M SO SORRY, BUFFY. I...I DON'T KNOW WHAT--
HOW'S DAWN?
SHE'S FINE... WELL, THAT'S IF YOU CONSIDER "FINE" AS IN BITTER, CONFUSED, AND RESENTFUL. TARA AND I LEFT HER IN MY ROOM. SHE DIDN'T WANT ANY BREAKFAST. GILES WAS GOING TO PICK HER UP--SHE'S PROBABLY AT THE MAGIC BOX NOW.
WHAT AM I GOING TO DO, WILLOW?
Um... DO YOU WANT TO COME TO SCHOOL? I MEAN SOMETIMES, WHEN I'M FEELING REALLY, REALLY DOWN I LIKE TO COME TO SCHOOL, EVEN IF IT'S LIKE SUNDAY, AND JUST HANG OUT.
NO, THAT'S OKAY. I CAN'T DEAL WITH SCHOOL FOR A LITTLE WHILE.

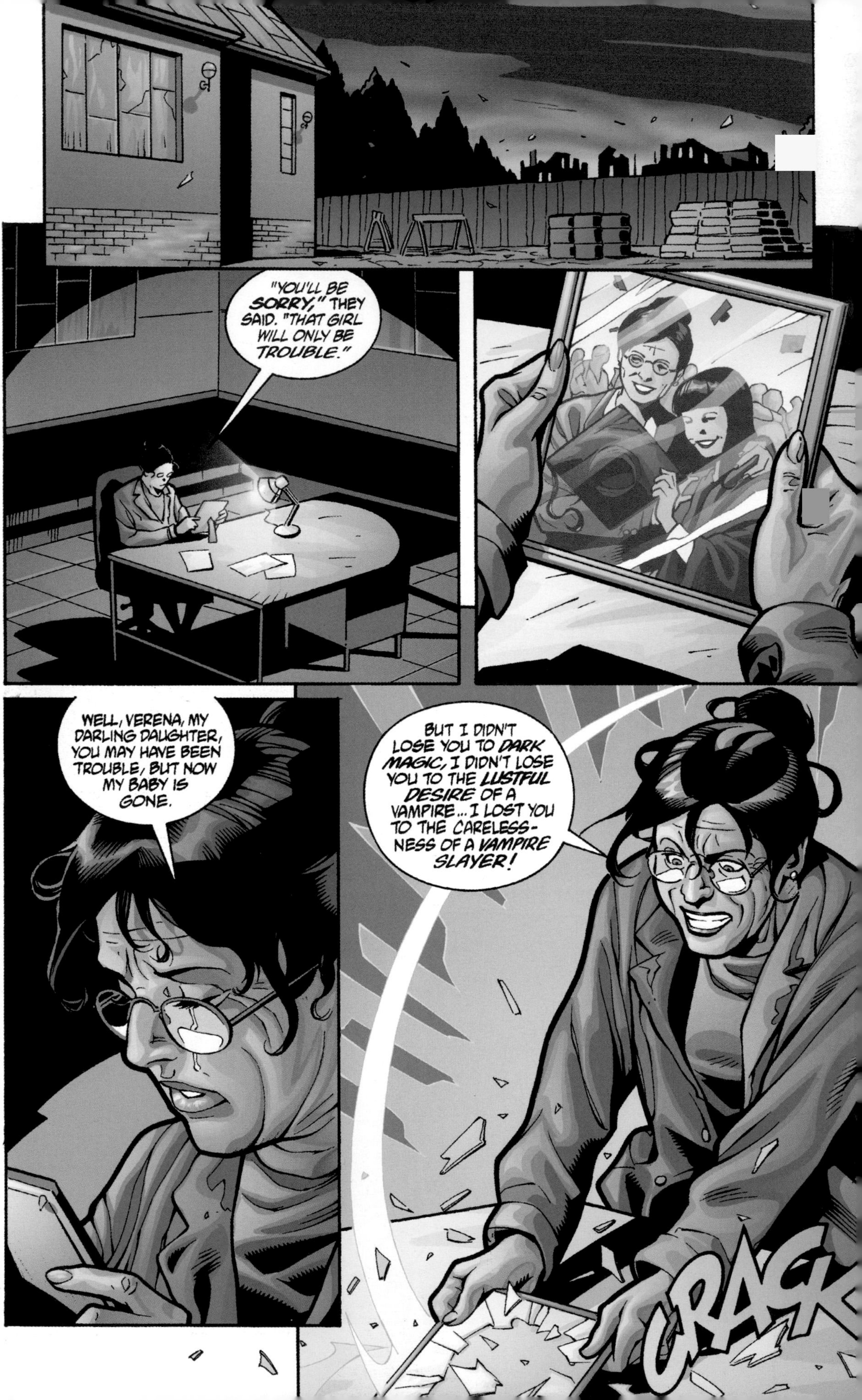

"YOU'LL BE SORRY," THEY SAID. "THAT GIRL WILL ONLY BE TROUBLE."
WELL, VERENA, MY DARLING DAUGHTER, YOU MAY HAVE BEEN TROUBLE, BUT NOW MY BABY IS GONE.
BUT I DIDN'T LOSE YOU TO DARK MAGIC, I DIDN'T LOSE YOU TO THE LUSTFUL DESIRE OF A VAMPIRE... I LOST YOU TO THE CARELESS-NESS OF A VAMPIRE SLAYER!
CRACK

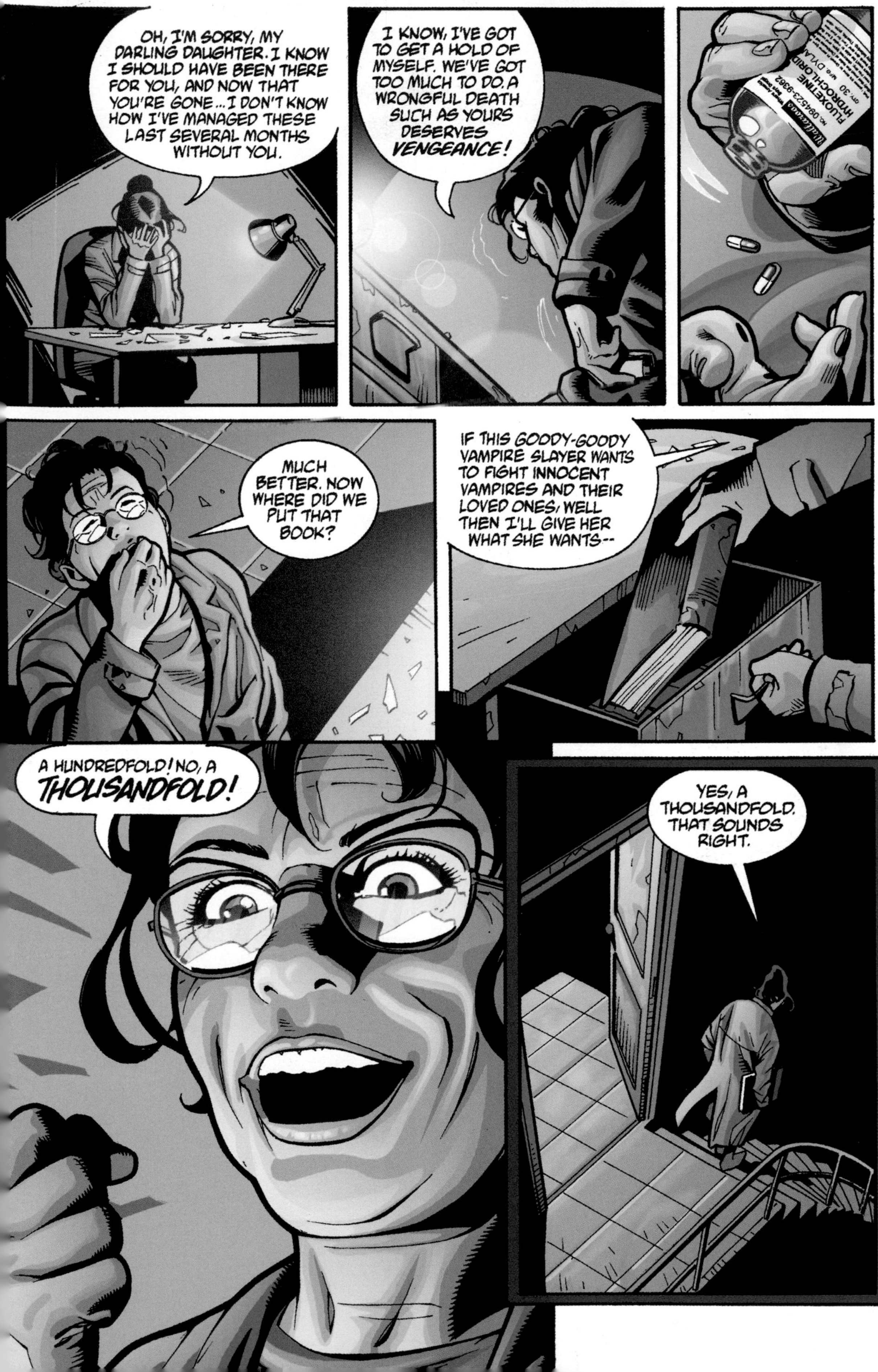
OH, I'M SORRY, MY DARLING DAUGHTER. I KNOW I SHOULD HAVE BEEN THERE FOR YOU, AND NOW THAT YOU'RE GONE... I DON'T KNOW HOW I'VE MANAGED THESE LAST SEVERAL MONTHS WITHOUT YOU.
I KNOW, I'VE GOT TO GET A HOLD OF MYSELF. WE'VE GOT TOO MUCH TO DO. A WRONGFUL DEATH SUCH AS YOURS DESERVES VENGEANCE!
MUCH BETTER. NOW WHERE DID WE PUT THAT BOOK?
IF THIS GOODY-GOODY VAMPIRE SLAYER WANTS TO FIGHT INNOCENT VAMPIRES AND THEIR LOVED ONES, WELL THEN I'LL GIVE HER WHAT SHE WANTS--
A HUNDREDFOLD! NO, A THOUSANDFOLD!
YES, A THOUSANDFOLD. THAT SOUNDS RIGHT.

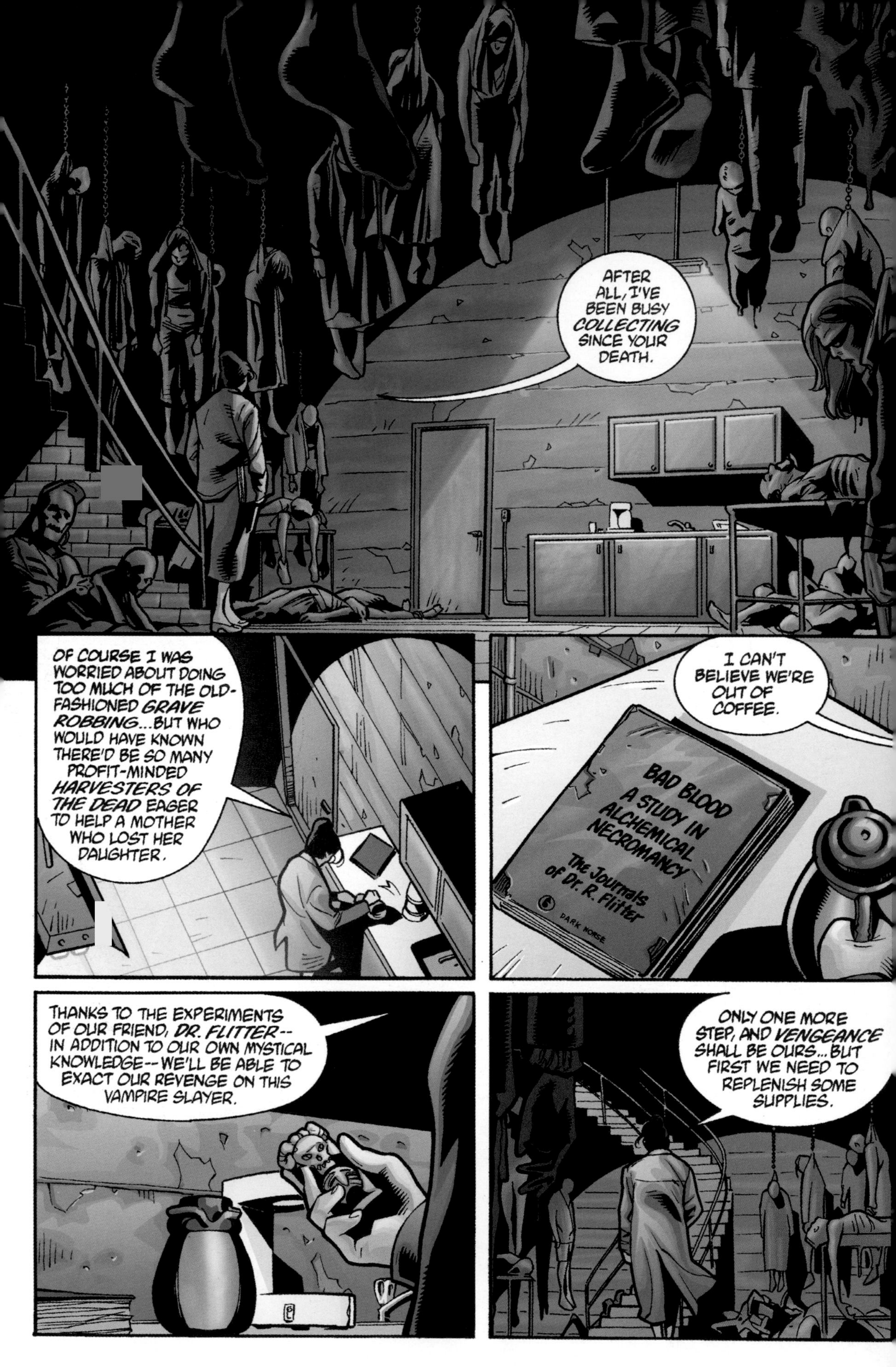

AFTER ALL, I'VE BEEN BUSY COLLECTING SINCE YOUR DEATH.
OF COURSE I WAS WORRIED ABOUT DOING TOO MUCH OF THE OLD-FASHIONED GRAVE ROBBING...BUT WHO WOULD HAVE KNOWN THERE'D BE SO MANY PROFIT-MINDED HARVESTERS OF THE DEAD EAGER TO HELP A MOTHER WHO LOST HER DAUGHTER.
I CAN'T BELIEVE WE'RE OUT OF COFFEE.
BAD BLOOD
A STUDY IN ALCHEMICAL NECROMANCY
The Journals of Dr. R. Flitter
DARK HORSE
THANKS TO THE EXPERIMENTS OF OUR FRIEND, DR. FLITTER-- IN ADDITION TO OUR OWN MYSTICAL KNOWLEDGE--WE'LL BE ABLE TO EXACT OUR REVENGE ON THIS VAMPIRE SLAYER.
ONLY ONE MORE STEP, AND VENGEANCE SHALL BE OURS...BUT FIRST WE NEED TO REPLENISH SOME SUPPLIES.

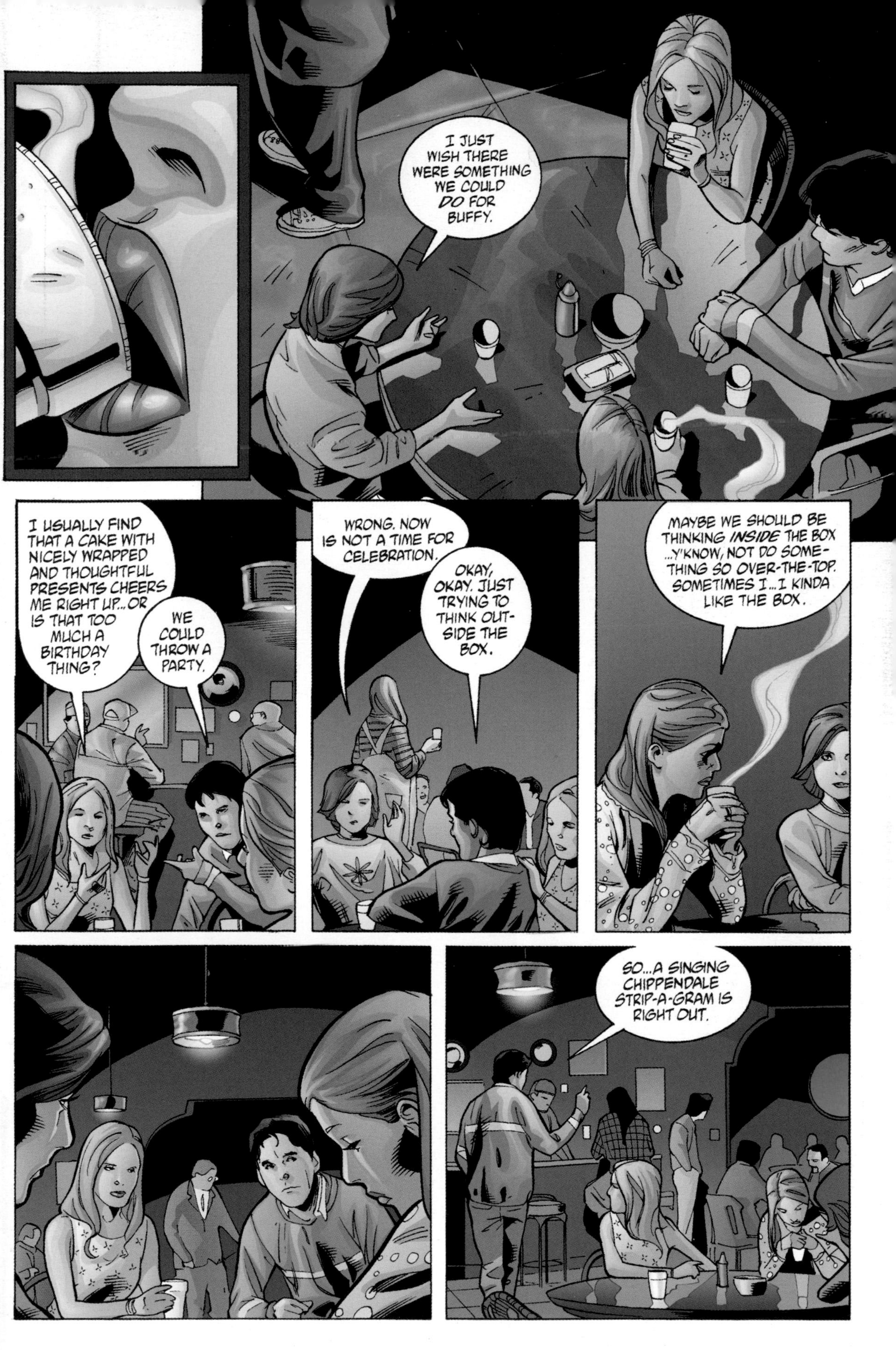
I JUST WISH THERE WERE SOMETHING WE COULD DO FOR BUFFY.
I USUALLY FIND THAT A CAKE WITH NICELY WRAPPED AND THOUGHTFUL PRESENTS CHEERS ME RIGHT UP...OR IS THAT TOO MUCH A BIRTHDAY THING?
WE COULD THROW A PARTY.
WRONG. NOW IS NOT A TIME FOR CELEBRATION.
OKAY, OKAY. JUST TRYING TO THINK OUT-SIDE THE BOX.
MAYBE WE SHOULD BE THINKING INSIDE THE BOX ...Y'KNOW, NOT DO SOME-THING SO OVER-THE-TOP. SOMETIMES I...I KINDA LIKE THE BOX.
SO...A SINGING CHIPPENDALE STRIP-A-GRAM IS RIGHT OUT.

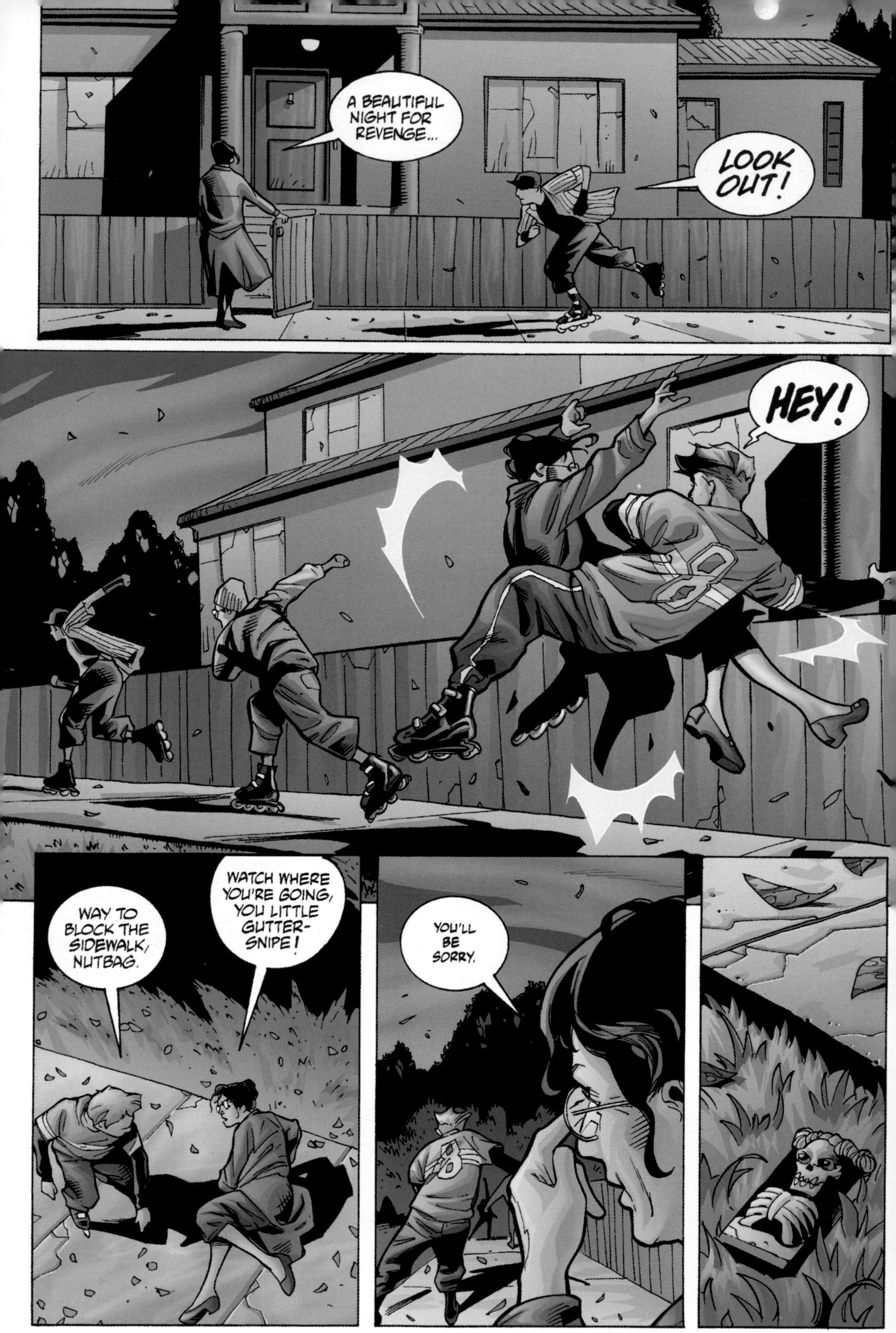
A BEAUTIFUL NIGHT FOR REVENGE...
LOOK OUT!
HEY!
WAY TO BLOCK THE SIDEWALK, NUTBAG.
WATCH WHERE YOU'RE GOING, YOU LITTLE GUTTER-SNIPE!
YOU'LL BE SORRY.

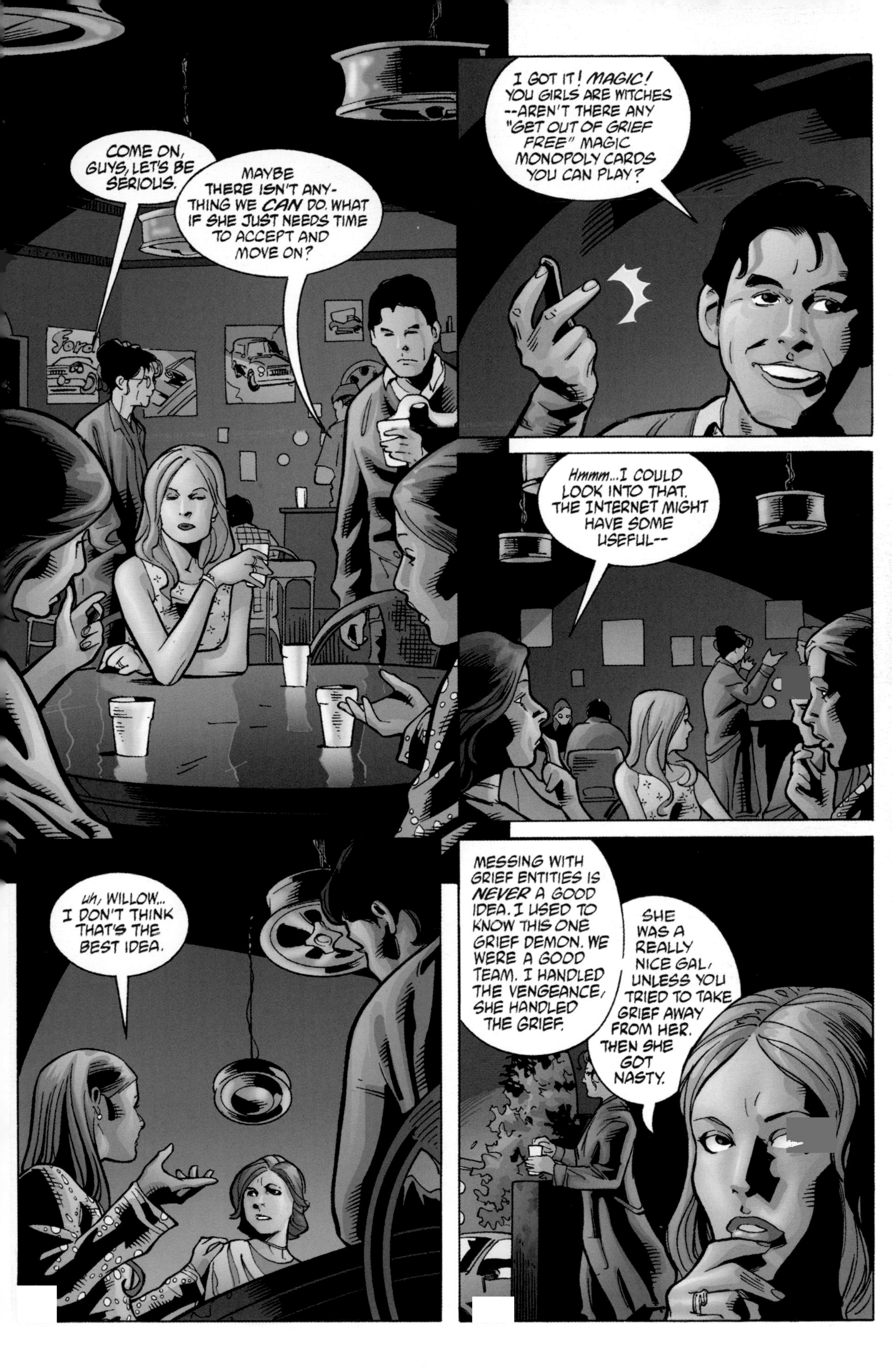
COME ON, GUYS, LET'S BE SERIOUS.
MAYBE THERE ISN'T ANY-THING WE *CAN* DO. WHAT IF SHE JUST NEEDS TIME TO ACCEPT AND MOVE ON?
I GOT IT! *MAGIC!* YOU GIRLS ARE WITCHES --AREN'T THERE ANY "*GET OUT OF GRIEF FREE*" MAGIC MONOPOLY CARDS YOU CAN PLAY?
Hmmm...I COULD LOOK INTO THAT. THE INTERNET MIGHT HAVE SOME USEFUL--
uh, WILLOW... I DON'T THINK THAT'S THE BEST IDEA.
MESSING WITH GRIEF ENTITIES IS ***NEVER*** A GOOD IDEA. I USED TO KNOW THIS ONE GRIEF DEMON. WE WERE A GOOD TEAM. I HANDLED THE VENGEANCE, SHE HANDLED THE GRIEF.
SHE WAS A REALLY NICE GAL, UNLESS YOU TRIED TO TAKE GRIEF AWAY FROM HER. THEN SHE GOT NASTY.

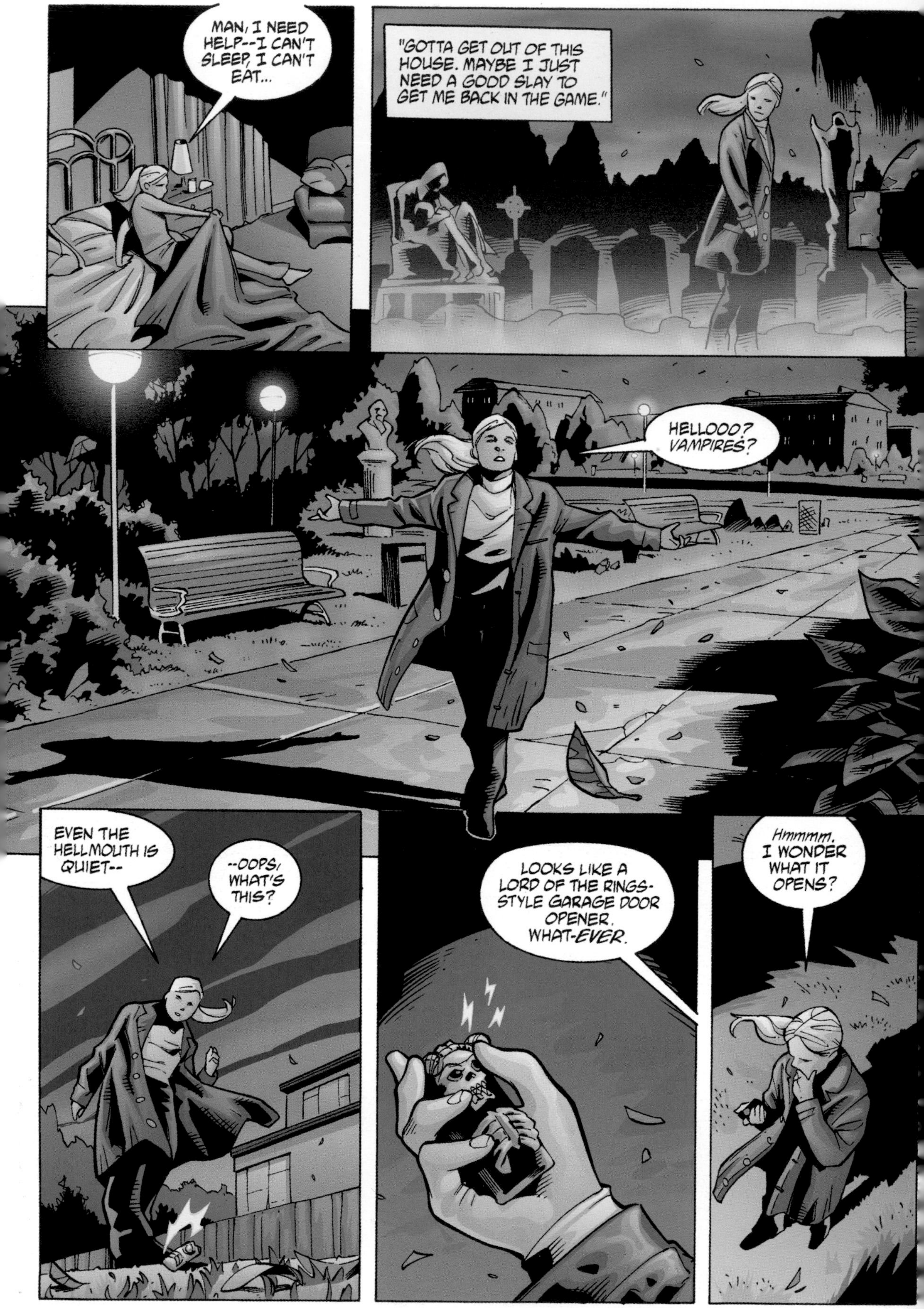
MAN, I NEED HELP--I CAN'T SLEEP, I CAN'T EAT...
"GOTTA GET OUT OF THIS HOUSE. MAYBE I JUST NEED A GOOD SLAY TO GET ME BACK IN THE GAME."
HELLOOO? VAMPIRES?
EVEN THE HELLMOUTH IS QUIET--
--OOPS, WHAT'S THIS?
LOOKS LIKE A LORD OF THE RINGS-STYLE GARAGE DOOR OPENER. WHAT-EVER.
Hmmmm. I WONDER WHAT IT OPENS?

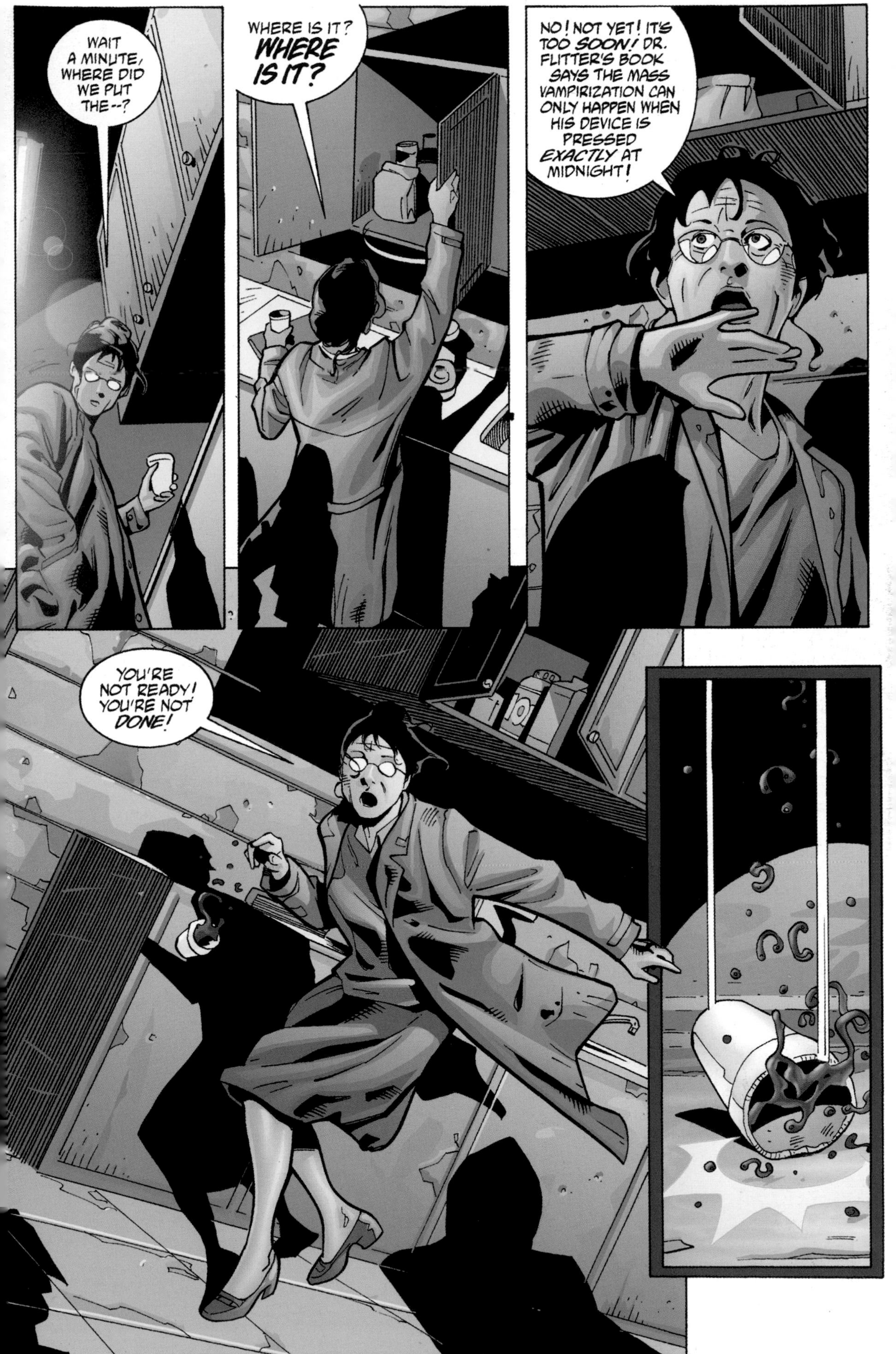
WAIT A MINUTE, WHERE DID WE PUT THE--?
WHERE IS IT? *WHERE IS IT?*
NO! NOT YET! IT'S TOO *SOON!* DR. FLITTER'S BOOK SAYS THE MASS VAMPIRIZATION CAN ONLY HAPPEN WHEN HIS DEVICE IS PRESSED *EXACTLY* AT MIDNIGHT!
YOU'RE NOT READY! YOU'RE NOT *DONE!*

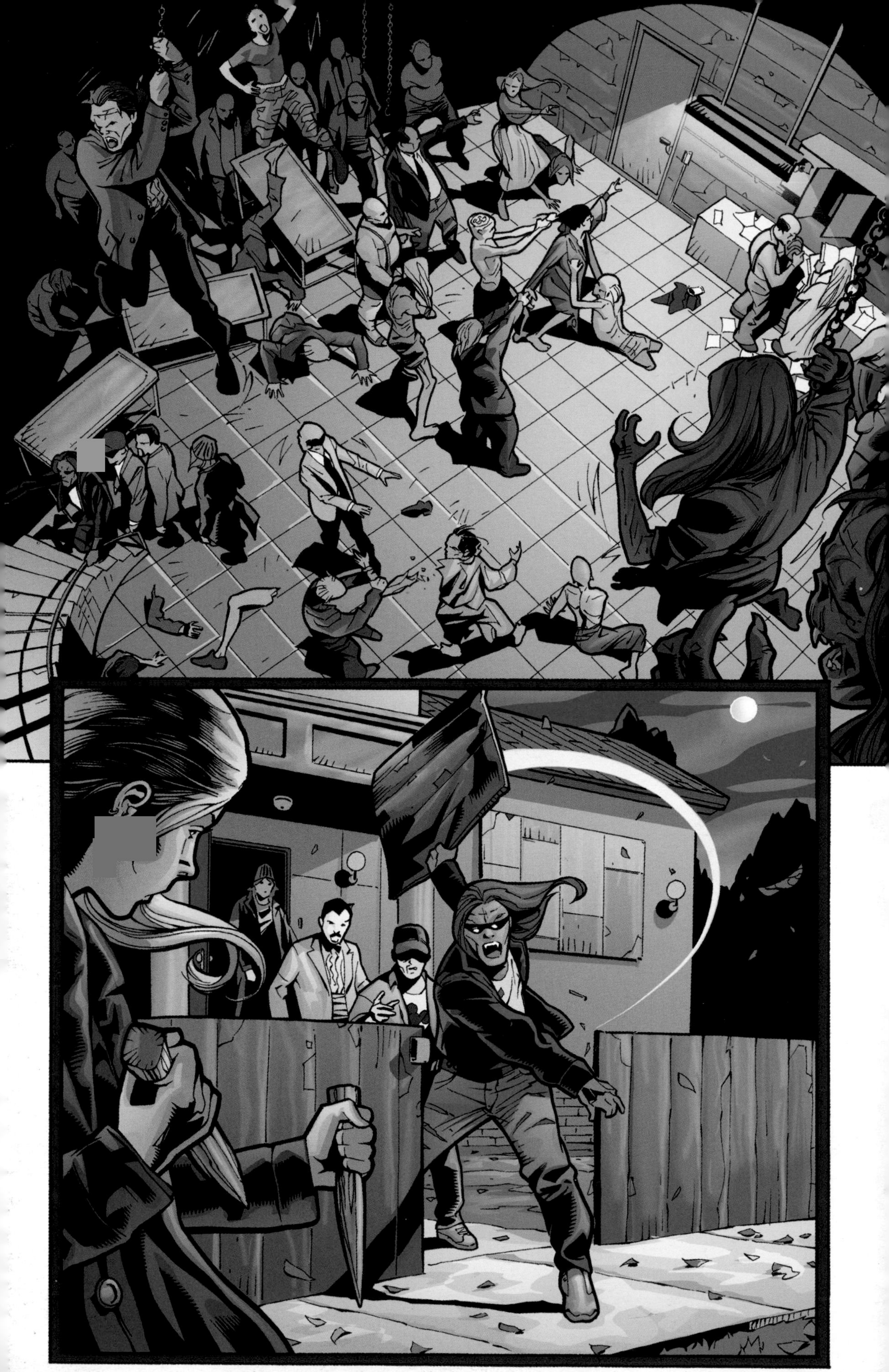

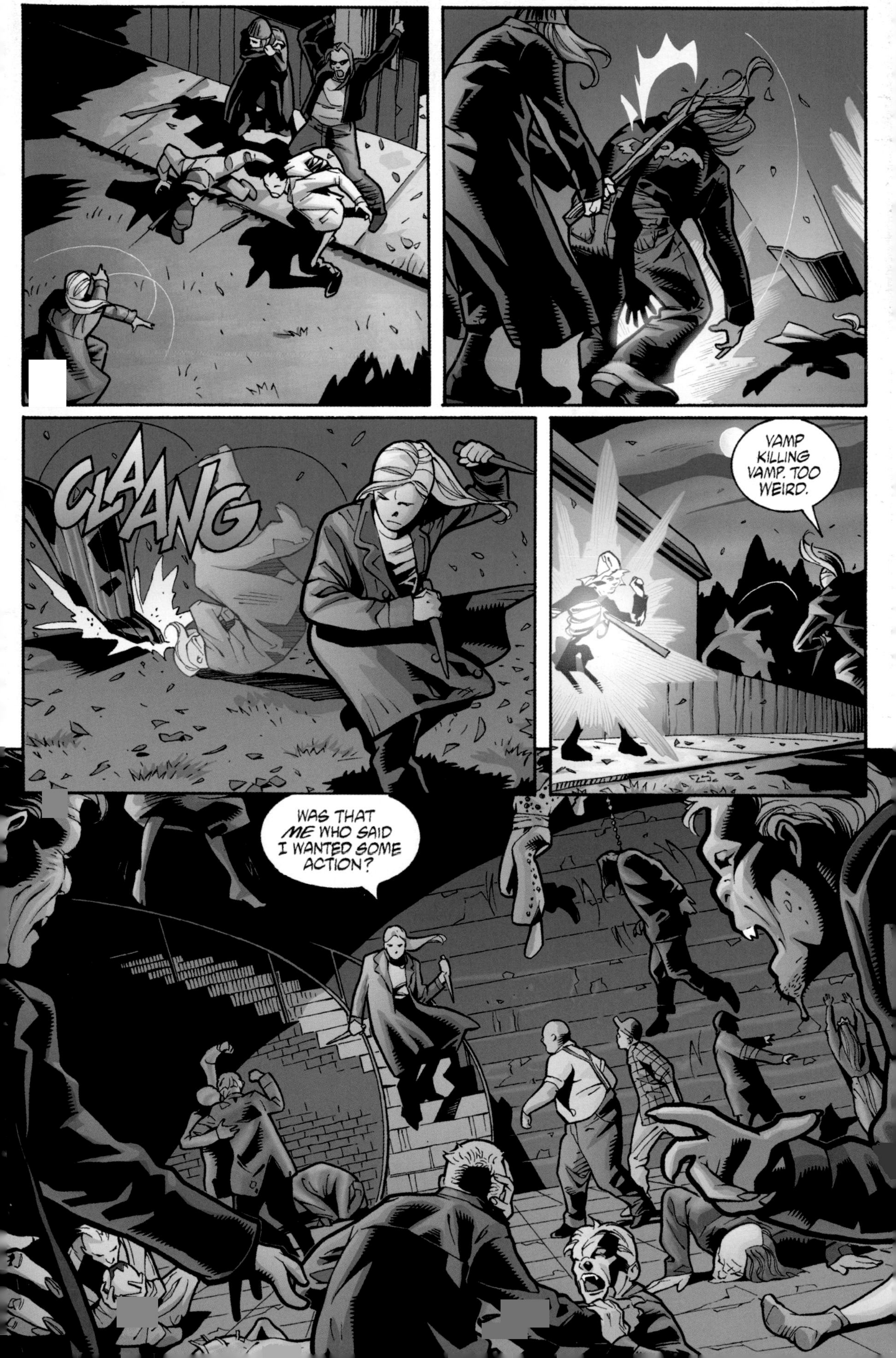
CLAANG
VAMP KILLING VAMP. TOO WEIRD.
WAS THAT ME WHO SAID I WANTED SOME ACTION?

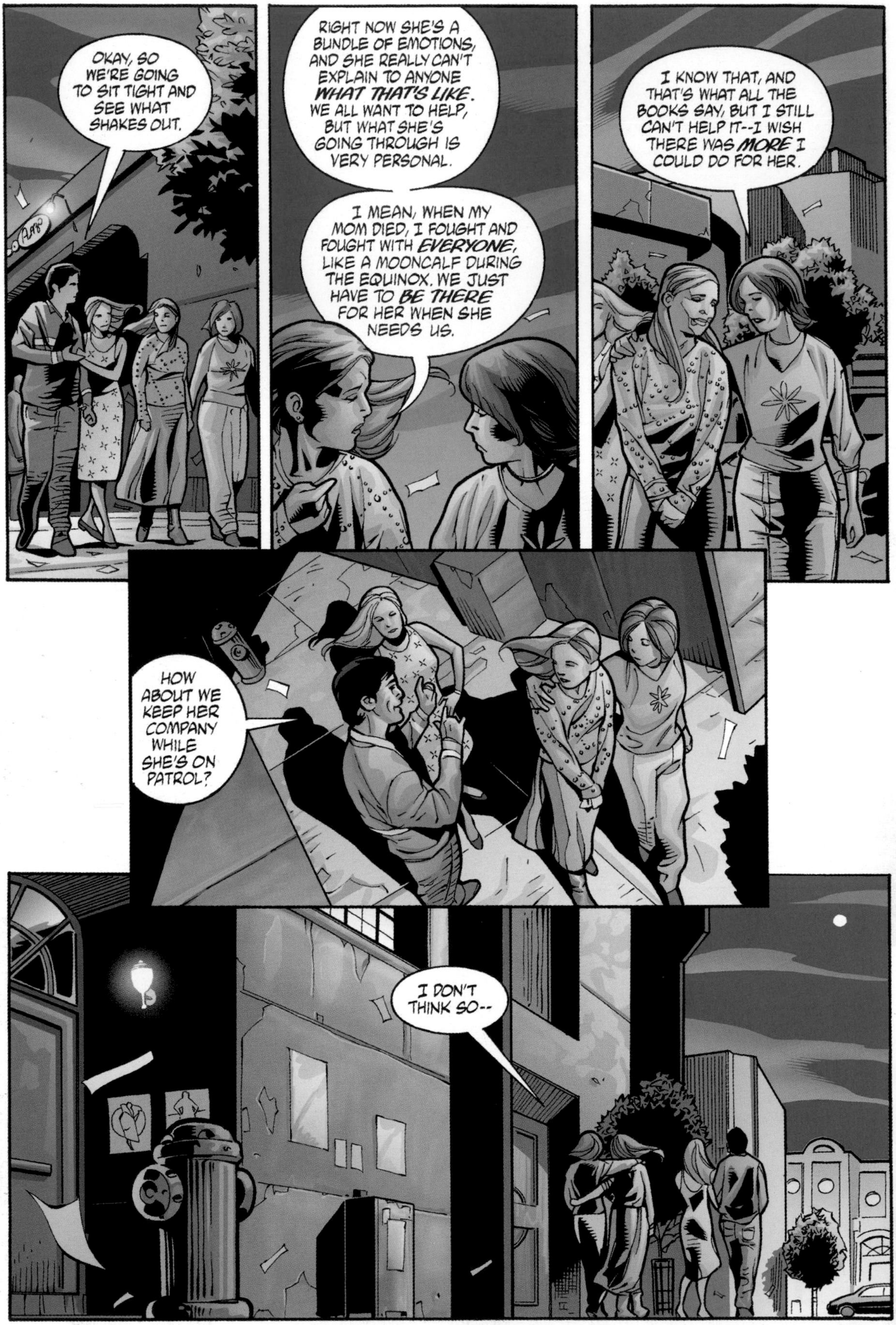
OKAY, SO WE'RE GOING TO SIT TIGHT AND SEE WHAT SHAKES OUT.
RIGHT NOW SHE'S A BUNDLE OF EMOTIONS, AND SHE REALLY CAN'T EXPLAIN TO ANYONE WHAT THAT'S LIKE. WE ALL WANT TO HELP, BUT WHAT SHE'S GOING THROUGH IS VERY PERSONAL.
I MEAN, WHEN MY MOM DIED, I FOUGHT AND FOUGHT WITH EVERYONE, LIKE A MOONCALF DURING THE EQUINOX. WE JUST HAVE TO BE THERE FOR HER WHEN SHE NEEDS US.
I KNOW THAT, AND THAT'S WHAT ALL THE BOOKS SAY, BUT I STILL CAN'T HELP IT--I WISH THERE WAS MORE I COULD DO FOR HER.
HOW ABOUT WE KEEP HER COMPANY WHILE SHE'S ON PATROL?
I DON'T THINK SO--

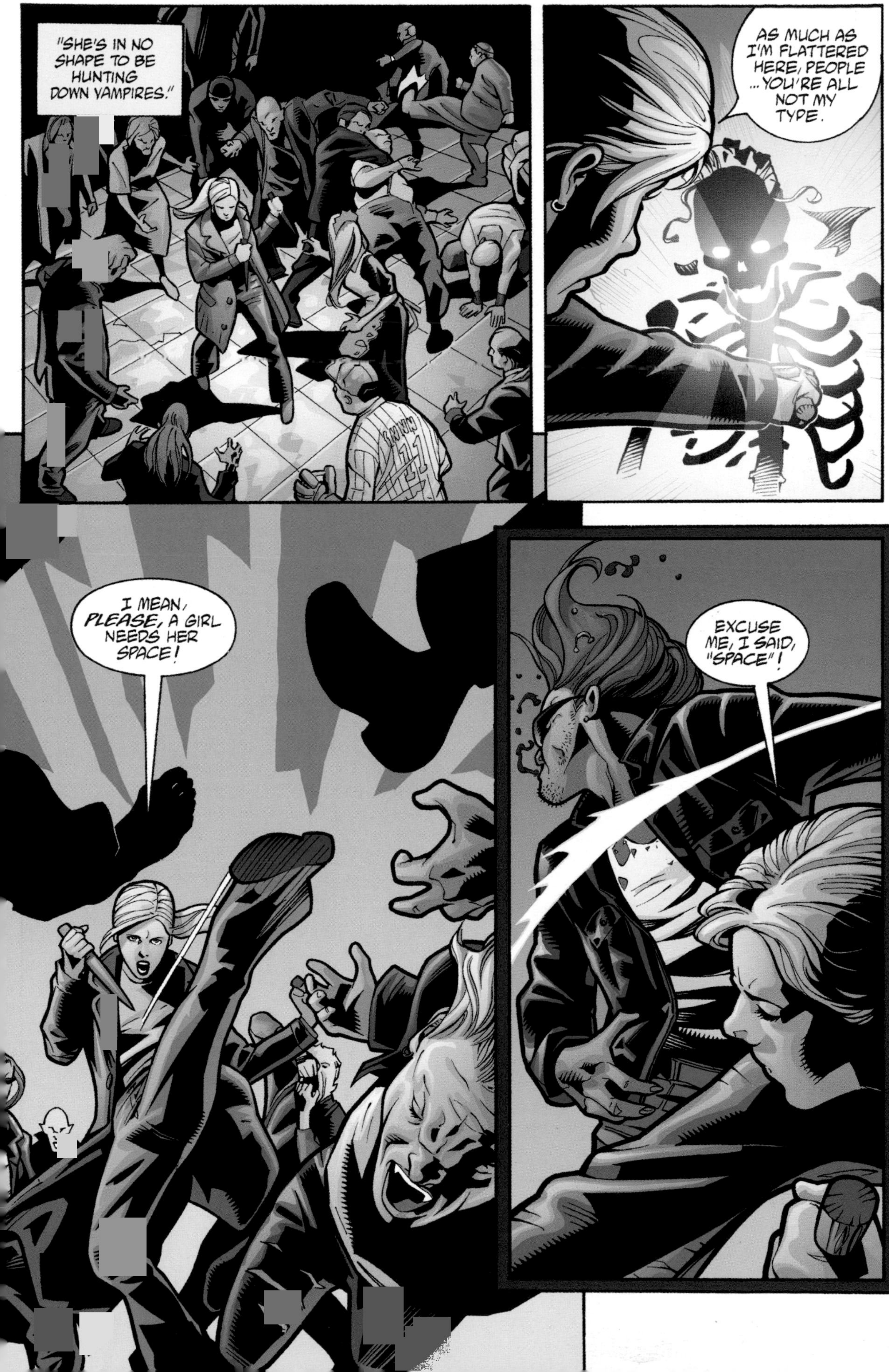
"SHE'S IN NO SHAPE TO BE HUNTING DOWN VAMPIRES."
AS MUCH AS I'M FLATTERED HERE, PEOPLE ...YOU'RE ALL NOT MY TYPE.
I MEAN, PLEASE, A GIRL NEEDS HER SPACE!
EXCUSE ME, I SAID, "SPACE"!

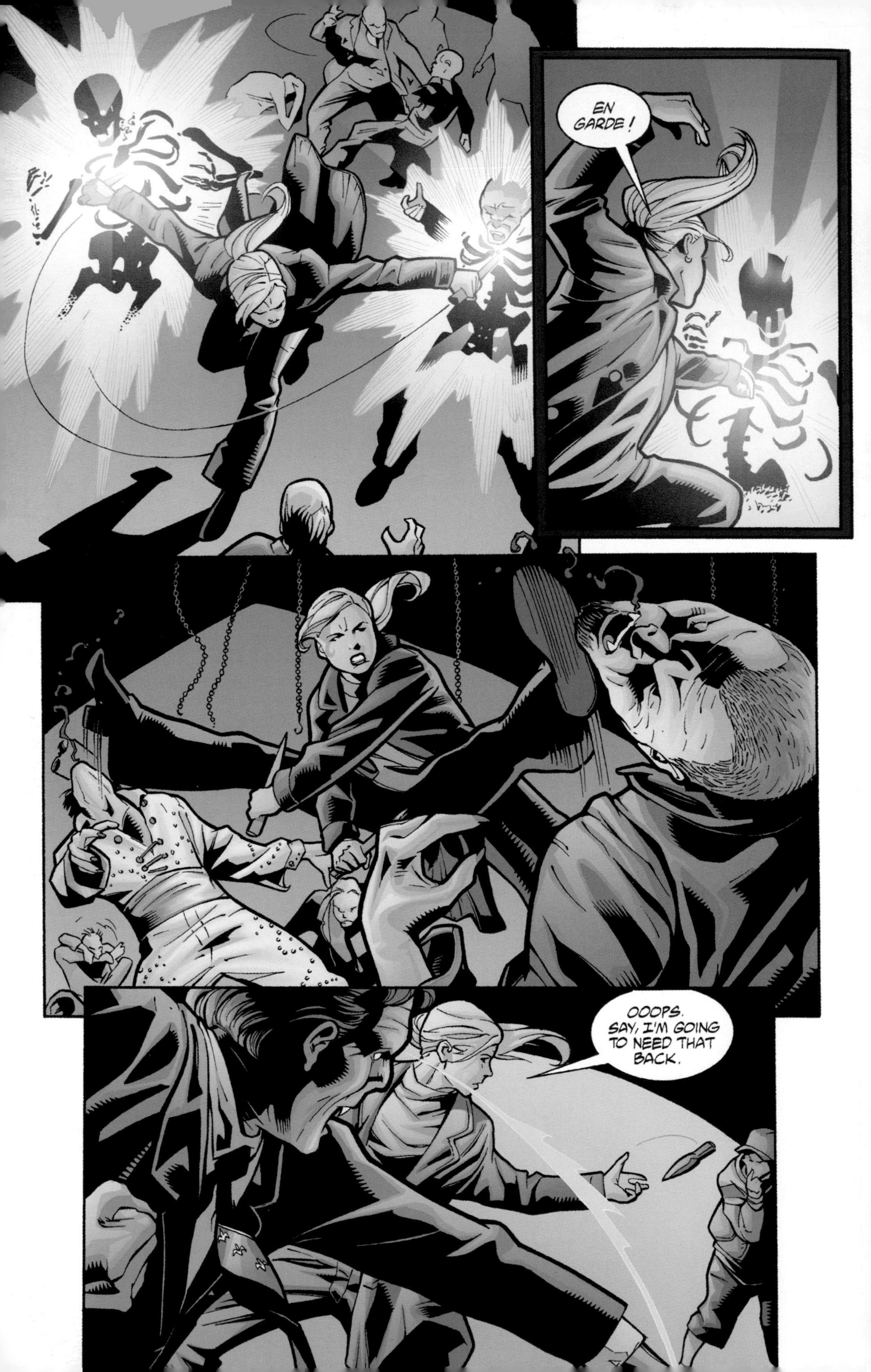
EN GARDE!
OOOPS. SAY, I'M GOING TO NEED THAT BACK.

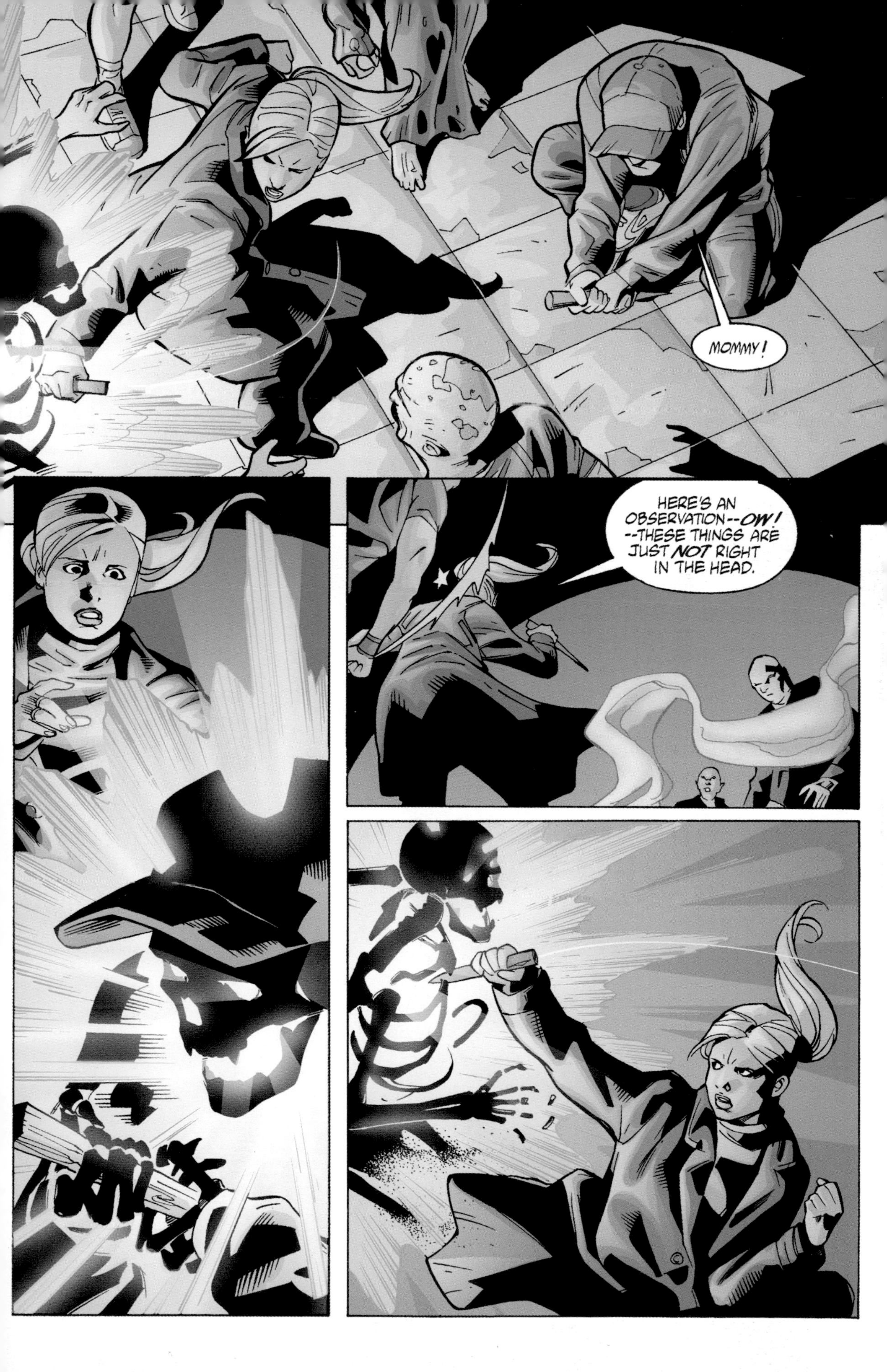
MOMMY!
HERE'S AN OBSERVATION--OW! --THESE THINGS ARE JUST NOT RIGHT IN THE HEAD.

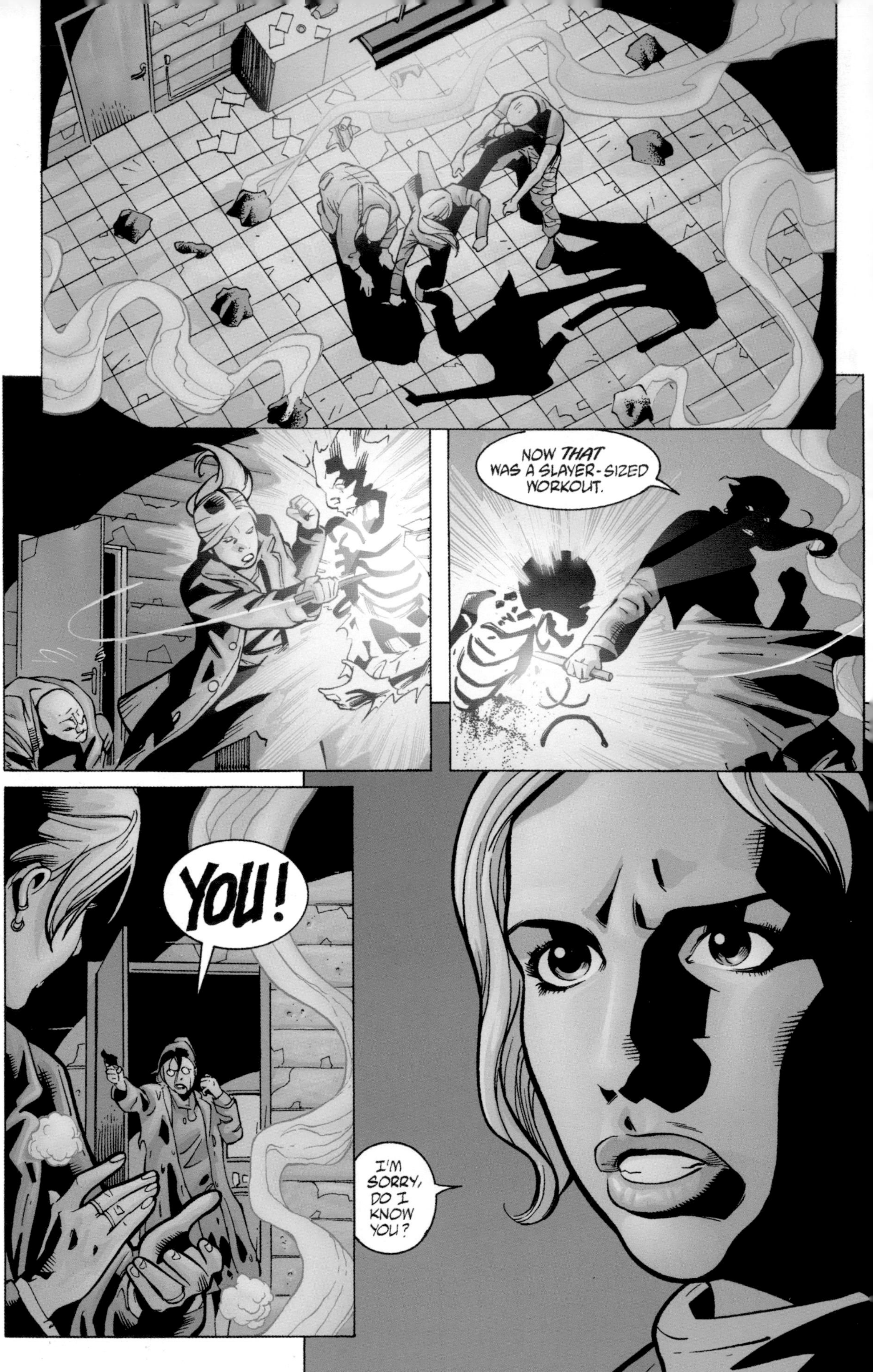
NOW THAT WAS A SLAYER-SIZED WORKOUT.
YOU!
I'M SORRY, DO I KNOW YOU?

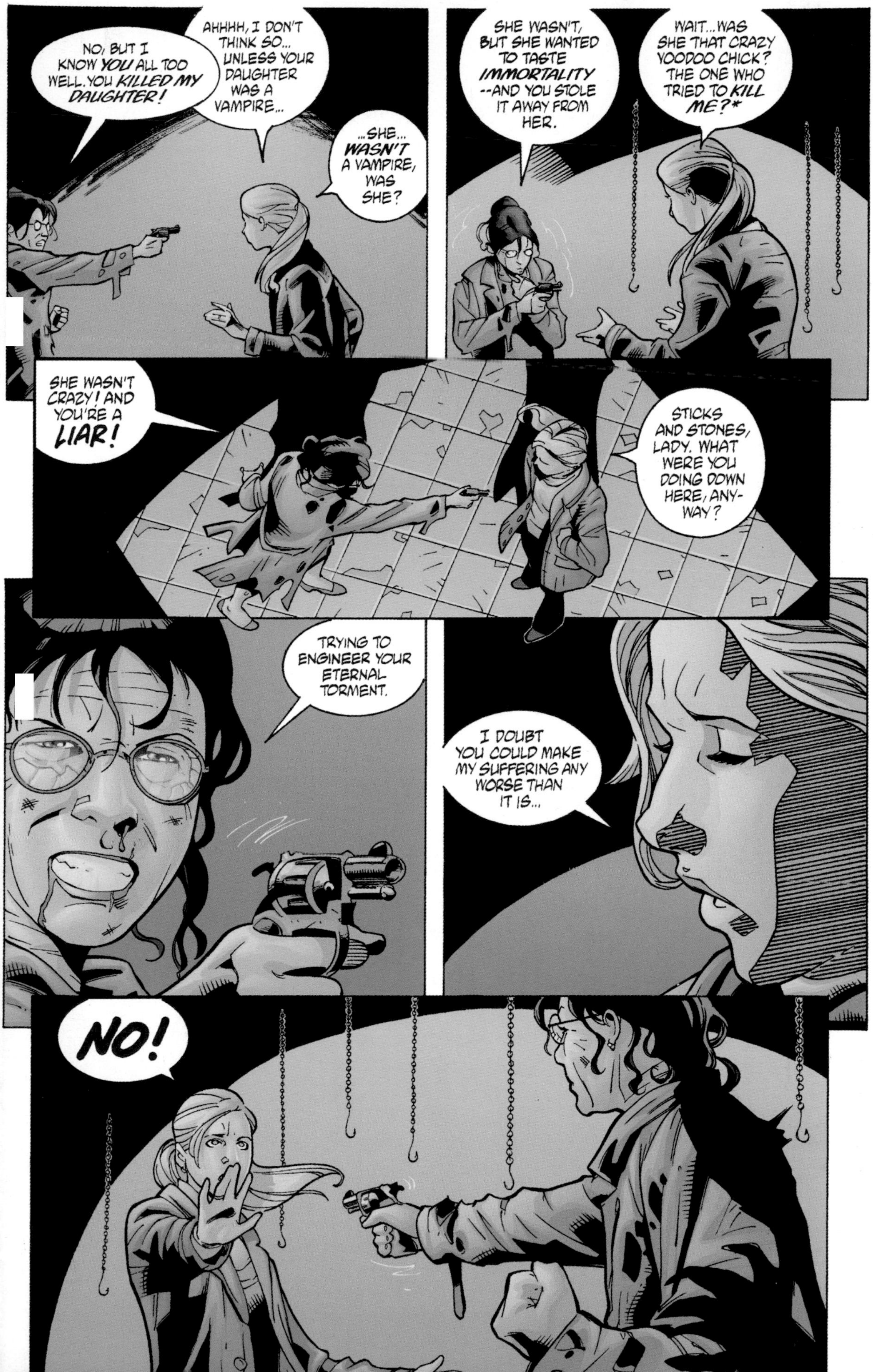
NO, BUT I KNOW YOU ALL TOO WELL. YOU KILLED MY DAUGHTER!
AHHHH, I DON'T THINK SO... UNLESS YOUR DAUGHTER WAS A VAMPIRE...
...SHE... WASN'T A VAMPIRE, WAS SHE?
SHE WASN'T, BUT SHE WANTED TO TASTE IMMORTALITY --AND YOU STOLE IT AWAY FROM HER.
WAIT...WAS SHE THAT CRAZY VOODOO CHICK? THE ONE WHO TRIED TO KILL ME?*
SHE WASN'T CRAZY! AND YOU'RE A LIAR!
STICKS AND STONES, LADY. WHAT WERE YOU DOING DOWN HERE, ANY-WAY?
TRYING TO ENGINEER YOUR ETERNAL TORMENT.
I DOUBT YOU COULD MAKE MY SUFFERING ANY WORSE THAN IT IS...
NO!

* BUFFY: AUTUMNALS (ISSUE #28)

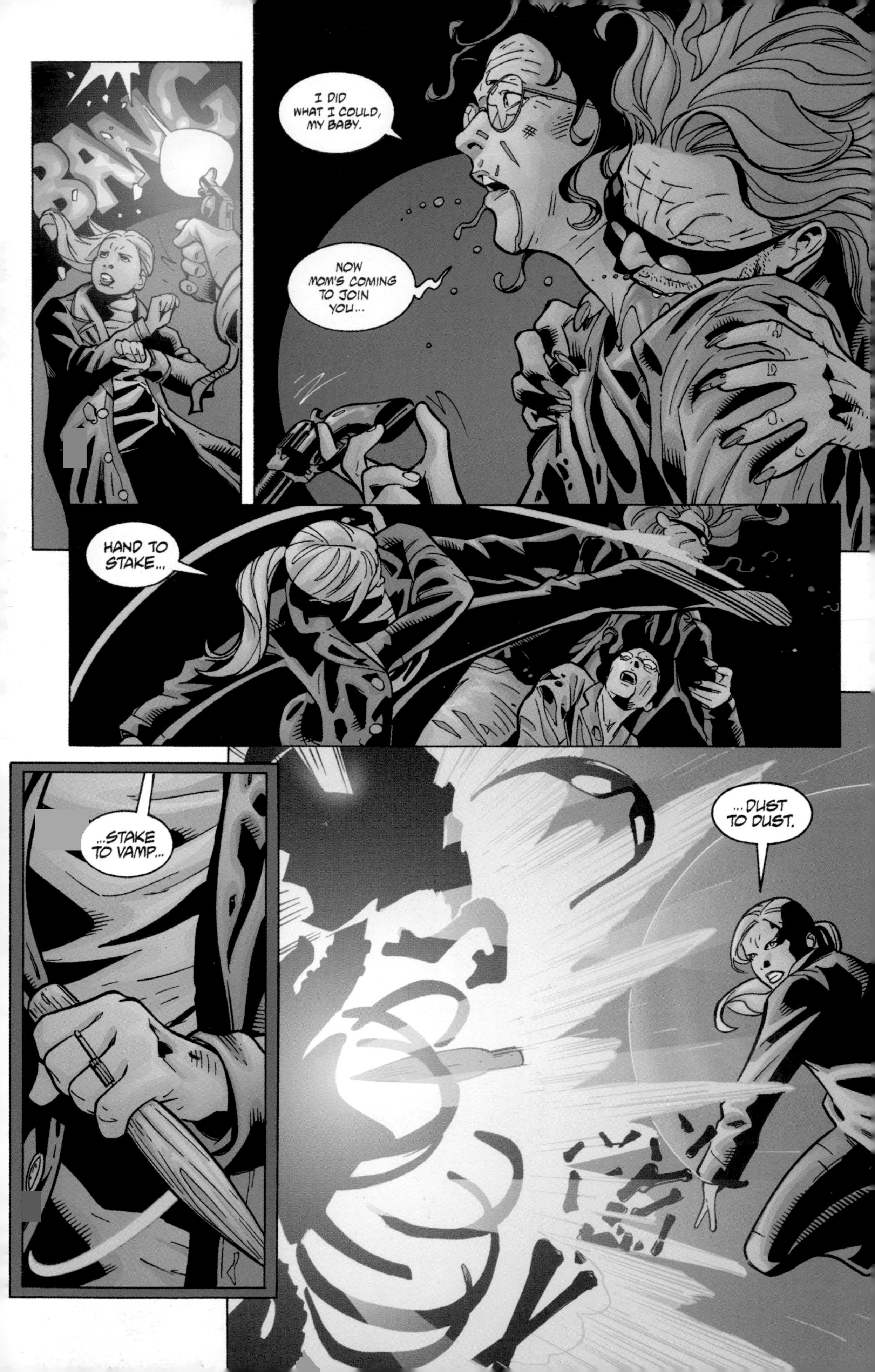
BANG
I DID WHAT I COULD, MY BABY.
NOW MOM'S COMING TO JOIN YOU...
HAND TO STAKE...
...STAKE TO VAMP...
...DUST TO DUST.

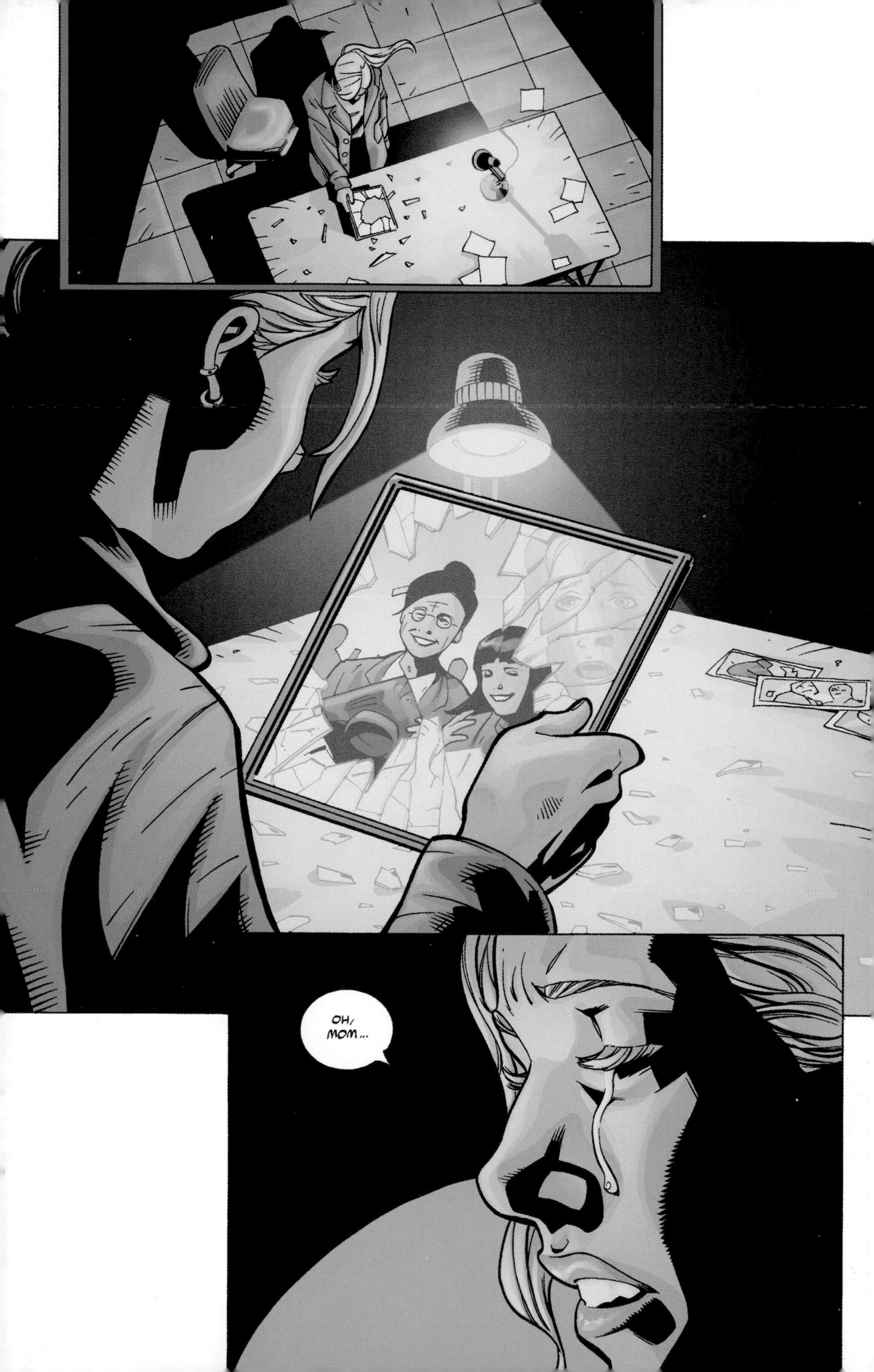
OH, MOM...

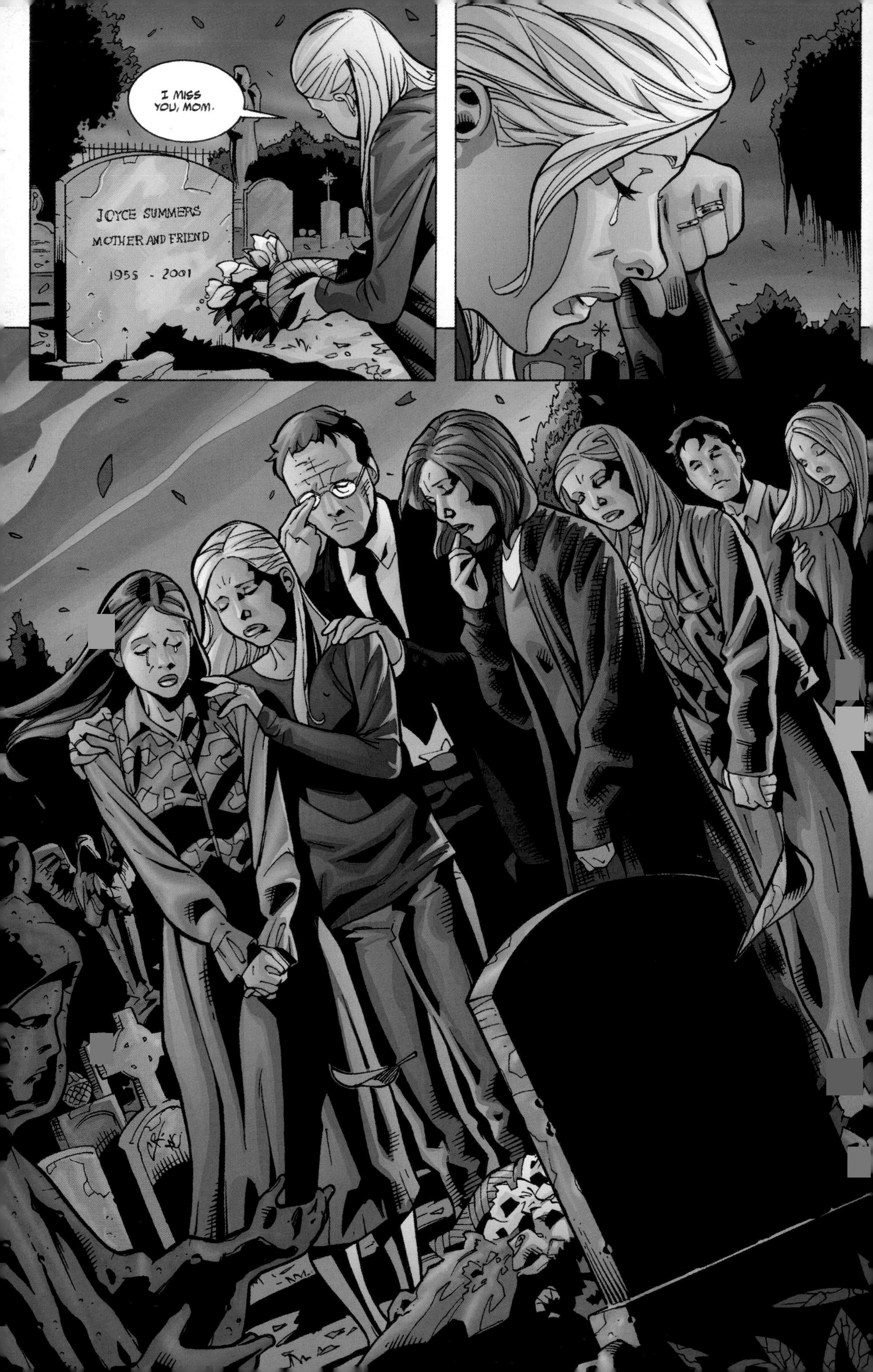
I MISS YOU, MOM.
JOYCE SUMMERS
MOTHER AND FRIEND
1955 - 2001

Buffy the Vampire Slayer™

Ugly Little Monsters

based on the television series created by
JOSS WHEDON

writers TOM FASSBENDER & JIM PASCOE

penciller CLIFF RICHARDS

inkers JOE PIMENTEL & WILL CONRAD

colorist DAVE MCCAIG

letterer CLEM ROBINS

This story takes place during Buffy the Vampire Slayer's *fifth season.*

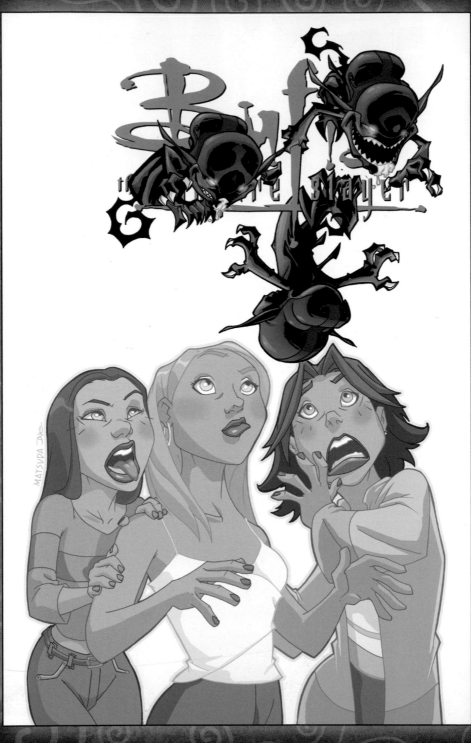

jeff matsuda with dave mccaig

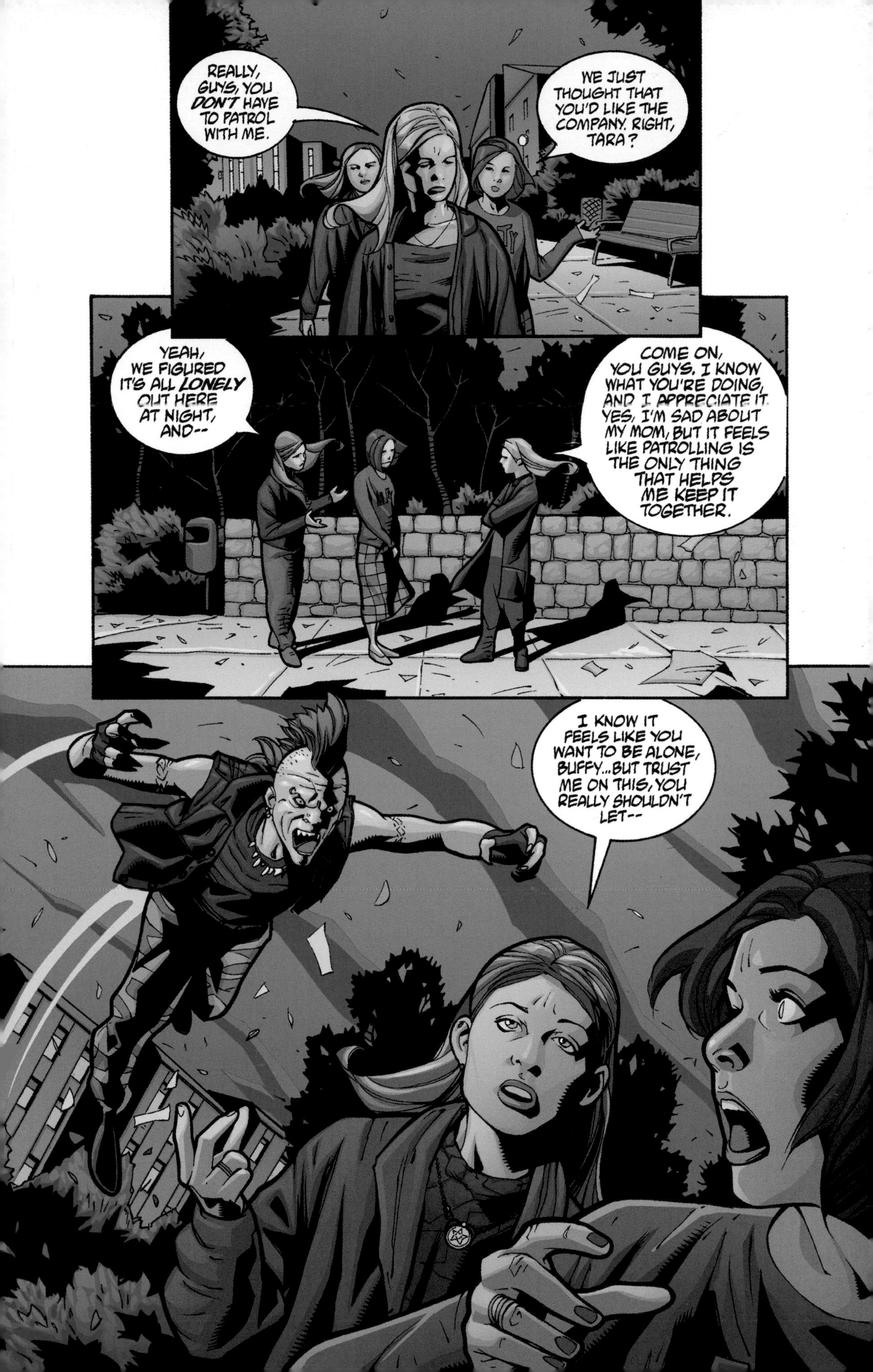
REALLY, GUYS, YOU DON'T HAVE TO PATROL WITH ME.
WE JUST THOUGHT THAT YOU'D LIKE THE COMPANY. RIGHT, TARA?
YEAH, WE FIGURED IT'S ALL LONELY OUT HERE AT NIGHT, AND--
COME ON, YOU GUYS. I KNOW WHAT YOU'RE DOING, AND I APPRECIATE IT. YES, I'M SAD ABOUT MY MOM, BUT IT FEELS LIKE PATROLLING IS THE ONLY THING THAT HELPS ME KEEP IT TOGETHER.
I KNOW IT FEELS LIKE YOU WANT TO BE ALONE, BUFFY...BUT TRUST ME ON THIS, YOU REALLY SHOULDN'T LET--

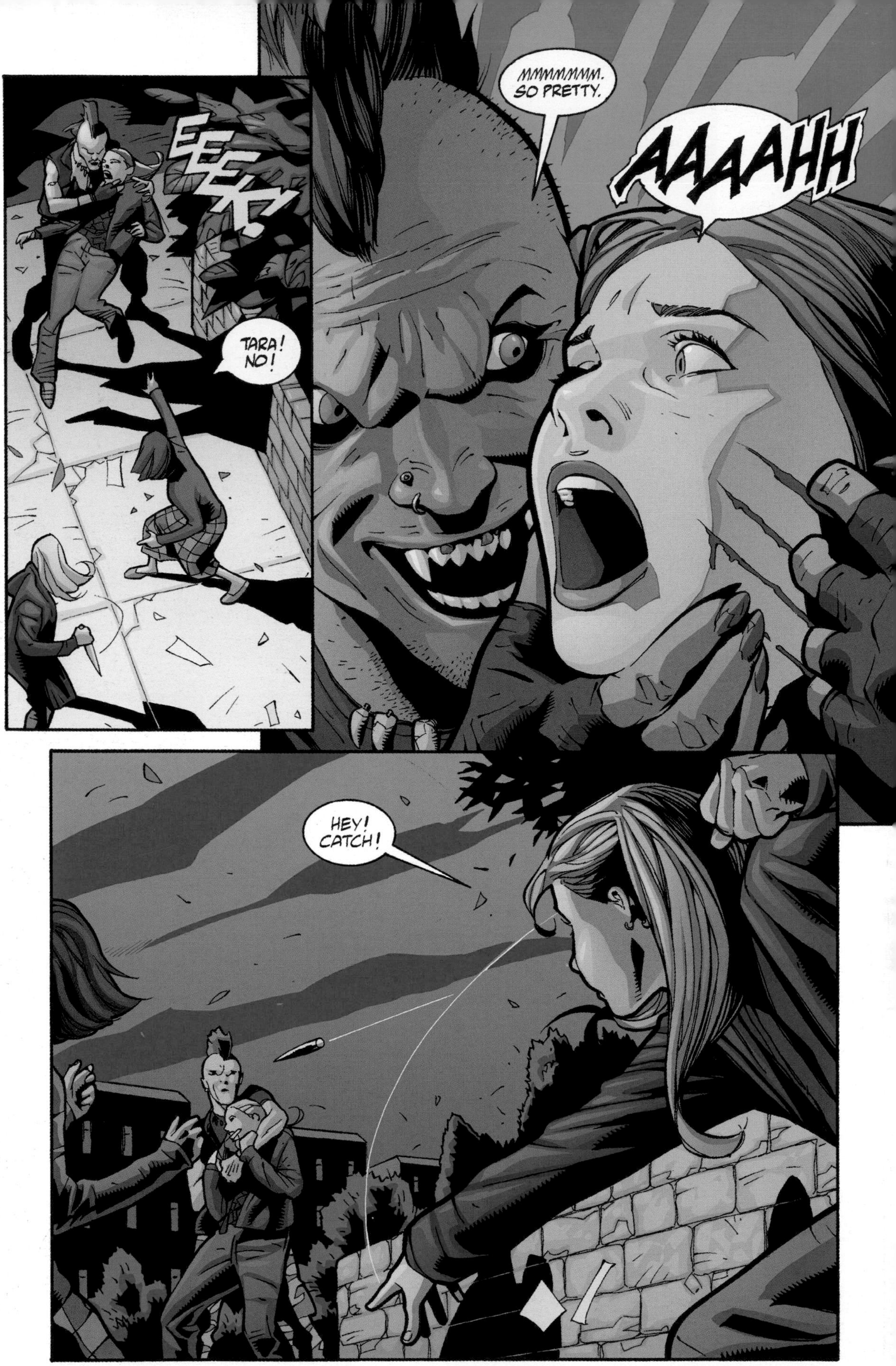
EEEK!
TARA! NO!
MMMMMMM. SO PRETTY.
AAAAHH
HEY! CATCH!

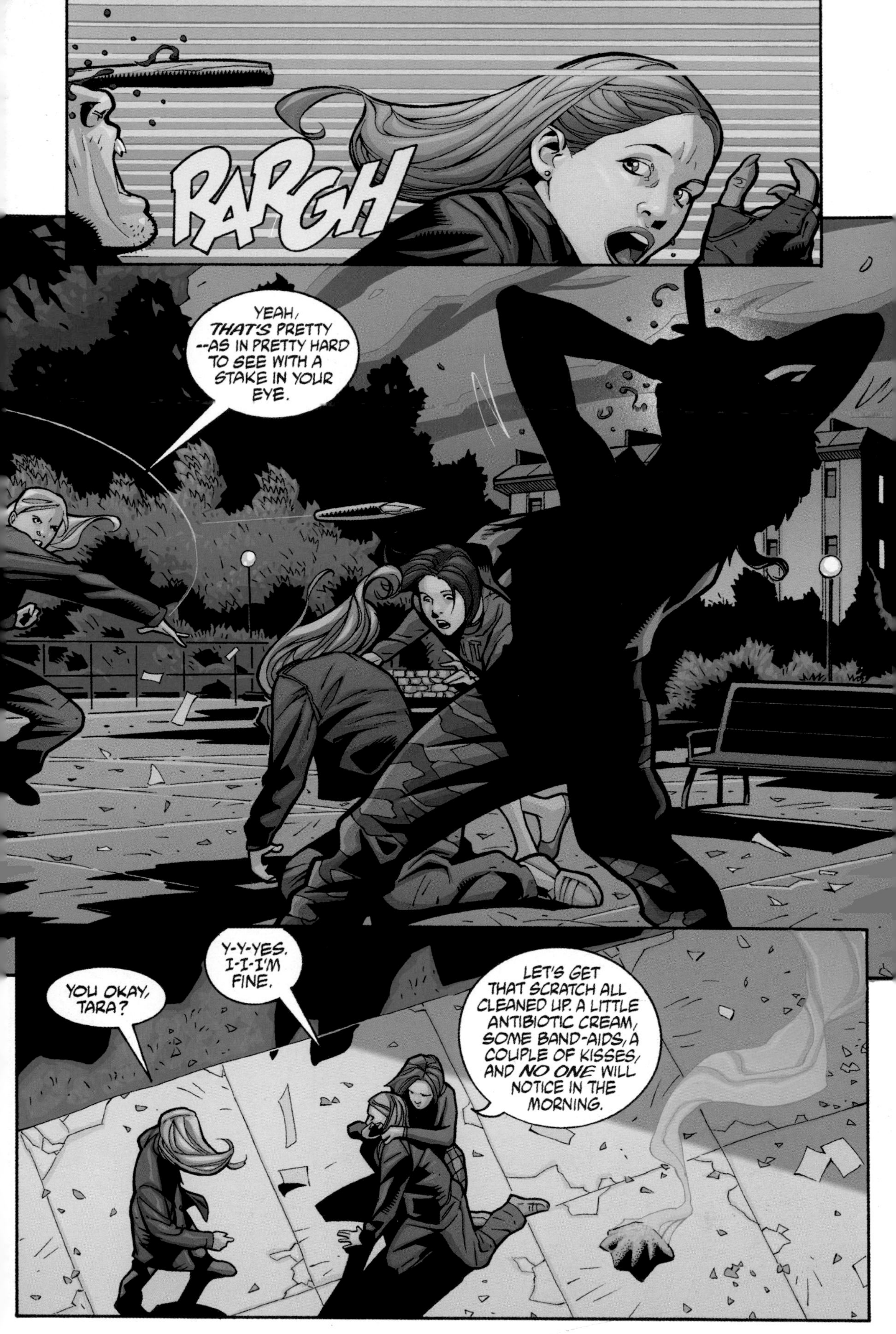
RARGH
YEAH, THAT'S PRETTY --AS IN PRETTY HARD TO SEE WITH A STAKE IN YOUR EYE.
YOU OKAY, TARA?
Y-Y-YES. I-I-I'M FINE.
LET'S GET THAT SCRATCH ALL CLEANED UP. A LITTLE ANTIBIOTIC CREAM, SOME BAND-AIDS, A COUPLE OF KISSES, AND NO ONE WILL NOTICE IN THE MORNING.

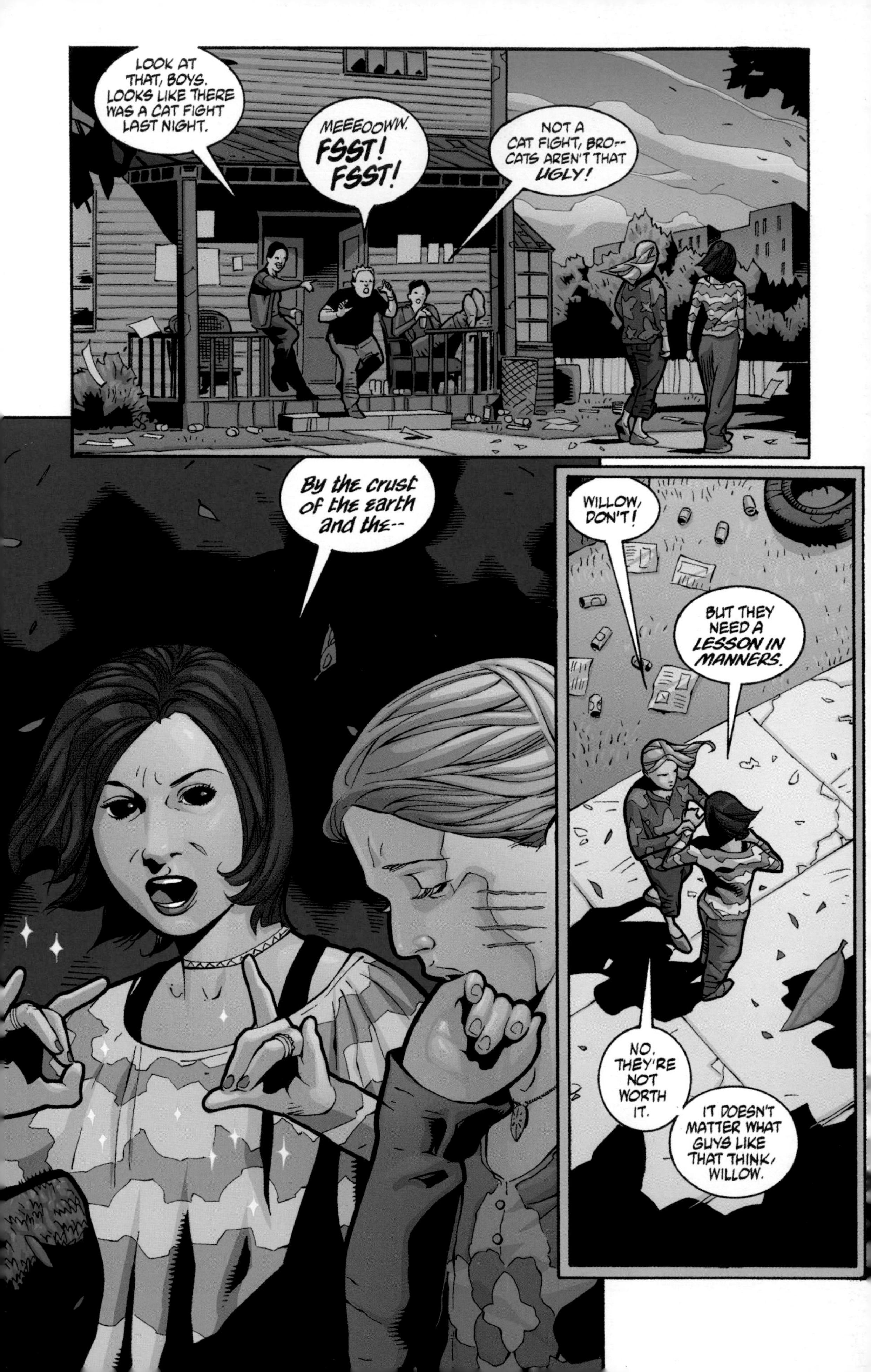
LOOK AT THAT, BOYS. LOOKS LIKE THERE WAS A CAT FIGHT LAST NIGHT.
MEEEOOWW. FSST! FSST!
NOT A CAT FIGHT, BRO-- CATS AREN'T THAT UGLY!
By the crust of the earth and the--
WILLOW, DON'T!
BUT THEY NEED A LESSON IN MANNERS.
NO. THEY'RE NOT WORTH IT.
IT DOESN'T MATTER WHAT GUYS LIKE THAT THINK, WILLOW.

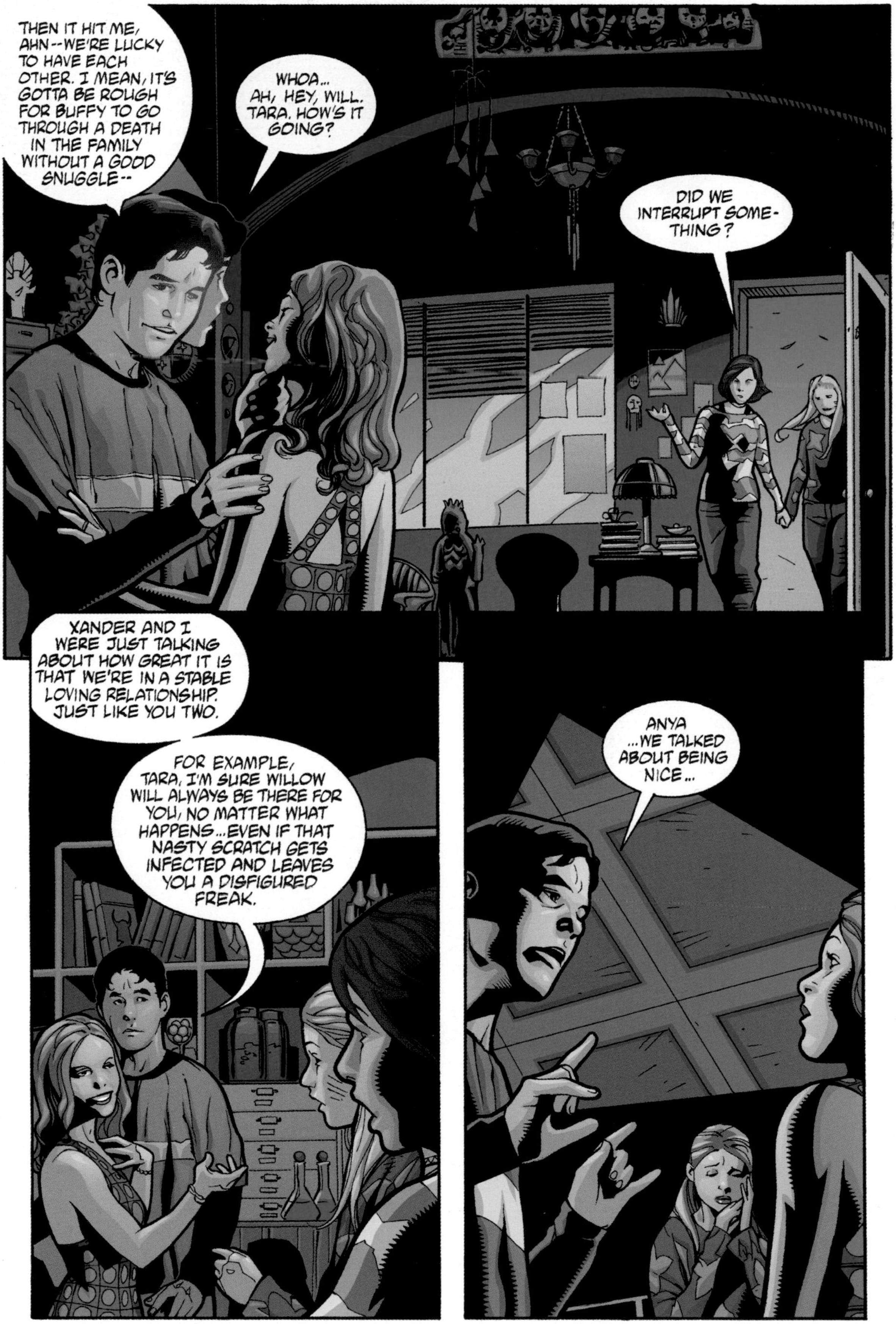

THEN IT HIT ME, AHN--WE'RE LUCKY TO HAVE EACH OTHER. I MEAN, IT'S GOTTA BE ROUGH FOR BUFFY TO GO THROUGH A DEATH IN THE FAMILY WITHOUT A GOOD SNUGGLE--
WHOA... AH, HEY, WILL. TARA. HOW'S IT GOING?
DID WE INTERRUPT SOME-THING?
XANDER AND I WERE JUST TALKING ABOUT HOW GREAT IT IS THAT WE'RE IN A STABLE LOVING RELATIONSHIP. JUST LIKE YOU TWO.
FOR EXAMPLE, TARA, I'M SURE WILLOW WILL ALWAYS BE THERE FOR YOU, NO MATTER WHAT HAPPENS...EVEN IF THAT NASTY SCRATCH GETS INFECTED AND LEAVES YOU A DISFIGURED FREAK.
ANYA ...WE TALKED ABOUT BEING NICE...

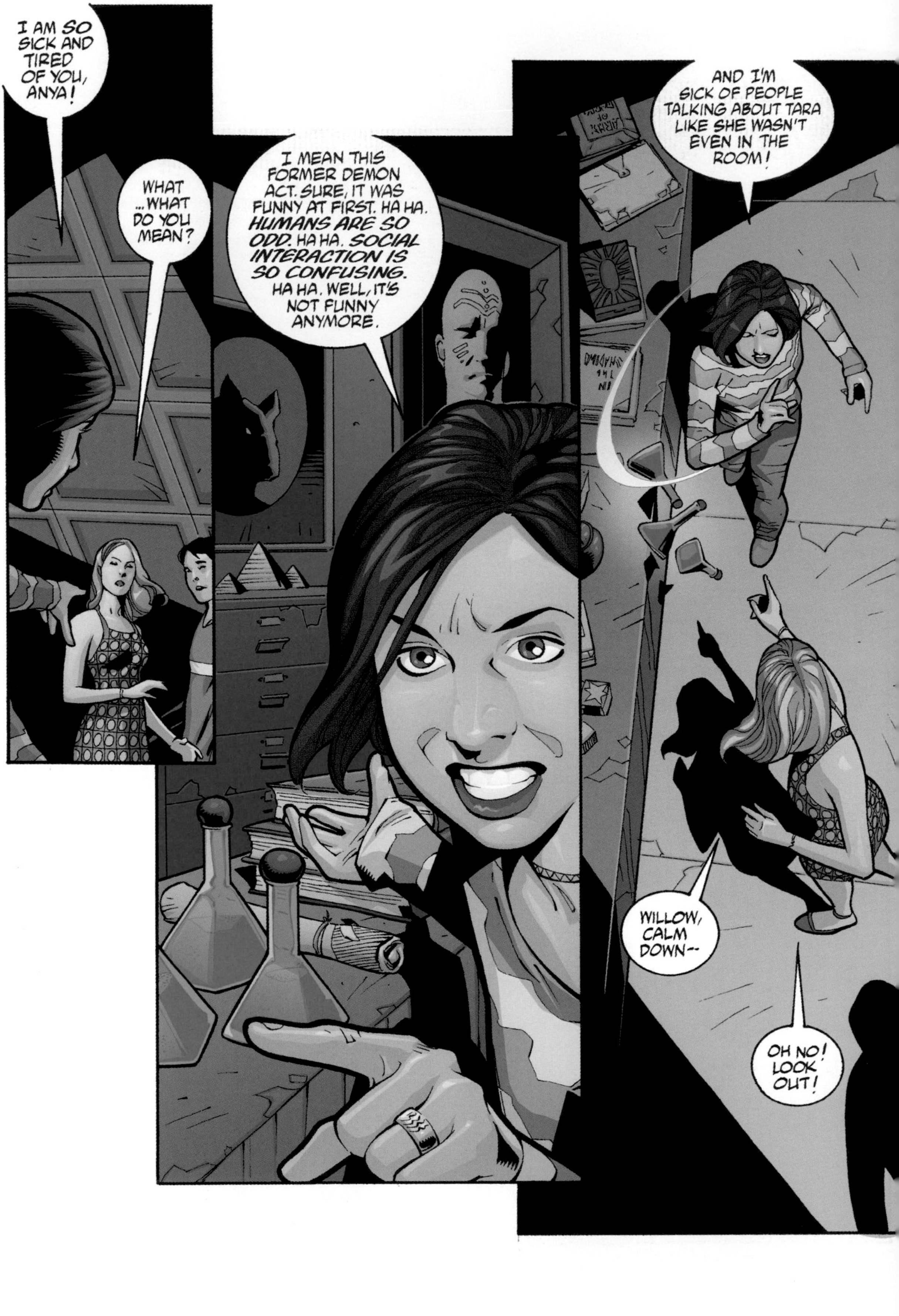
I AM SO SICK AND TIRED OF YOU, ANYA!
WHAT ...WHAT DO YOU MEAN?
I MEAN THIS FORMER DEMON ACT. SURE, IT WAS FUNNY AT FIRST. HA HA. HUMANS ARE SO ODD. HA HA. SOCIAL INTERACTION IS SO CONFUSING. HA HA. WELL, IT'S NOT FUNNY ANYMORE.
AND I'M SICK OF PEOPLE TALKING ABOUT TARA LIKE SHE WASN'T EVEN IN THE ROOM!
WILLOW, CALM DOWN--
OH NO! LOOK OUT!

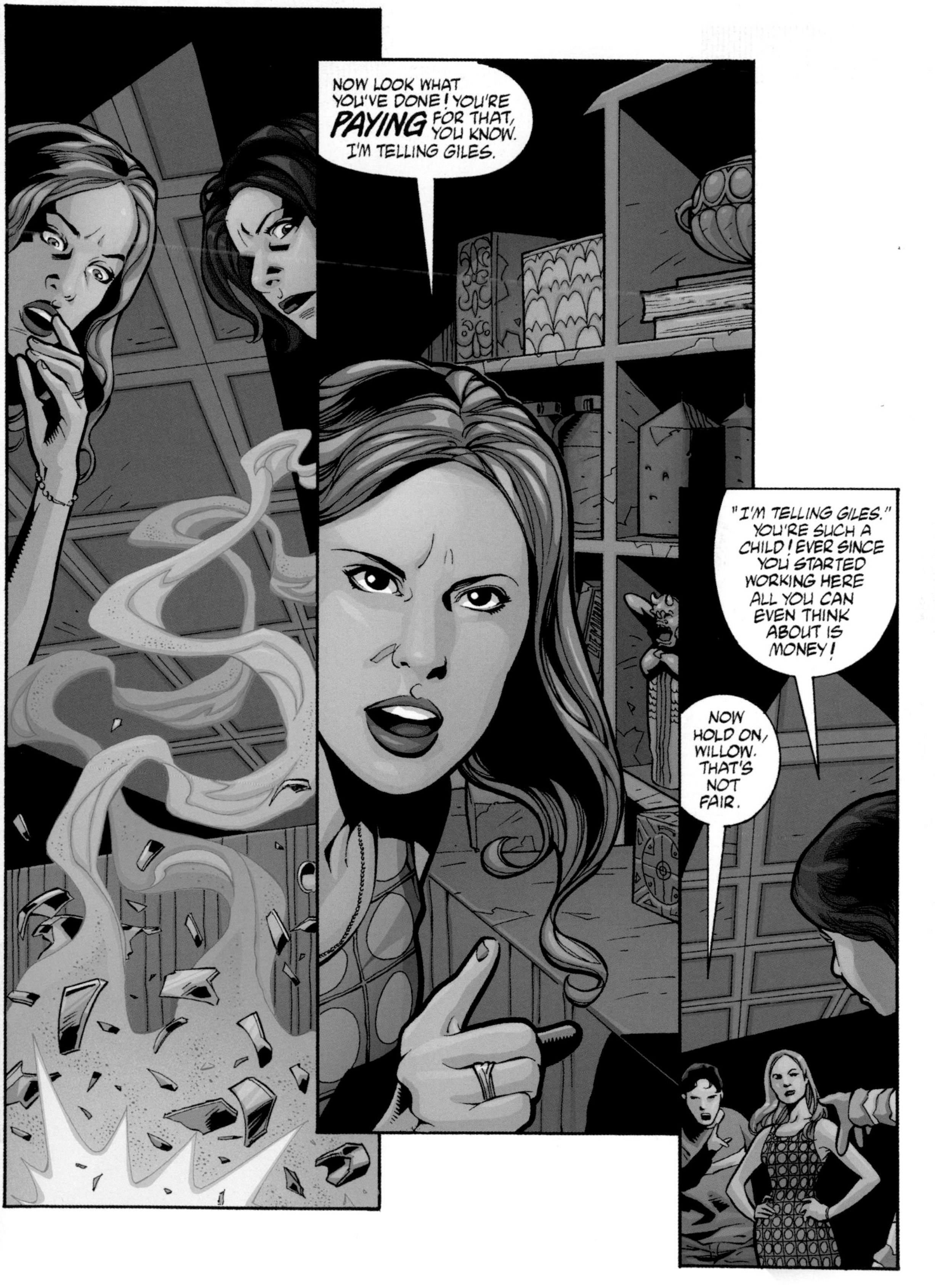
NOW LOOK WHAT YOU'VE DONE! YOU'RE PAYING FOR THAT, YOU KNOW. I'M TELLING GILES.
"I'M TELLING GILES." YOU'RE SUCH A CHILD! EVER SINCE YOU STARTED WORKING HERE ALL YOU CAN EVEN THINK ABOUT IS MONEY!
NOW HOLD ON, WILLOW. THAT'S NOT FAIR.

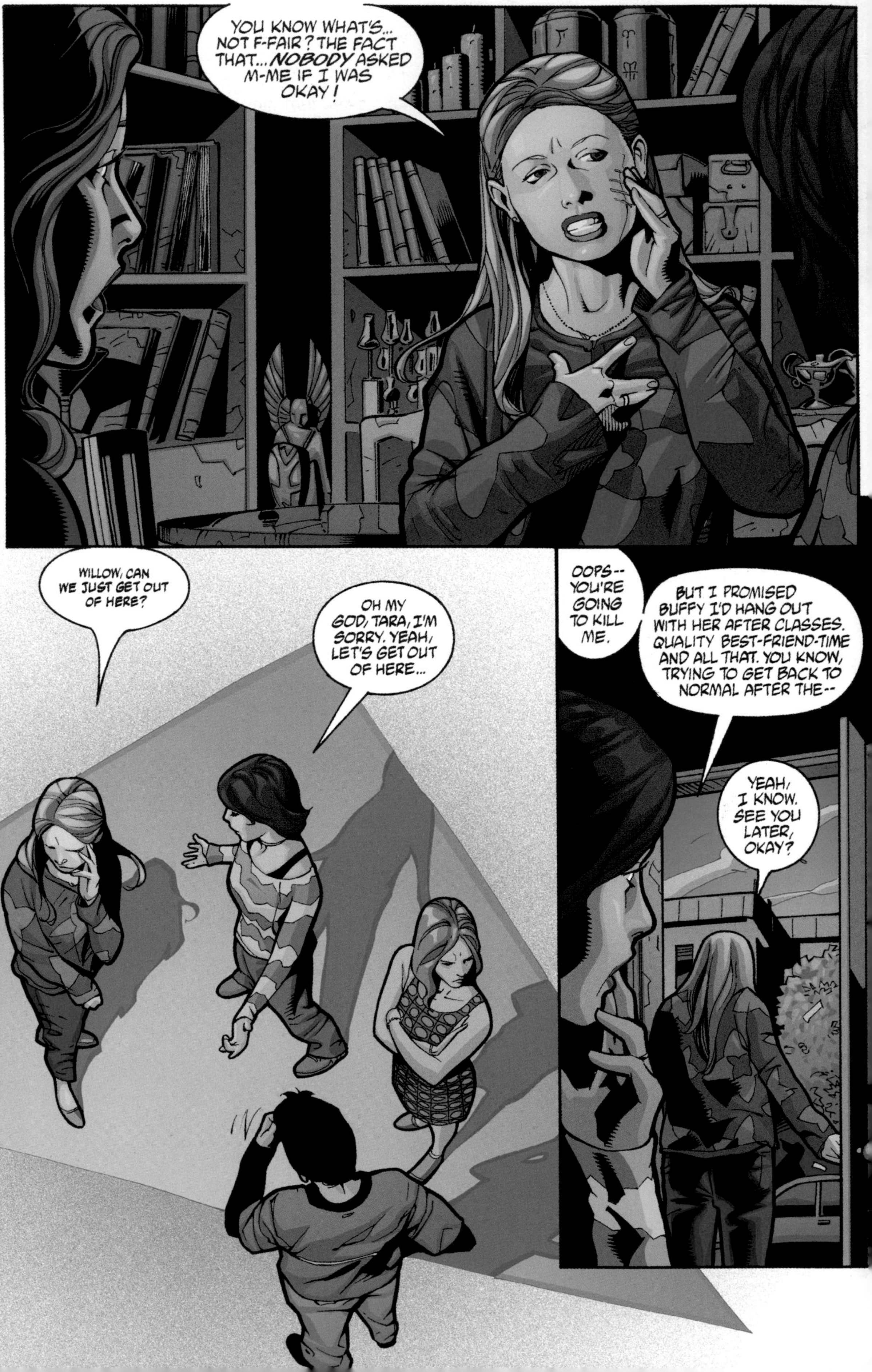
YOU KNOW WHAT'S... NOT F-FAIR? THE FACT THAT... NOBODY ASKED M-ME IF I WAS OKAY!
WILLOW, CAN WE JUST GET OUT OF HERE?
OH MY GOD, TARA, I'M SORRY. YEAH, LET'S GET OUT OF HERE...
OOPS-- YOU'RE GOING TO KILL ME.
BUT I PROMISED BUFFY I'D HANG OUT WITH HER AFTER CLASSES. QUALITY BEST-FRIEND-TIME AND ALL THAT. YOU KNOW, TRYING TO GET BACK TO NORMAL AFTER THE--
YEAH, I KNOW. SEE YOU LATER, OKAY?

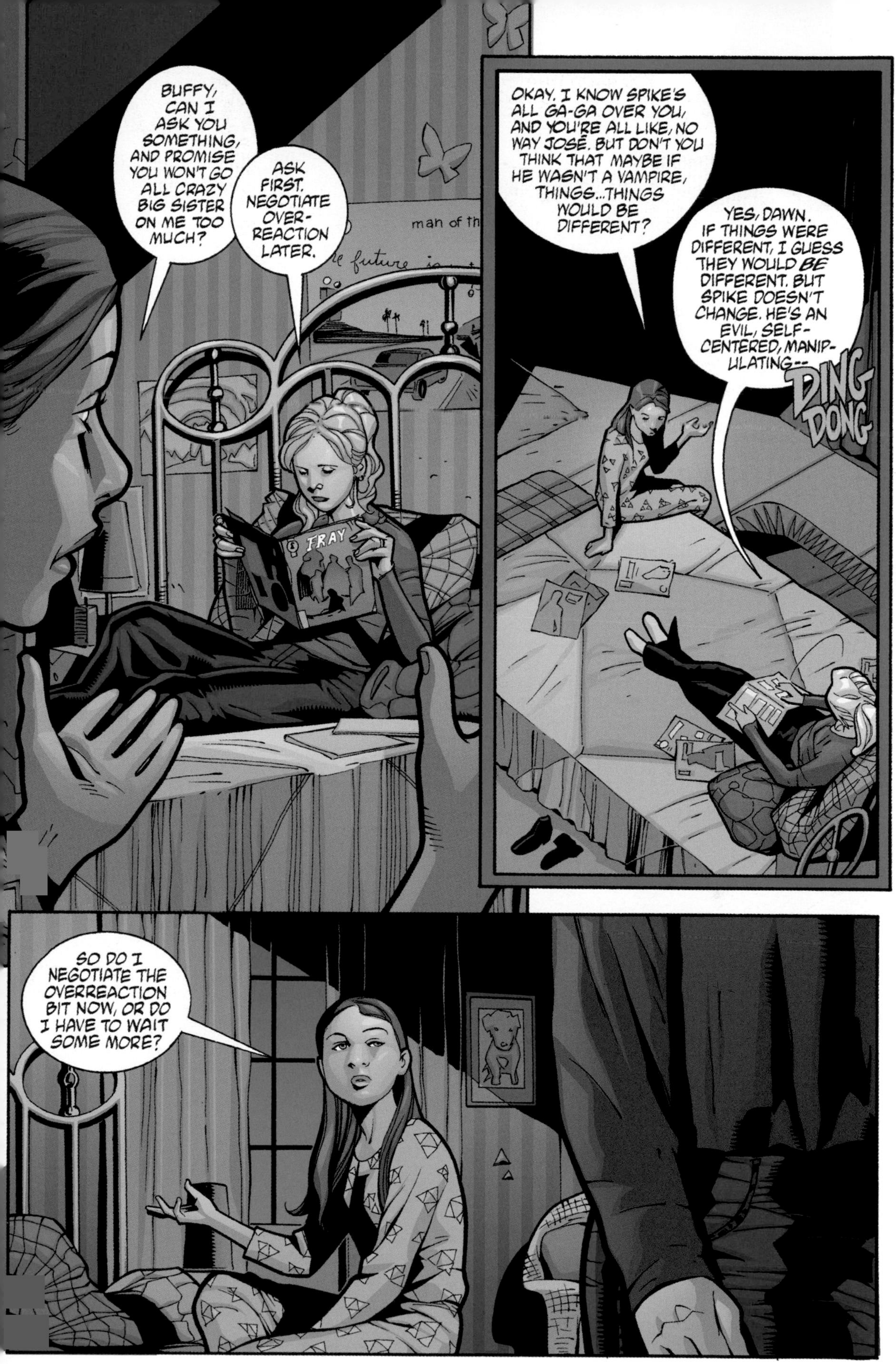

BUFFY, CAN I ASK YOU SOMETHING, AND PROMISE YOU WON'T GO ALL CRAZY BIG SISTER ON ME TOO MUCH?
ASK FIRST. NEGOTIATE OVER-REACTION LATER.
FRAY
OKAY. I KNOW SPIKE'S ALL GA-GA OVER YOU, AND YOU'RE ALL LIKE, NO WAY JOSÉ. BUT DON'T YOU THINK THAT MAYBE IF HE WASN'T A VAMPIRE, THINGS...THINGS WOULD BE DIFFERENT?
YES, DAWN. IF THINGS WERE DIFFERENT, I GUESS THEY WOULD *BE* DIFFERENT. BUT SPIKE DOESN'T CHANGE. HE'S AN EVIL, SELF-CENTERED, MANIP-ULATING--
DING DONG
SO DO I NEGOTIATE THE OVERREACTION BIT NOW, OR DO I HAVE TO WAIT SOME MORE?

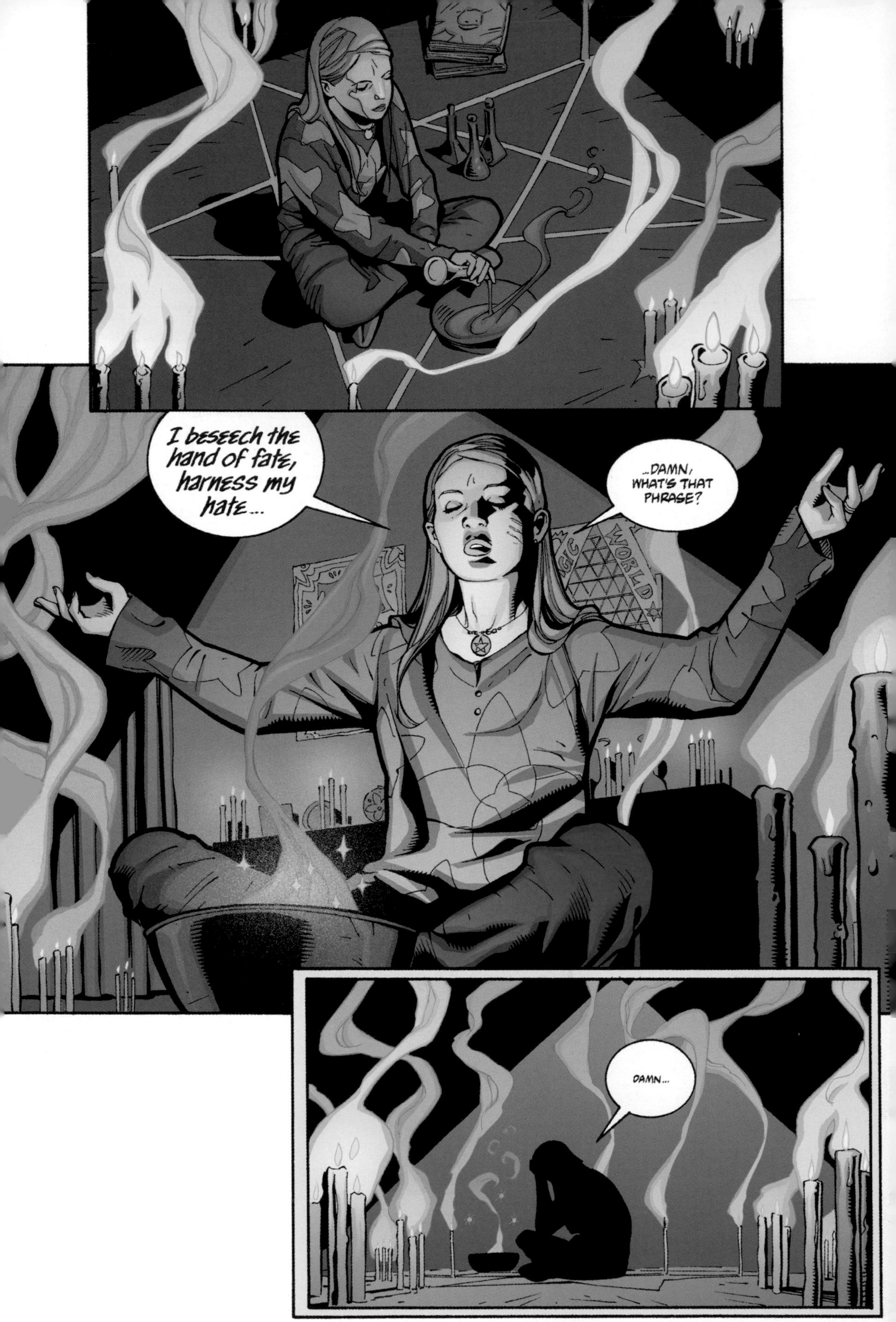
I beseech the hand of fate, harness my hate...
...DAMN, WHAT'S THAT PHRASE?
DAMN...

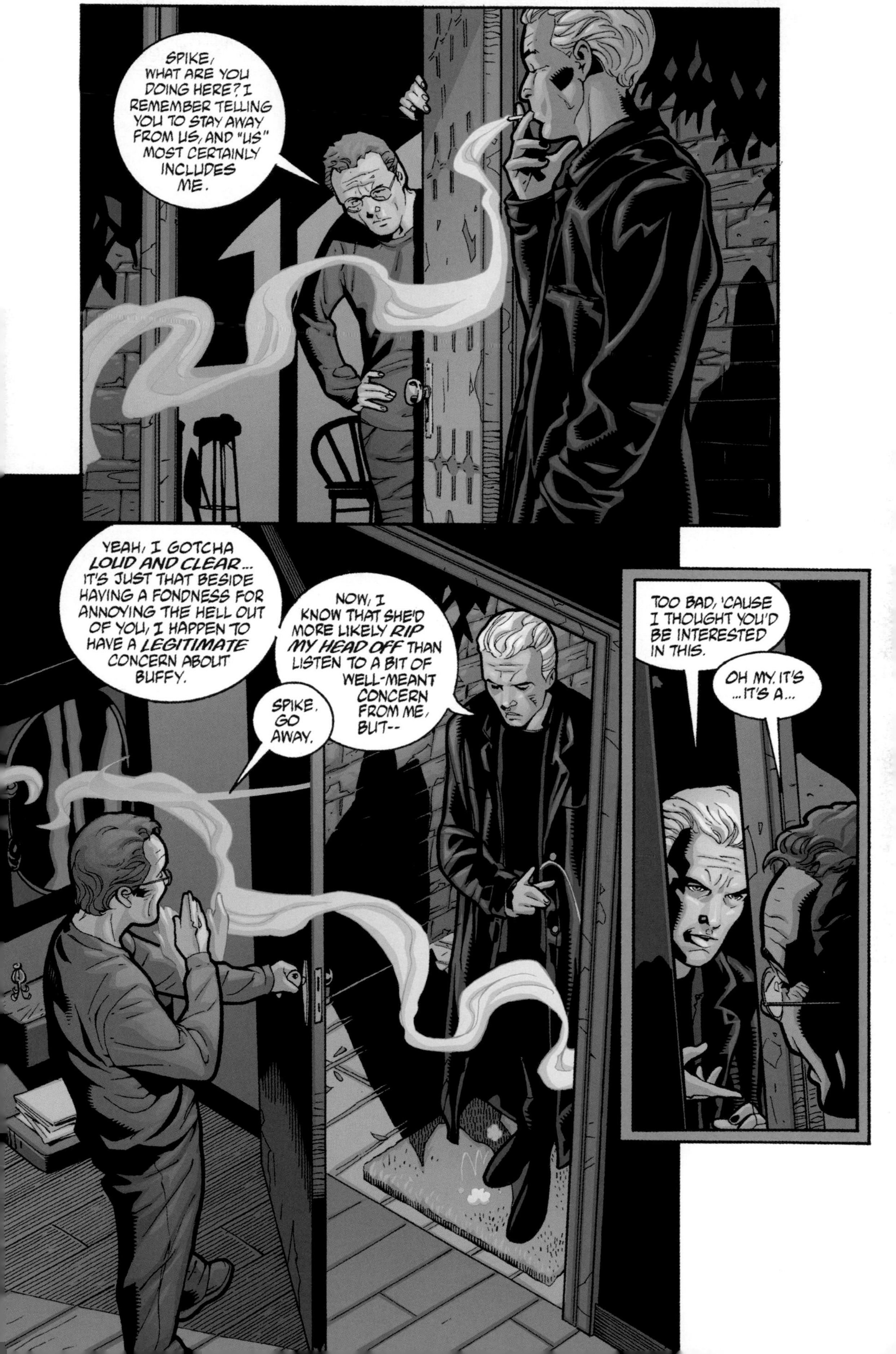
SPIKE, WHAT ARE YOU DOING HERE? I REMEMBER TELLING YOU TO STAY AWAY FROM US, AND "US" MOST CERTAINLY INCLUDES ME.
YEAH, I GOTCHA LOUD AND CLEAR... IT'S JUST THAT BESIDE HAVING A FONDNESS FOR ANNOYING THE HELL OUT OF YOU, I HAPPEN TO HAVE A LEGITIMATE CONCERN ABOUT BUFFY.
NOW, I KNOW THAT SHE'D MORE LIKELY RIP MY HEAD OFF THAN LISTEN TO A BIT OF WELL-MEANT CONCERN FROM ME, BUT--
SPIKE. GO AWAY.
TOO BAD, 'CAUSE I THOUGHT YOU'D BE INTERESTED IN THIS.
OH MY. IT'S ...IT'S A...

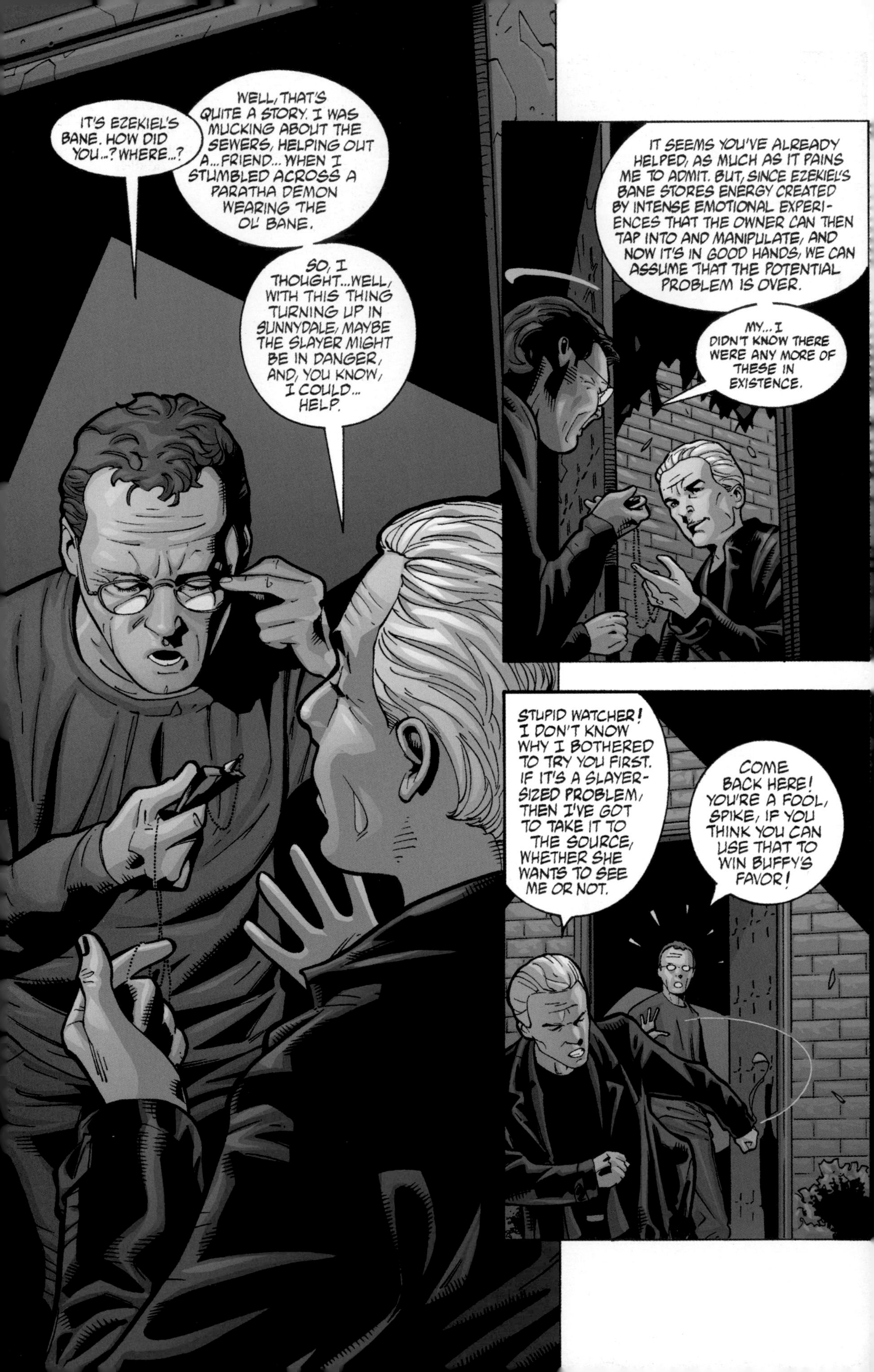
IT'S EZEKIEL'S BANE. HOW DID YOU...? WHERE...?
WELL, THAT'S QUITE A STORY. I WAS MUCKING ABOUT THE SEWERS, HELPING OUT A...FRIEND... WHEN I STUMBLED ACROSS A PARATHA DEMON WEARING THE OL' BANE.
SO, I THOUGHT...WELL, WITH THIS THING TURNING UP IN SUNNYDALE, MAYBE THE SLAYER MIGHT BE IN DANGER, AND, YOU KNOW, I COULD... HELP.
IT SEEMS YOU'VE ALREADY HELPED, AS MUCH AS IT PAINS ME TO ADMIT. BUT, SINCE EZEKIEL'S BANE STORES ENERGY CREATED BY INTENSE EMOTIONAL EXPERI- ENCES THAT THE OWNER CAN THEN TAP INTO AND MANIPULATE, AND NOW IT'S IN GOOD HANDS, WE CAN ASSUME THAT THE POTENTIAL PROBLEM IS OVER.
MY... I DIDN'T KNOW THERE WERE ANY MORE OF THESE IN EXISTENCE.
STUPID WATCHER! I DON'T KNOW WHY I BOTHERED TO TRY YOU FIRST. IF IT'S A SLAYER- SIZED PROBLEM, THEN I'VE GOT TO TAKE IT TO THE SOURCE, WHETHER SHE WANTS TO SEE ME OR NOT.
COME BACK HERE! YOU'RE A FOOL, SPIKE, IF YOU THINK YOU CAN USE THAT TO WIN BUFFY'S FAVOR!

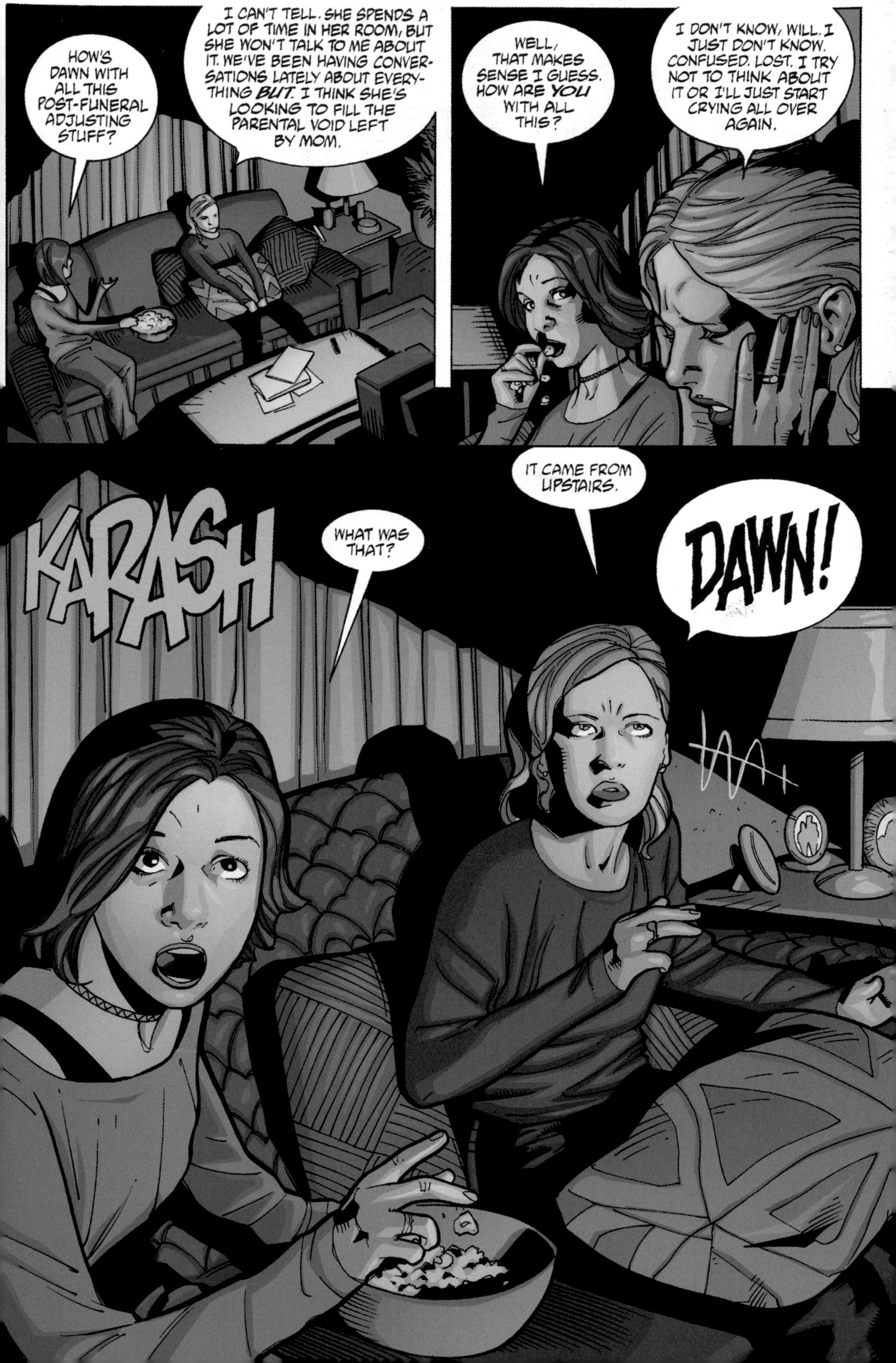
HOW'S DAWN WITH ALL THIS POST-FUNERAL ADJUSTING STUFF?
I CAN'T TELL. SHE SPENDS A LOT OF TIME IN HER ROOM, BUT SHE WON'T TALK TO ME ABOUT IT. WE'VE BEEN HAVING CONVERSATIONS LATELY ABOUT EVERYTHING BUT. I THINK SHE'S LOOKING TO FILL THE PARENTAL VOID LEFT BY MOM.
WELL, THAT MAKES SENSE I GUESS. HOW ARE YOU WITH ALL THIS?
I DON'T KNOW, WILL. I JUST DON'T KNOW. CONFUSED. LOST. I TRY NOT TO THINK ABOUT IT OR I'LL JUST START CRYING ALL OVER AGAIN.
KARASH
WHAT WAS THAT?
IT CAME FROM UPSTAIRS.
DAWN!

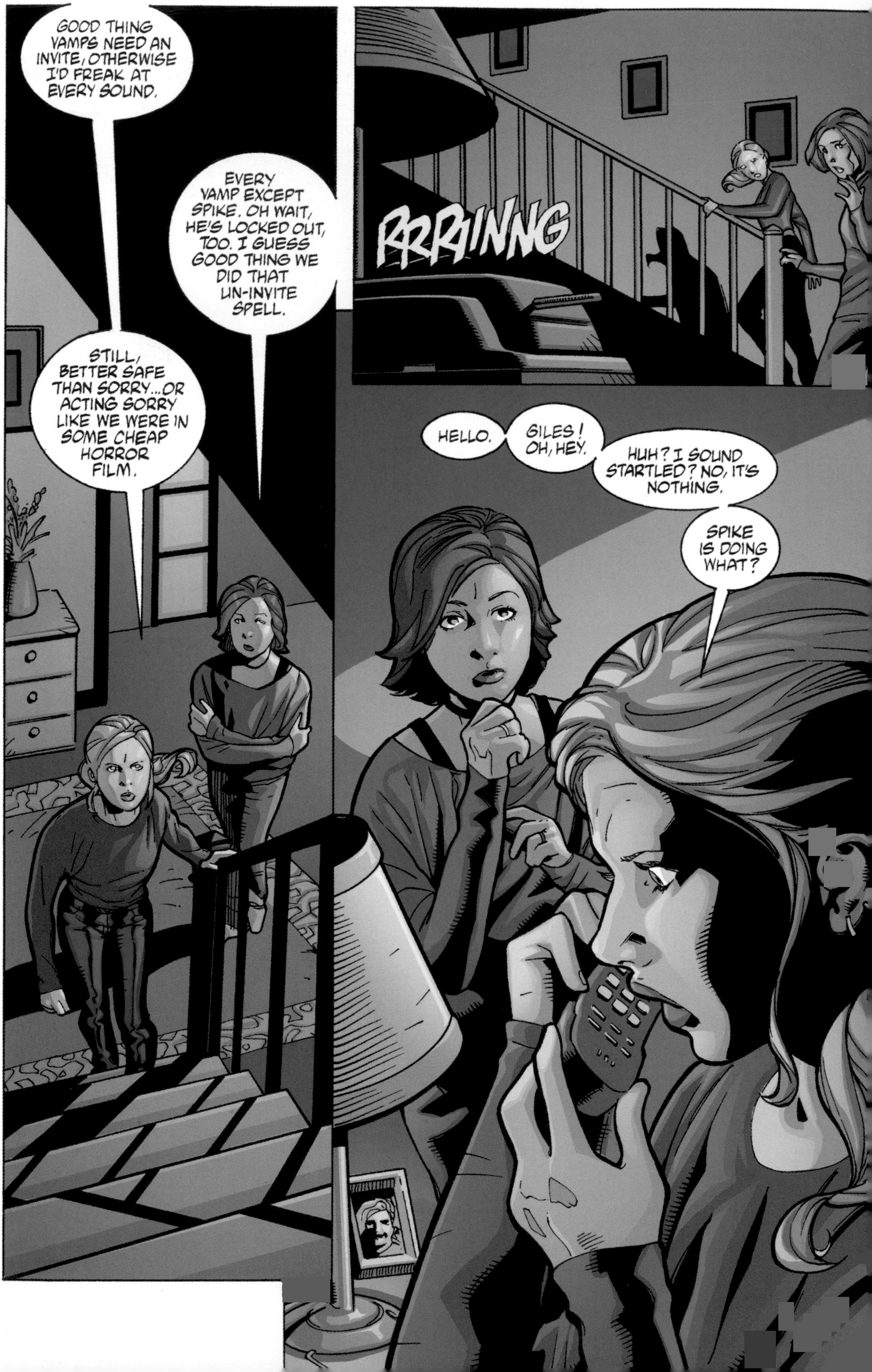
GOOD THING VAMPS NEED AN INVITE, OTHERWISE I'D FREAK AT EVERY SOUND.
EVERY VAMP EXCEPT SPIKE. OH WAIT, HE'S LOCKED OUT, TOO. I GUESS GOOD THING WE DID THAT UN-INVITE SPELL.
STILL, BETTER SAFE THAN SORRY...OR ACTING SORRY LIKE WE WERE IN SOME CHEAP HORROR FILM.
RRRIINNG
HELLO.
GILES! OH, HEY.
HUH? I SOUND STARTLED? NO, IT'S NOTHING.
SPIKE IS DOING WHAT?

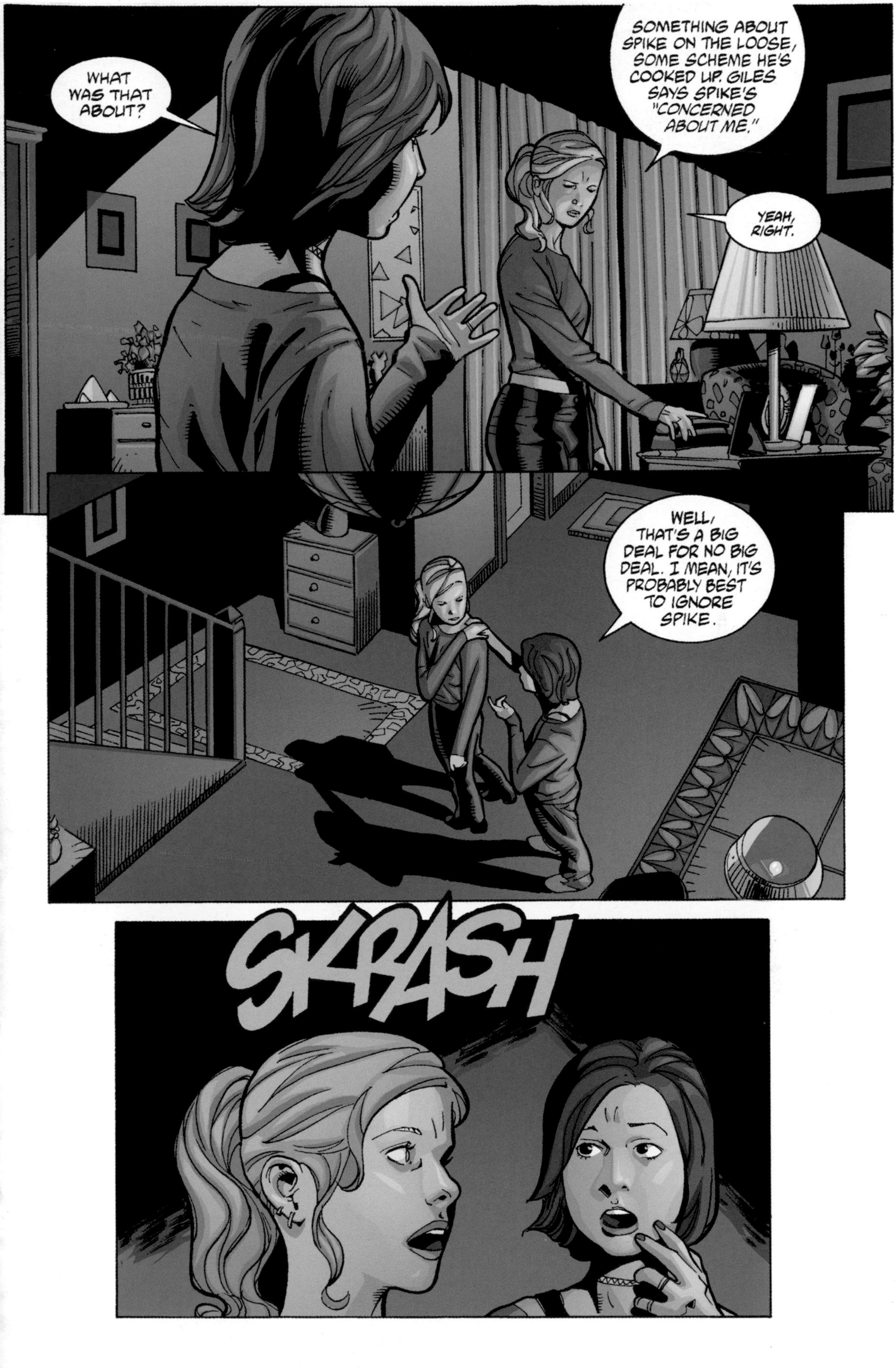
WHAT WAS THAT ABOUT?
SOMETHING ABOUT SPIKE ON THE LOOSE, SOME SCHEME HE'S COOKED UP. GILES SAYS SPIKE'S "CONCERNED ABOUT ME."
YEAH, RIGHT.
WELL, THAT'S A BIG DEAL FOR NO BIG DEAL. I MEAN, IT'S PROBABLY BEST TO IGNORE SPIKE.
SKRASH

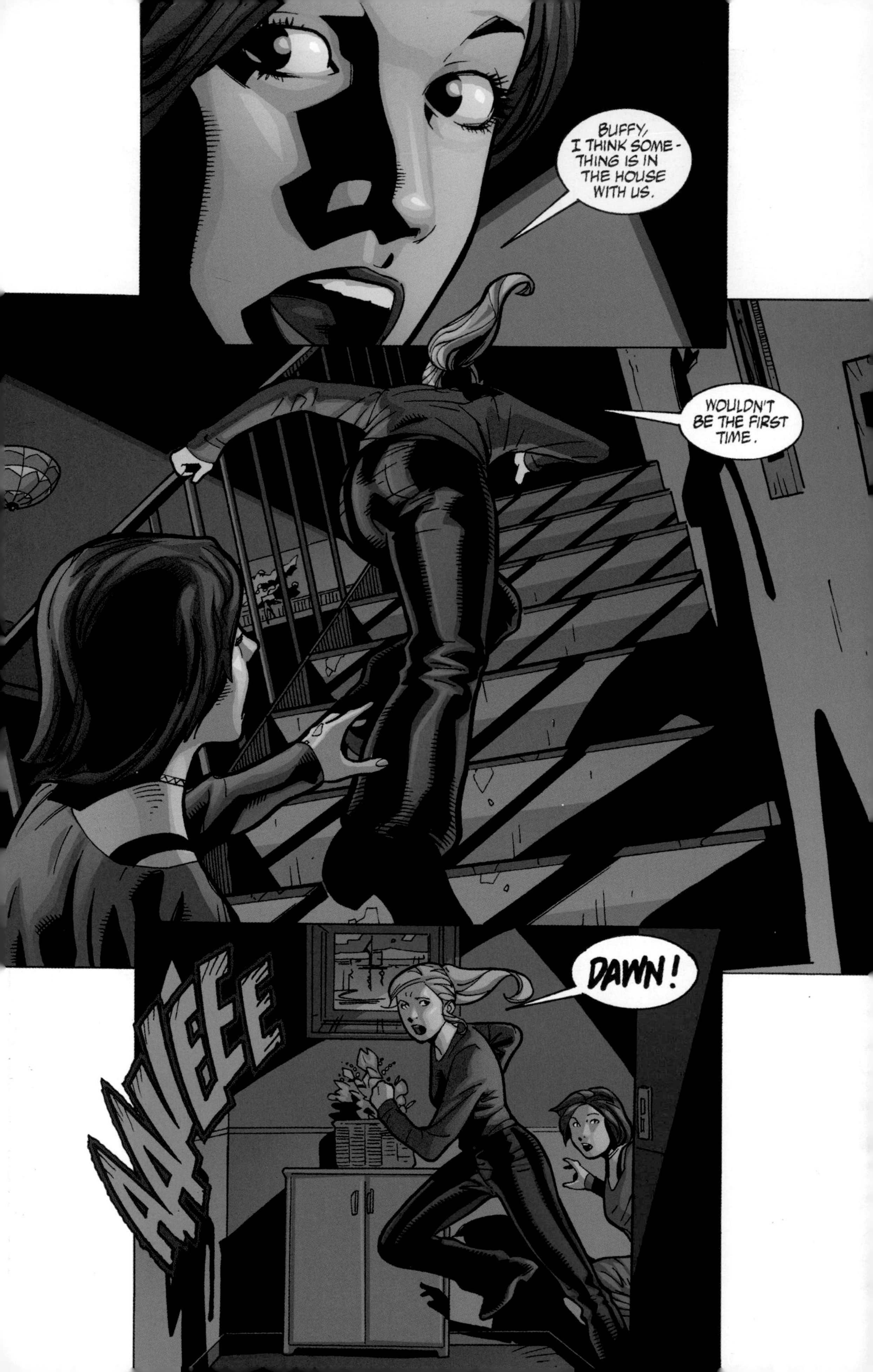
BUFFY, I THINK SOME-THING IS IN THE HOUSE WITH US.
WOULDN'T BE THE FIRST TIME.
AAWEEE
DAWN!

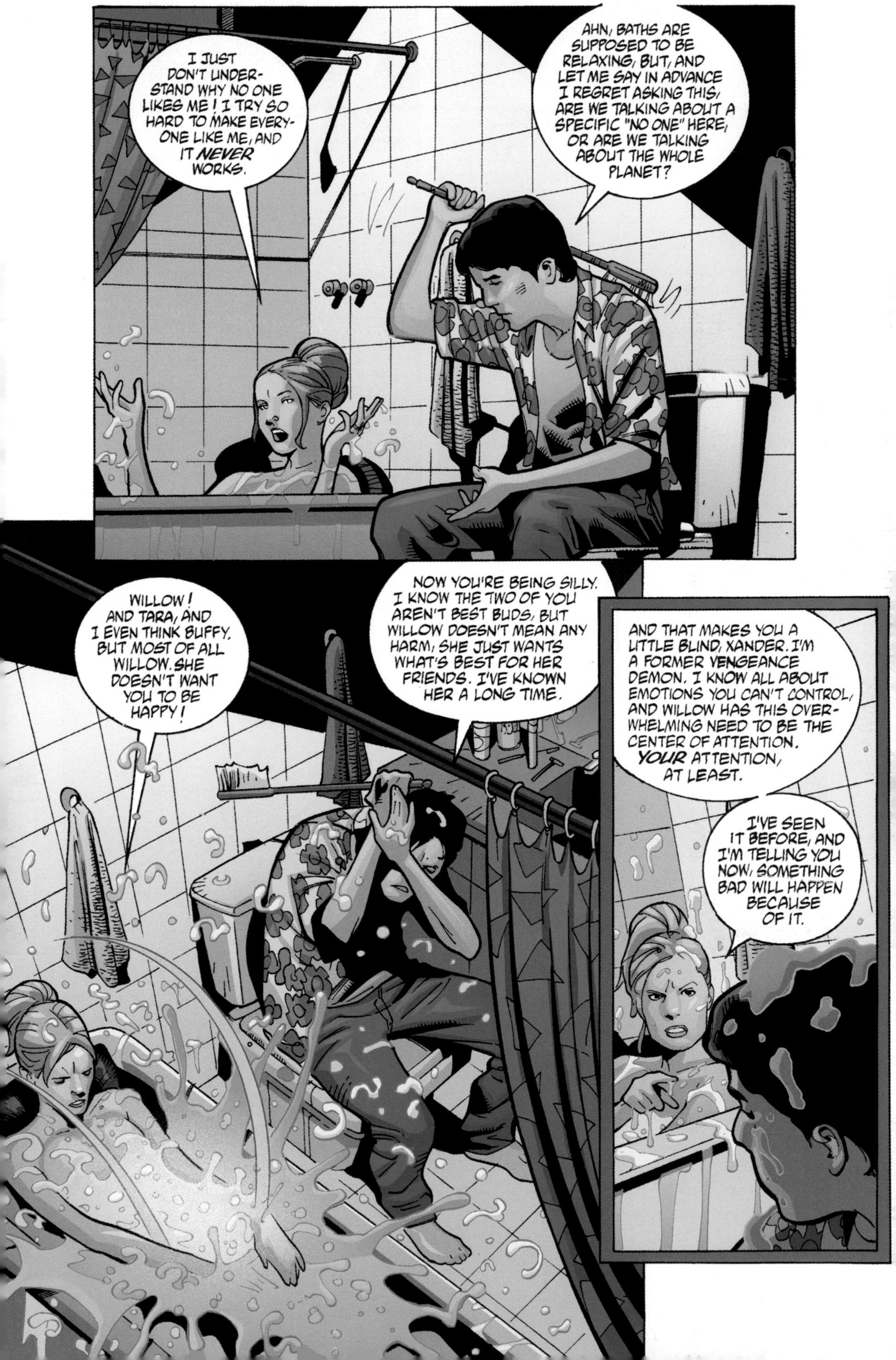
I JUST DON'T UNDER-STAND WHY NO ONE LIKES ME! I TRY SO HARD TO MAKE EVERY-ONE LIKE ME, AND IT NEVER WORKS.
AHN, BATHS ARE SUPPOSED TO BE RELAXING, BUT, AND LET ME SAY IN ADVANCE I REGRET ASKING THIS, ARE WE TALKING ABOUT A SPECIFIC "NO ONE" HERE, OR ARE WE TALKING ABOUT THE WHOLE PLANET?
WILLOW! AND TARA, AND I EVEN THINK BUFFY. BUT MOST OF ALL WILLOW. SHE DOESN'T WANT YOU TO BE HAPPY!
NOW YOU'RE BEING SILLY. I KNOW THE TWO OF YOU AREN'T BEST BUDS, BUT WILLOW DOESN'T MEAN ANY HARM; SHE JUST WANTS WHAT'S BEST FOR HER FRIENDS. I'VE KNOWN HER A LONG TIME.
AND THAT MAKES YOU A LITTLE BLIND, XANDER. I'M A FORMER VENGEANCE DEMON. I KNOW ALL ABOUT EMOTIONS YOU CAN'T CONTROL, AND WILLOW HAS THIS OVER-WHELMING NEED TO BE THE CENTER OF ATTENTION. YOUR ATTENTION, AT LEAST.
I'VE SEEN IT BEFORE, AND I'M TELLING YOU NOW, SOMETHING BAD WILL HAPPEN BECAUSE OF IT.

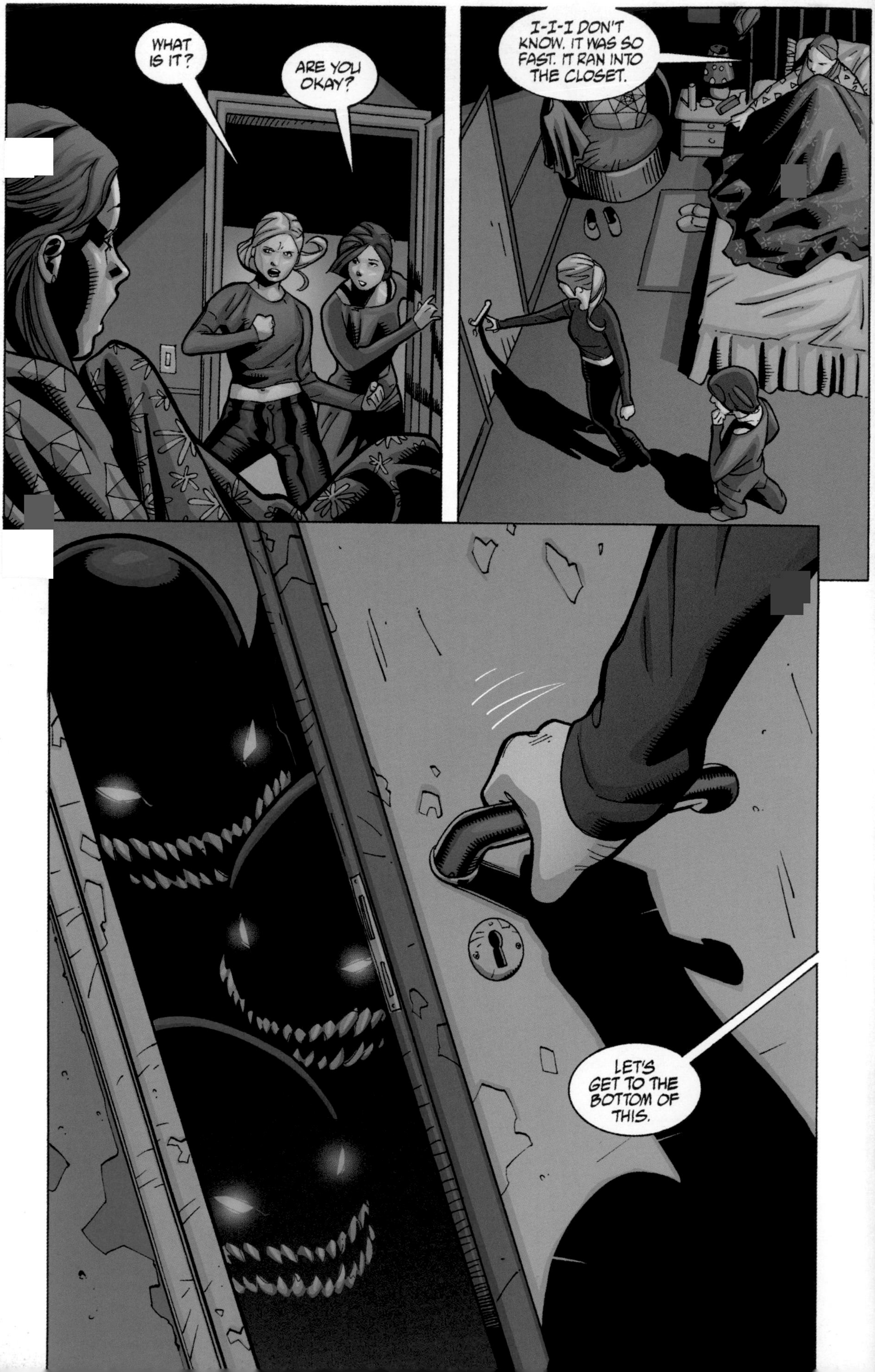
WHAT IS IT?
ARE YOU OKAY?
I-I-I DON'T KNOW. IT WAS SO FAST. IT RAN INTO THE CLOSET.
LET'S GET TO THE BOTTOM OF THIS.

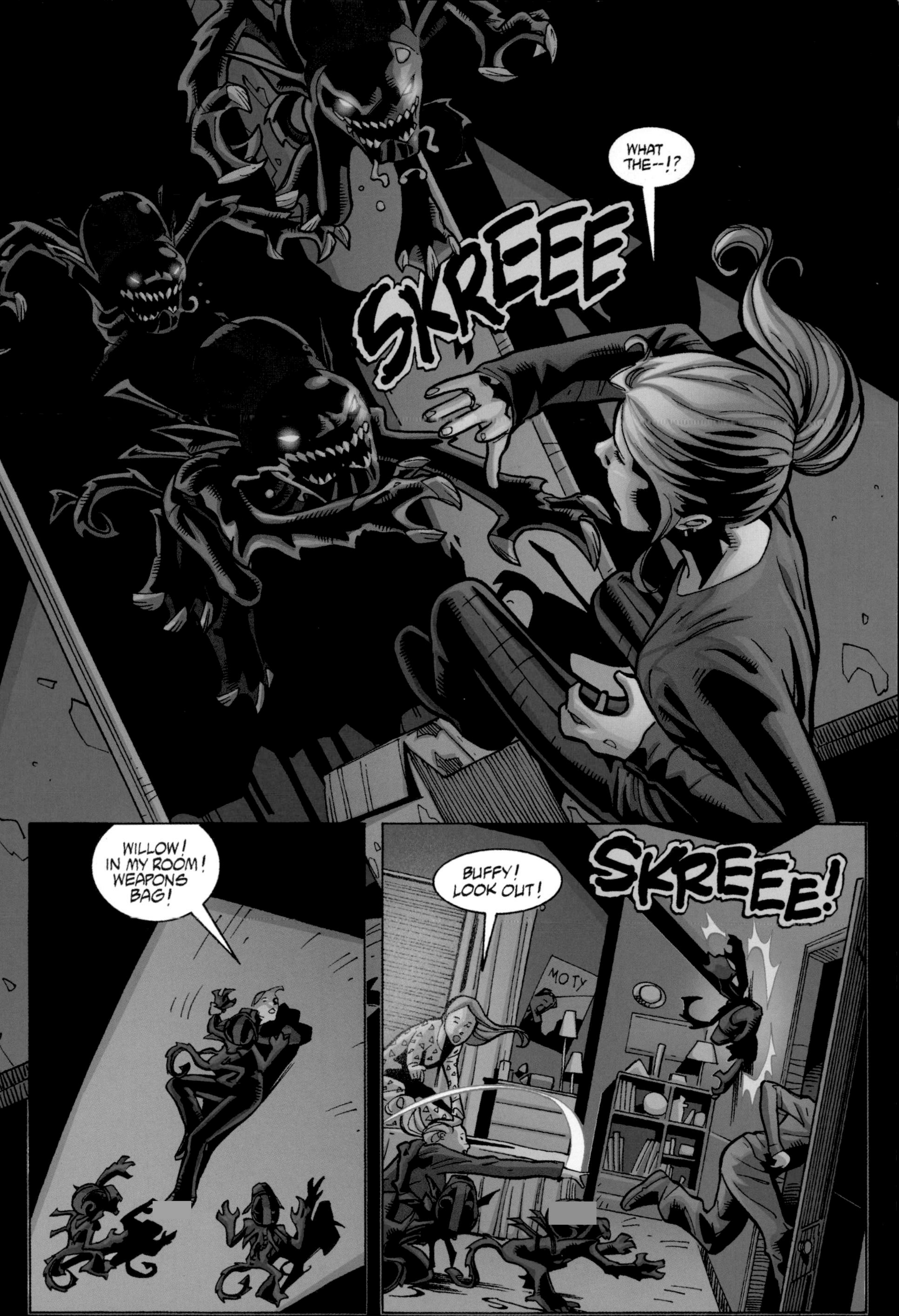
WHAT THE--!?
SKREEE
WILLOW! IN MY ROOM! WEAPONS BAG!
BUFFY! LOOK OUT!
SKREEEE!
MOTY

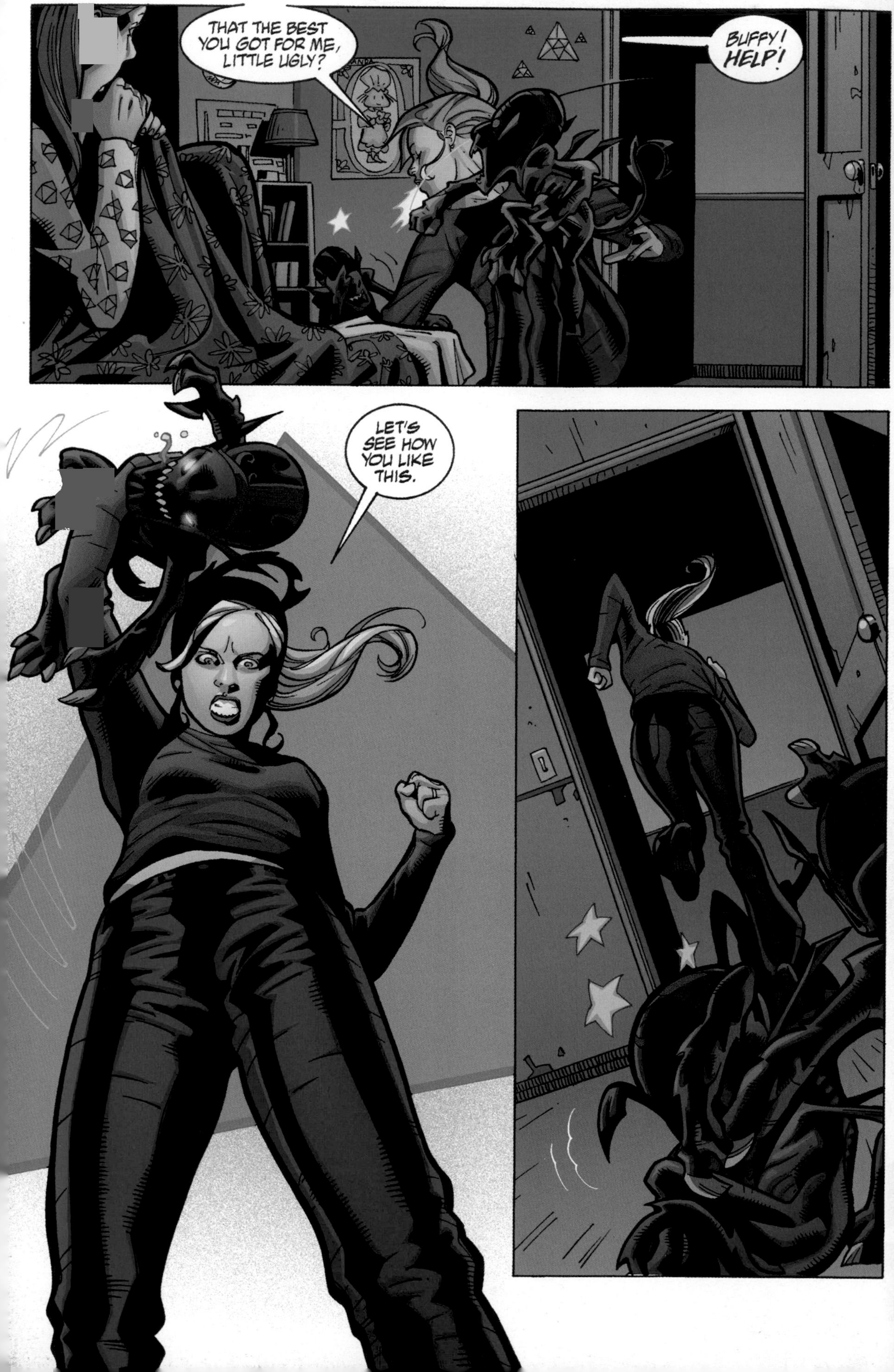
THAT THE BEST YOU GOT FOR ME, LITTLE UGLY?
BUFFY! HELP!
LET'S SEE HOW YOU LIKE THIS.

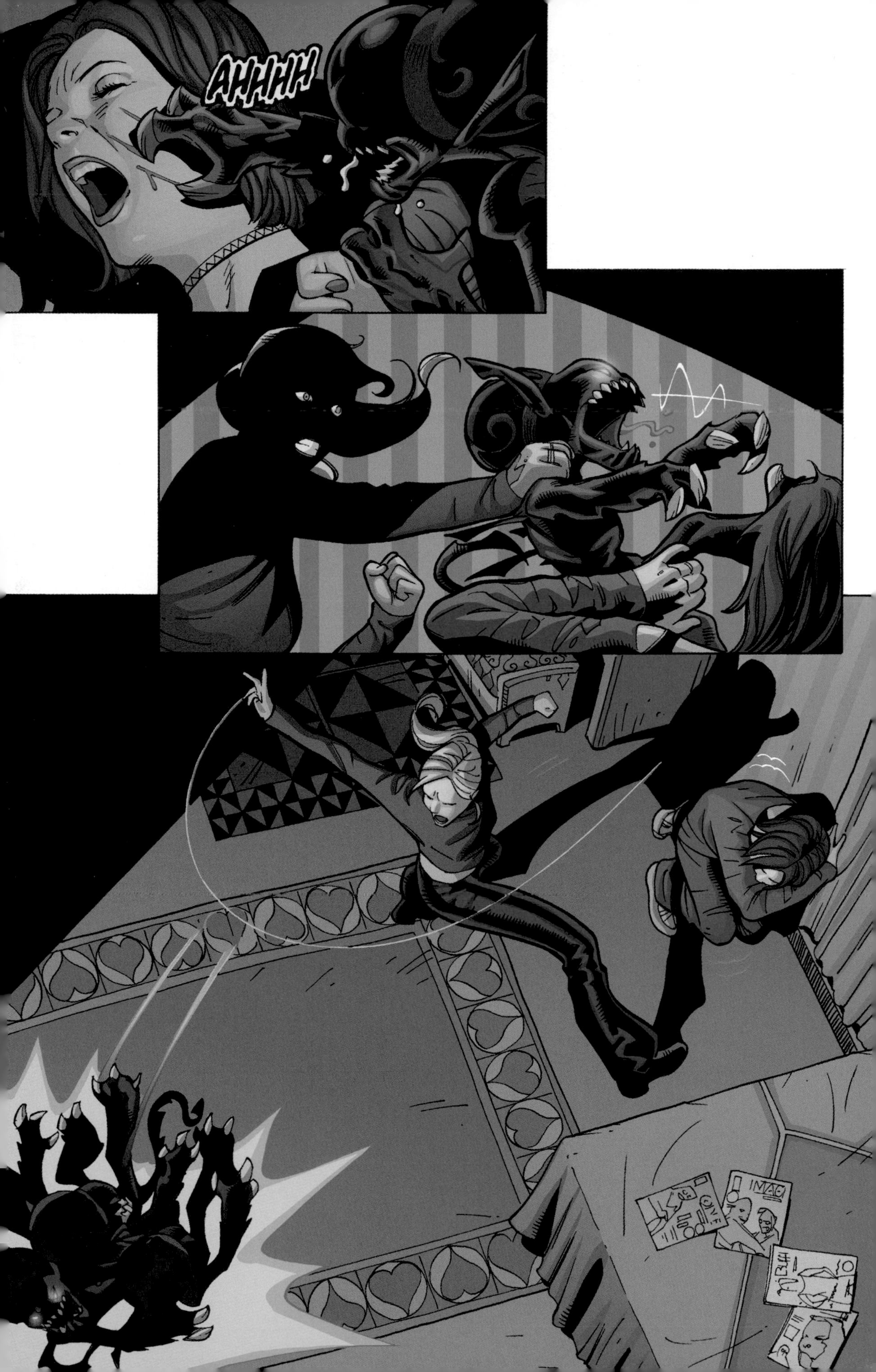
AHHHH

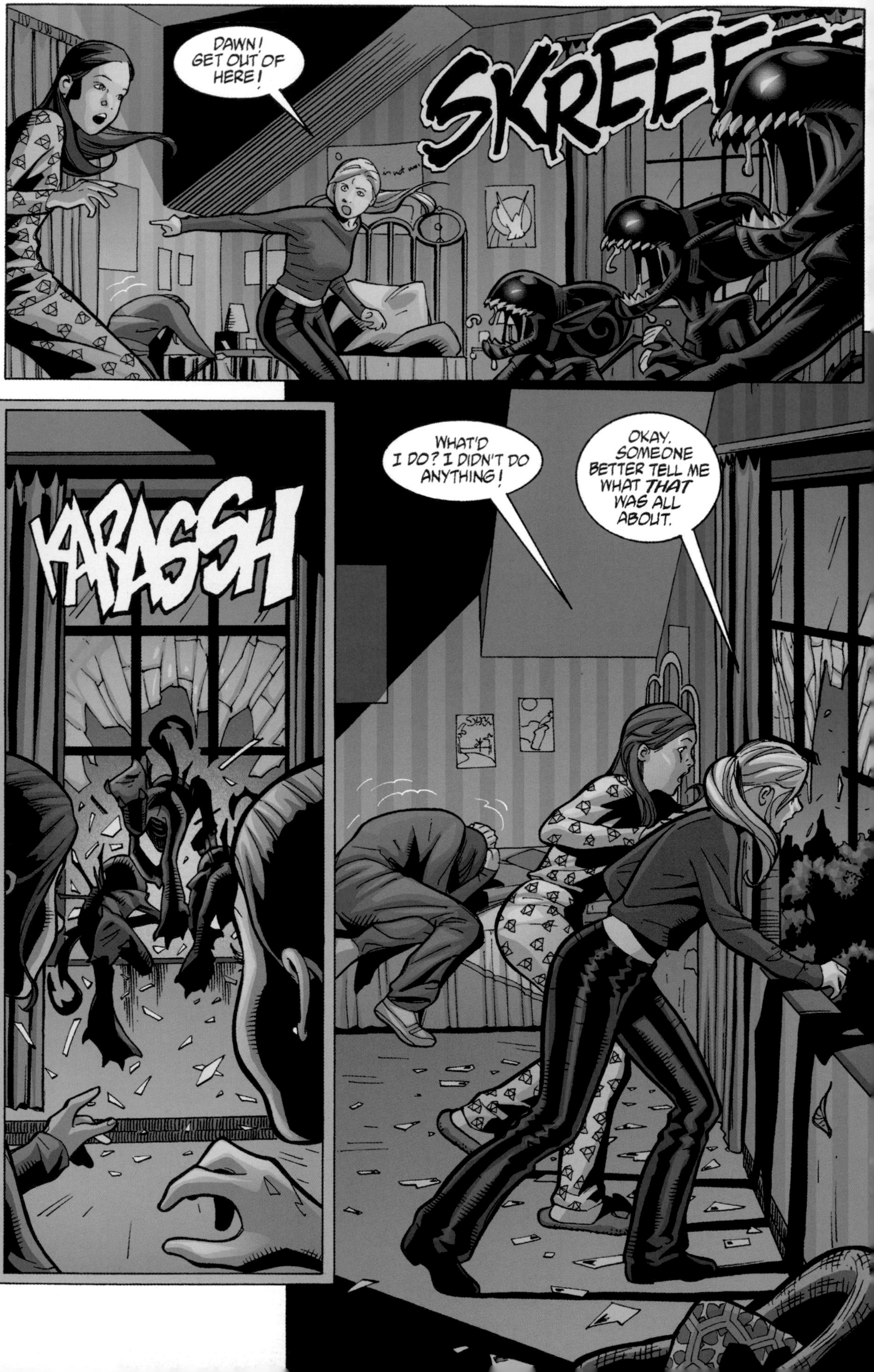
DAWN! GET OUT OF HERE!
SKREEE
KARASSH
WHAT'D I DO? I DIDN'T DO ANYTHING!
OKAY. SOMEONE BETTER TELL ME WHAT THAT WAS ALL ABOUT.

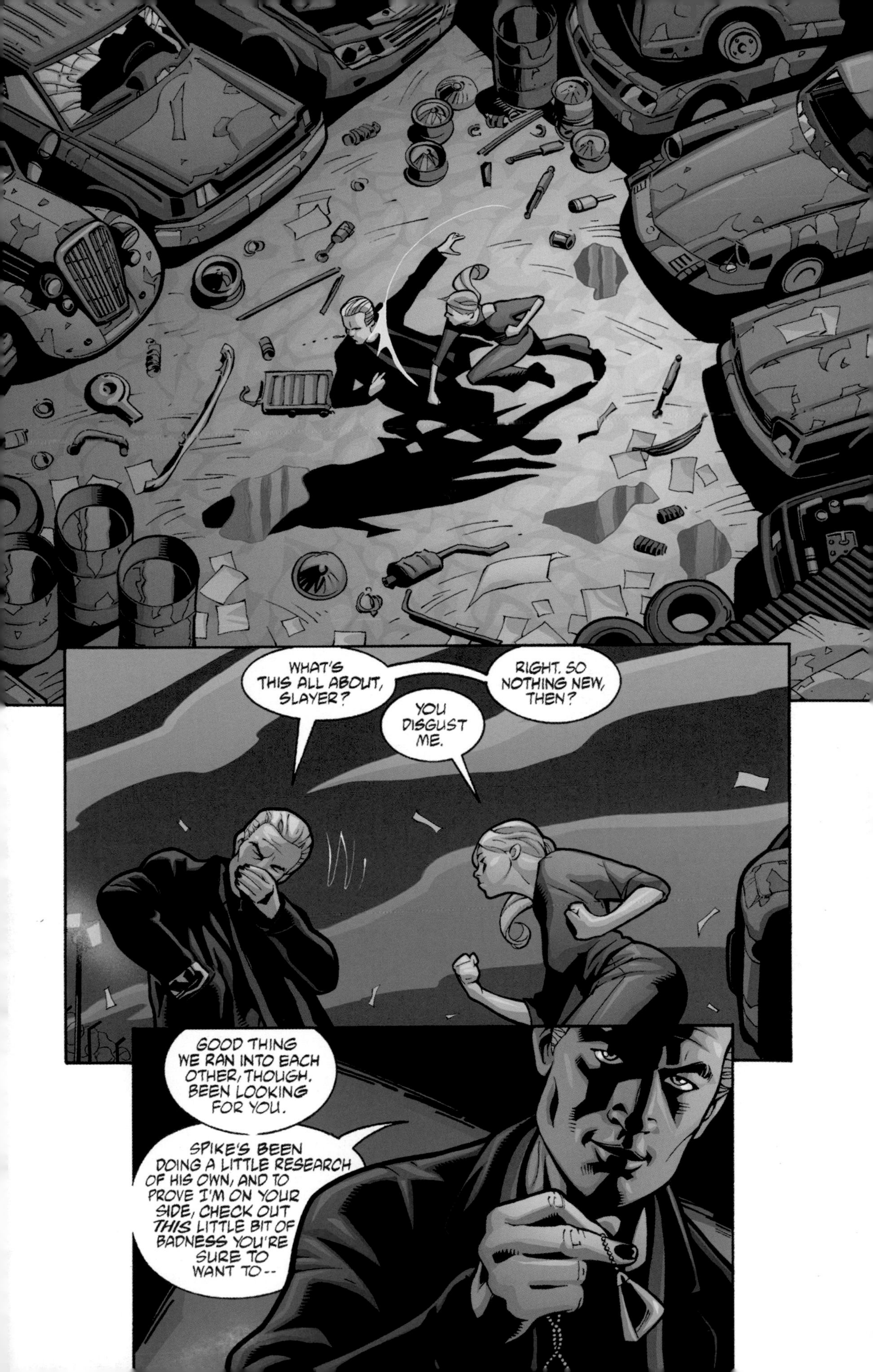
WHAT'S THIS ALL ABOUT, SLAYER?
YOU DISGUST ME.
RIGHT. SO NOTHING NEW, THEN?
GOOD THING WE RAN INTO EACH OTHER, THOUGH. BEEN LOOKING FOR YOU.
SPIKE'S BEEN DOING A LITTLE RESEARCH OF HIS OWN, AND TO PROVE I'M ON YOUR SIDE, CHECK OUT *THIS* LITTLE BIT OF BADNESS YOU'RE SURE TO WANT TO--

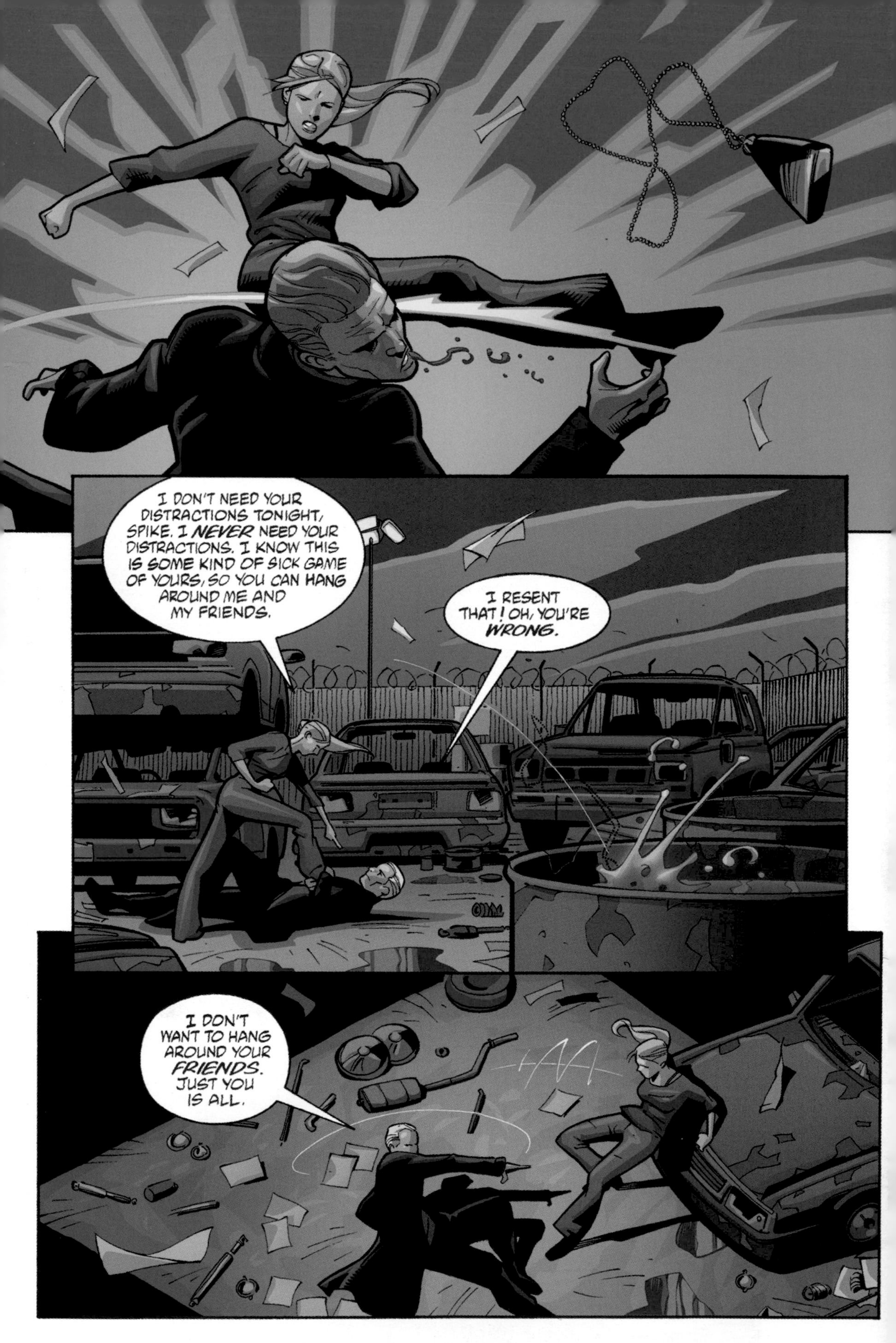
I DON'T NEED YOUR DISTRACTIONS TONIGHT, SPIKE. I NEVER NEED YOUR DISTRACTIONS. I KNOW THIS IS SOME KIND OF SICK GAME OF YOURS, SO YOU CAN HANG AROUND ME AND MY FRIENDS.
I RESENT THAT! OH, YOU'RE WRONG.
I DON'T WANT TO HANG AROUND YOUR FRIENDS. JUST YOU IS ALL.

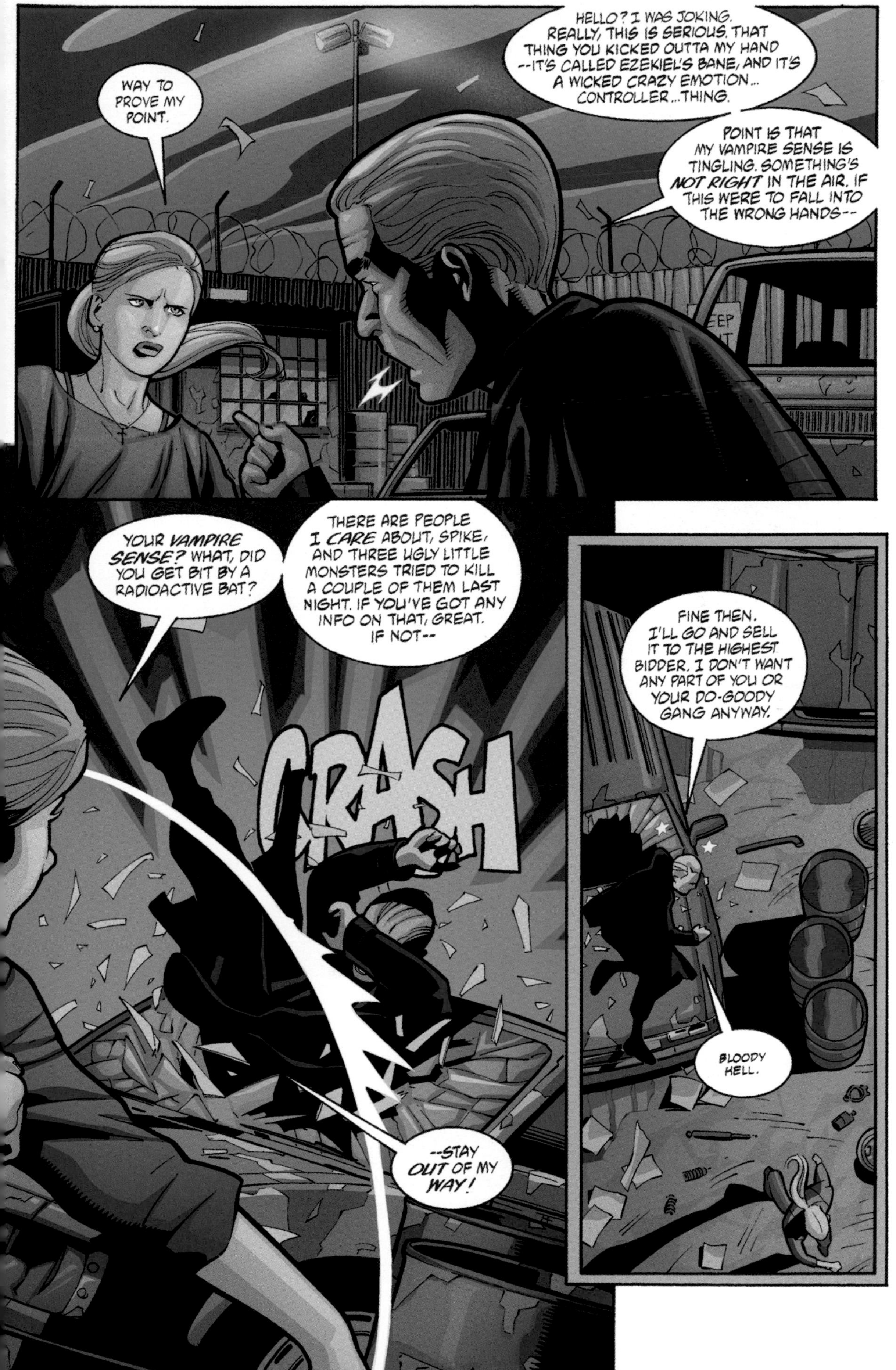
WAY TO PROVE MY POINT.
HELLO? I WAS JOKING. REALLY, THIS IS SERIOUS. THAT THING YOU KICKED OUTTA MY HAND --IT'S CALLED EZEKIEL'S BANE, AND IT'S A WICKED CRAZY EMOTION... CONTROLLER...THING.
POINT IS THAT MY VAMPIRE SENSE IS TINGLING. SOMETHING'S NOT RIGHT IN THE AIR. IF THIS WERE TO FALL INTO THE WRONG HANDS--
YOUR VAMPIRE SENSE? WHAT, DID YOU GET BIT BY A RADIOACTIVE BAT?
THERE ARE PEOPLE I CARE ABOUT, SPIKE, AND THREE UGLY LITTLE MONSTERS TRIED TO KILL A COUPLE OF THEM LAST NIGHT. IF YOU'VE GOT ANY INFO ON THAT, GREAT. IF NOT--
CRASH
--STAY OUT OF MY WAY!
FINE THEN. I'LL GO AND SELL IT TO THE HIGHEST BIDDER. I DON'T WANT ANY PART OF YOU OR YOUR DO-GOODY GANG ANYWAY.
BLOODY HELL.

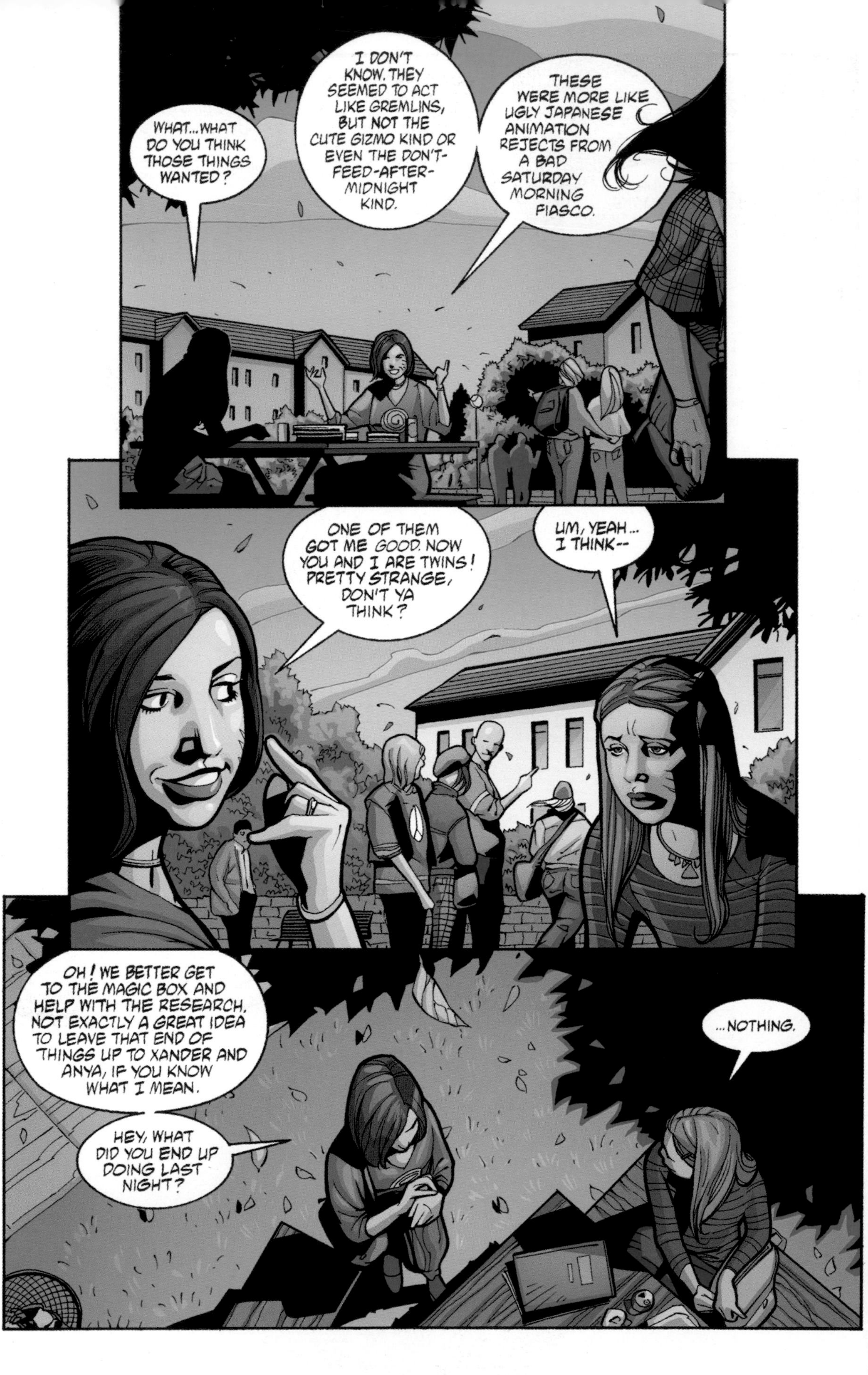
WHAT...WHAT DO YOU THINK THOSE THINGS WANTED?
I DON'T KNOW. THEY SEEMED TO ACT LIKE GREMLINS, BUT NOT THE CUTE GIZMO KIND OR EVEN THE DON'T-FEED-AFTER-MIDNIGHT KIND.
THESE WERE MORE LIKE UGLY JAPANESE ANIMATION REJECTS FROM A BAD SATURDAY MORNING FIASCO.
ONE OF THEM GOT ME GOOD. NOW YOU AND I ARE TWINS! PRETTY STRANGE, DON'T YA THINK?
UM, YEAH... I THINK--
OH! WE BETTER GET TO THE MAGIC BOX AND HELP WITH THE RESEARCH. NOT EXACTLY A GREAT IDEA TO LEAVE THAT END OF THINGS UP TO XANDER AND ANYA, IF YOU KNOW WHAT I MEAN.
HEY, WHAT DID YOU END UP DOING LAST NIGHT?
...NOTHING.

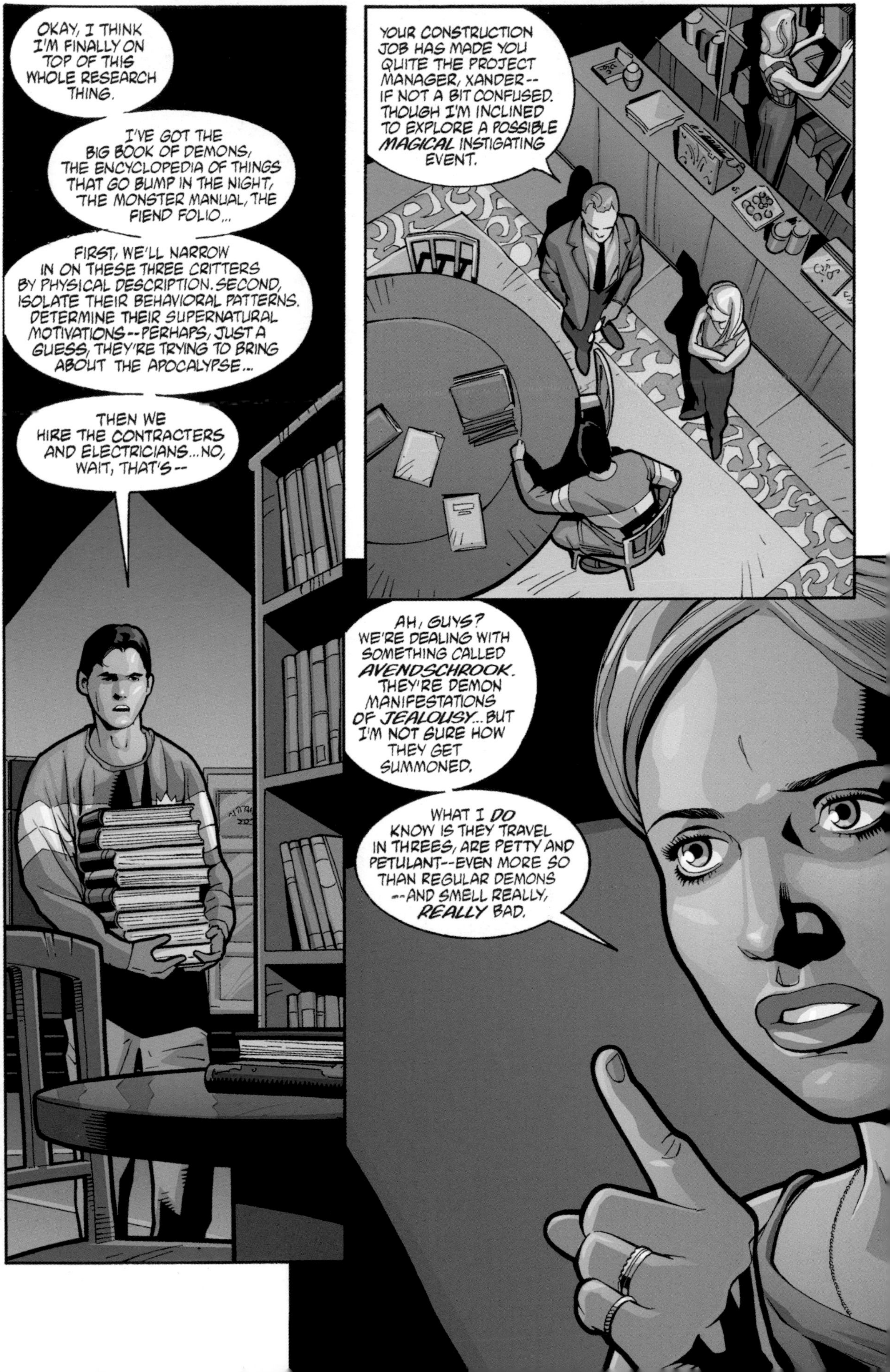
OKAY, I THINK I'M FINALLY ON TOP OF THIS WHOLE RESEARCH THING.
I'VE GOT THE BIG BOOK OF DEMONS, THE ENCYCLOPEDIA OF THINGS THAT GO BUMP IN THE NIGHT, THE MONSTER MANUAL, THE FIEND FOLIO...
FIRST, WE'LL NARROW IN ON THESE THREE CRITTERS BY PHYSICAL DESCRIPTION. SECOND, ISOLATE THEIR BEHAVIORAL PATTERNS. DETERMINE THEIR SUPERNATURAL MOTIVATIONS--PERHAPS, JUST A GUESS, THEY'RE TRYING TO BRING ABOUT THE APOCALYPSE...
THEN WE HIRE THE CONTRACTERS AND ELECTRICIANS...NO, WAIT, THAT'S--
YOUR CONSTRUCTION JOB HAS MADE YOU QUITE THE PROJECT MANAGER, XANDER-- IF NOT A BIT CONFUSED. THOUGH I'M INCLINED TO EXPLORE A POSSIBLE *MAGICAL* INSTIGATING EVENT.
AH, GUYS? WE'RE DEALING WITH SOMETHING CALLED ***AVENDSCHROOK***. THEY'RE DEMON MANIFESTATIONS OF ***JEALOUSY***...BUT I'M NOT SURE HOW THEY GET SUMMONED.
WHAT I *DO* KNOW IS THEY TRAVEL IN THREES, ARE PETTY AND PETULANT--EVEN MORE SO THAN REGULAR DEMONS --AND SMELL REALLY, ***REALLY*** BAD.

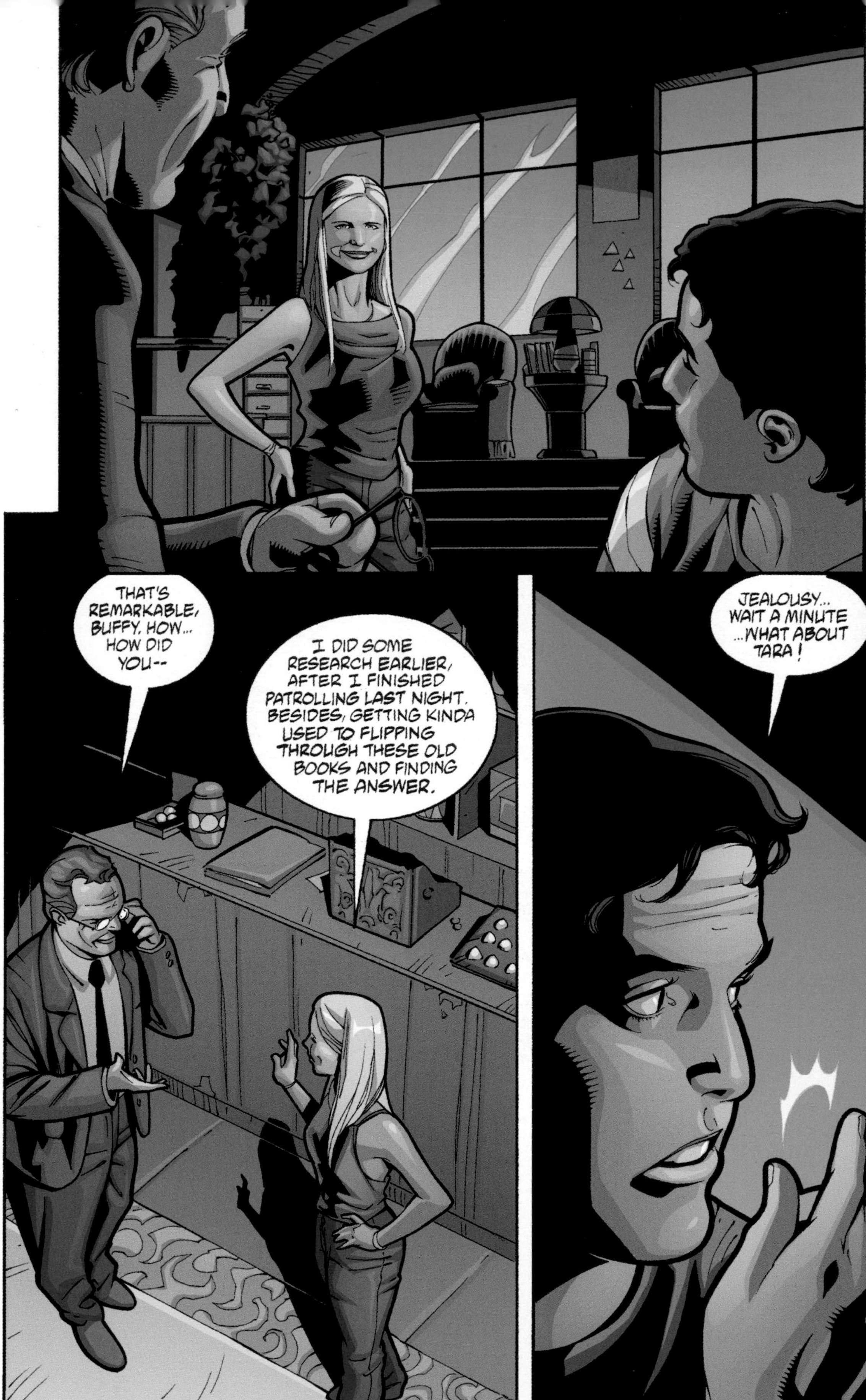
THAT'S REMARKABLE, BUFFY. HOW... HOW DID YOU--
I DID SOME RESEARCH EARLIER, AFTER I FINISHED PATROLLING LAST NIGHT. BESIDES, GETTING KINDA USED TO FLIPPING THROUGH THESE OLD BOOKS AND FINDING THE ANSWER.
JEALOUSY... WAIT A MINUTE ...WHAT ABOUT TARA!

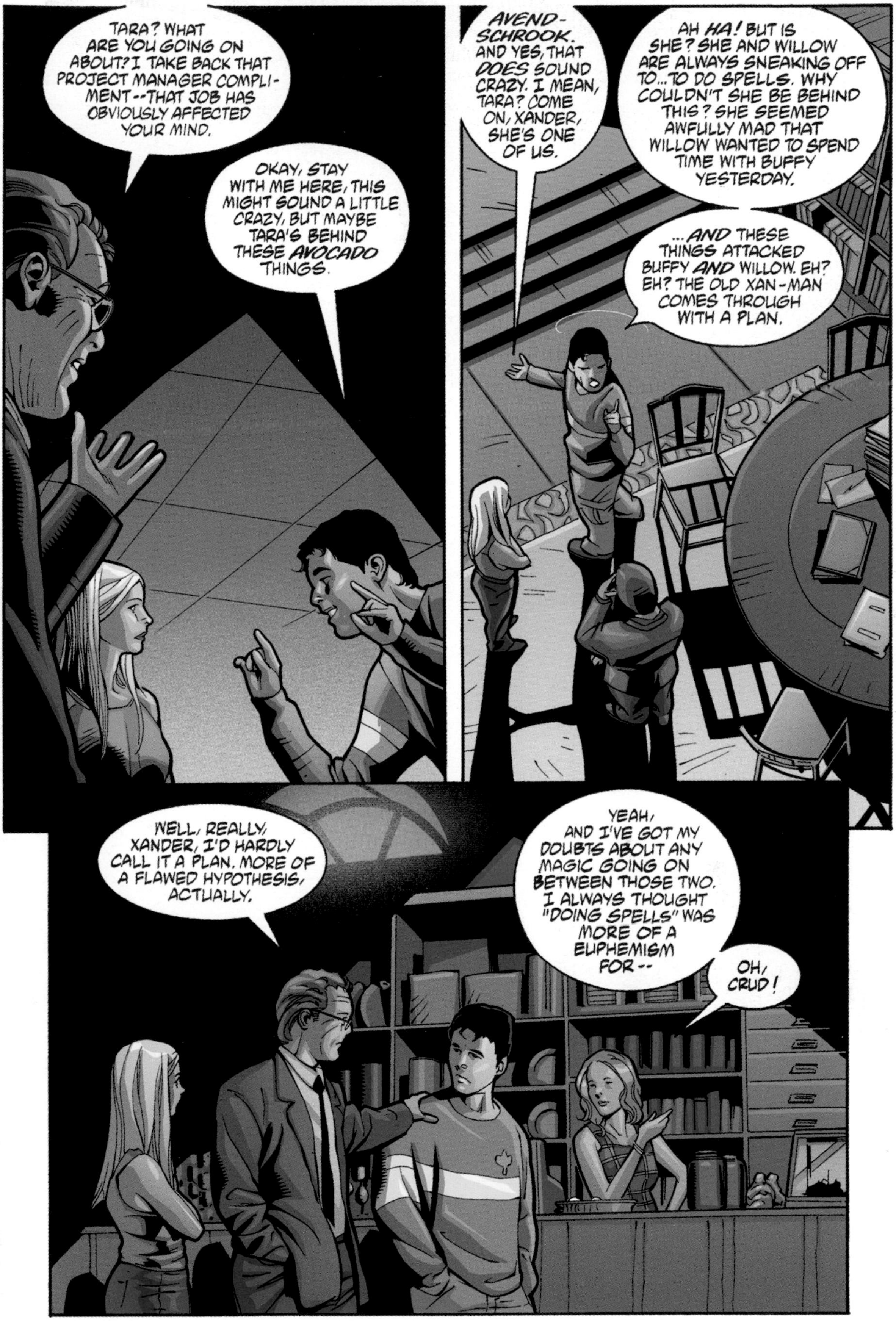
TARA? WHAT ARE YOU GOING ON ABOUT? I TAKE BACK THAT PROJECT MANAGER COMPLIMENT--THAT JOB HAS OBVIOUSLY AFFECTED YOUR MIND.
OKAY, STAY WITH ME HERE, THIS MIGHT SOUND A LITTLE CRAZY, BUT MAYBE TARA'S BEHIND THESE AVOCADO THINGS.
AVEND-SCHROOK. AND YES, THAT DOES SOUND CRAZY. I MEAN, TARA? COME ON, XANDER, SHE'S ONE OF US.
AH HA! BUT IS SHE? SHE AND WILLOW ARE ALWAYS SNEAKING OFF TO...TO DO SPELLS. WHY COULDN'T SHE BE BEHIND THIS? SHE SEEMED AWFULLY MAD THAT WILLOW WANTED TO SPEND TIME WITH BUFFY YESTERDAY.
...AND THESE THINGS ATTACKED BUFFY AND WILLOW. EH? EH? THE OLD XAN-MAN COMES THROUGH WITH A PLAN.
WELL, REALLY, XANDER, I'D HARDLY CALL IT A PLAN. MORE OF A FLAWED HYPOTHESIS, ACTUALLY.
YEAH, AND I'VE GOT MY DOUBTS ABOUT ANY MAGIC GOING ON BETWEEN THOSE TWO. I ALWAYS THOUGHT "DOING SPELLS" WAS MORE OF A EUPHEMISM FOR--
OH, CRUD!

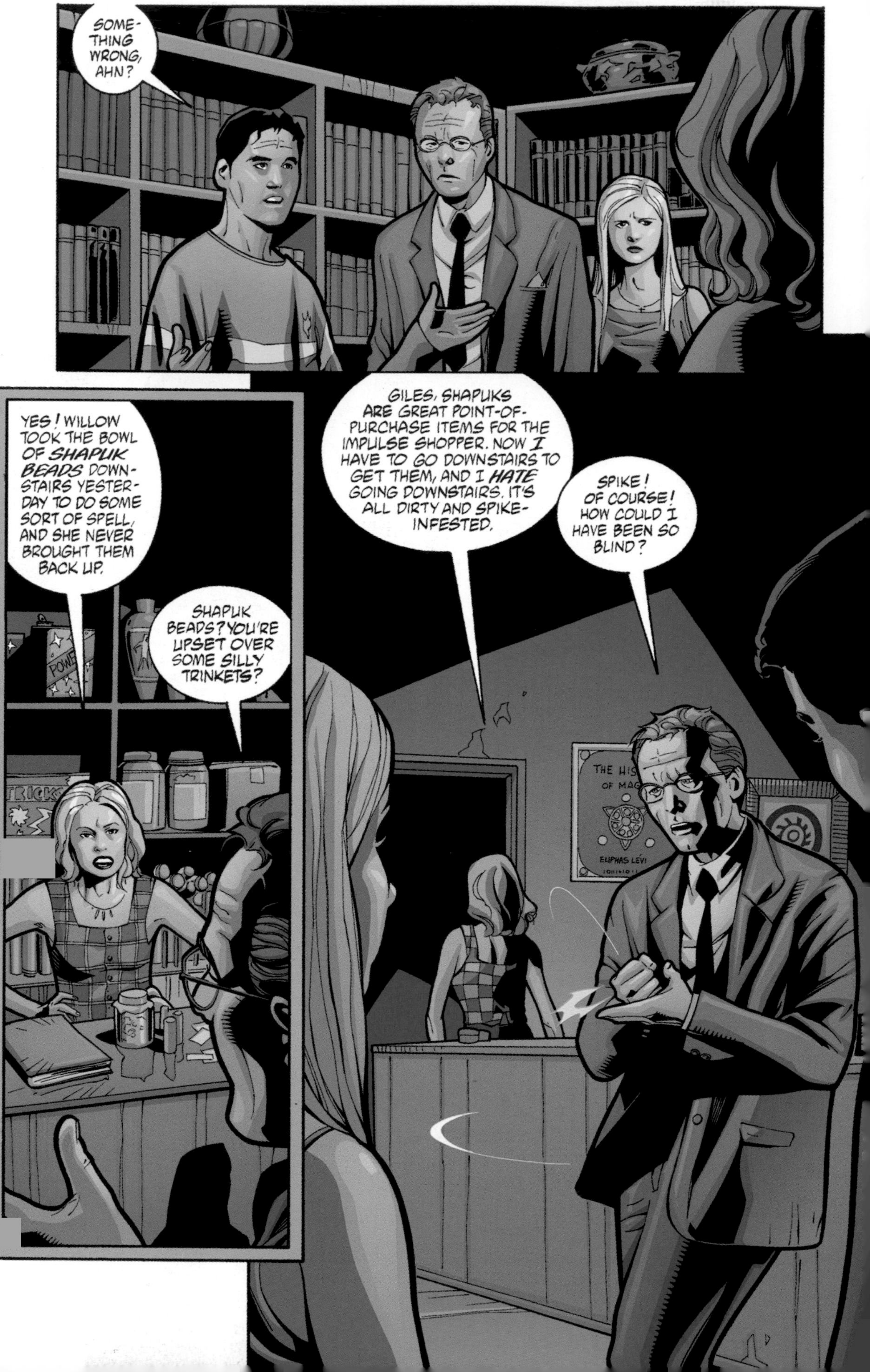
SOME-THING WRONG, AHN?
YES! WILLOW TOOK THE BOWL OF SHAPUK BEADS DOWN-STAIRS YESTER-DAY TO DO SOME SORT OF SPELL, AND SHE NEVER BROUGHT THEM BACK UP.
SHAPUK BEADS? YOU'RE UPSET OVER SOME SILLY TRINKETS?
GILES, SHAPUKS ARE GREAT POINT-OF-PURCHASE ITEMS FOR THE IMPULSE SHOPPER. NOW I HAVE TO GO DOWNSTAIRS TO GET THEM, AND I HATE GOING DOWNSTAIRS. IT'S ALL DIRTY AND SPIKE-INFESTED.
SPIKE! OF COURSE! HOW COULD I HAVE BEEN SO BLIND?
THE HIS OF MAG
ELIPHAS LEVI
TRICKS
POWE

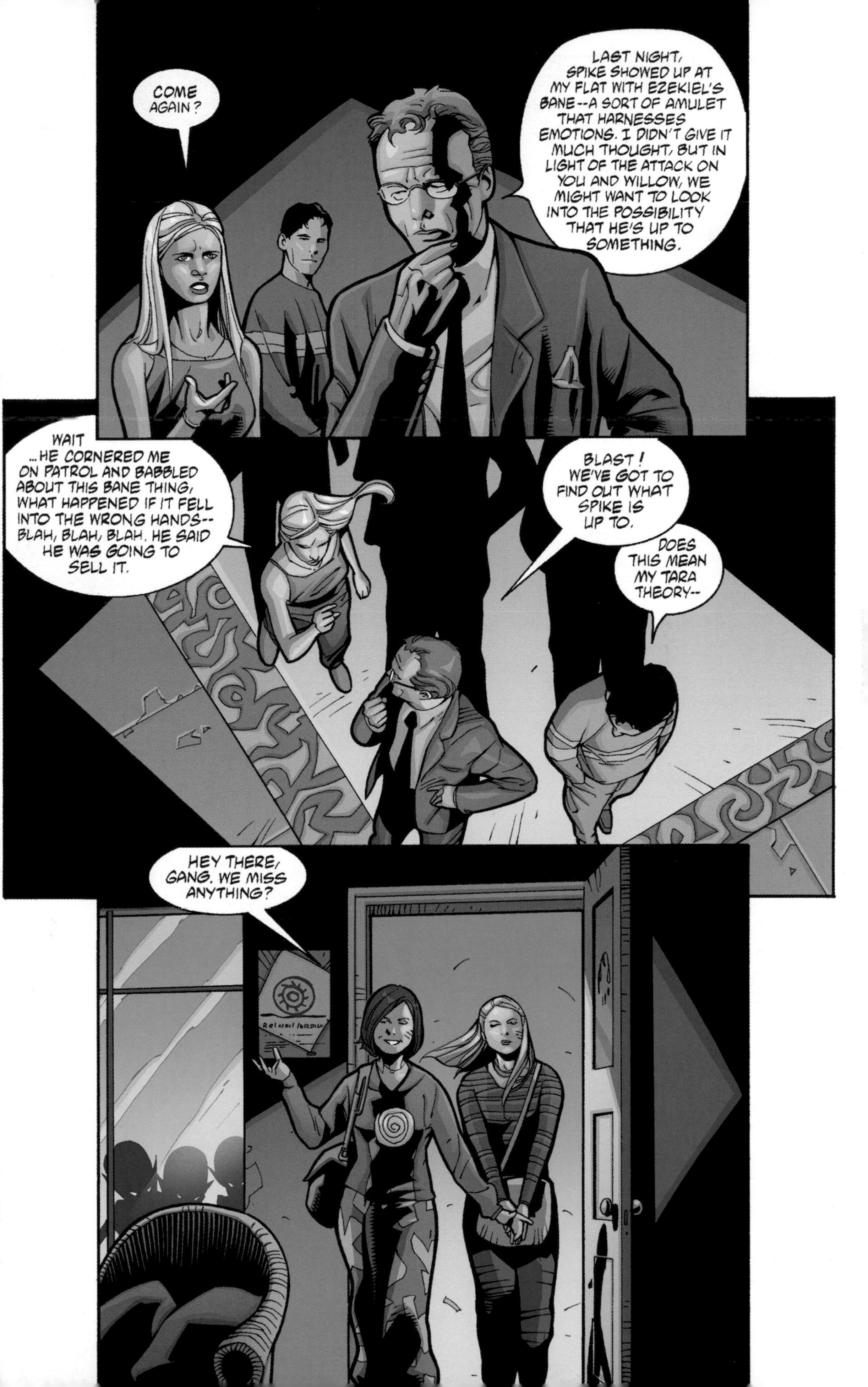
COME AGAIN?
LAST NIGHT, SPIKE SHOWED UP AT MY FLAT WITH EZEKIEL'S BANE--A SORT OF AMULET THAT HARNESSES EMOTIONS. I DIDN'T GIVE IT MUCH THOUGHT, BUT IN LIGHT OF THE ATTACK ON YOU AND WILLOW, WE MIGHT WANT TO LOOK INTO THE POSSIBILITY THAT HE'S UP TO SOMETHING.
WAIT ...HE CORNERED ME ON PATROL AND BABBLED ABOUT THIS BANE THING, WHAT HAPPENED IF IT FELL INTO THE WRONG HANDS--BLAH, BLAH, BLAH. HE SAID HE WAS GOING TO SELL IT.
BLAST! WE'VE GOT TO FIND OUT WHAT SPIKE IS UP TO.
DOES THIS MEAN MY TARA THEORY--
HEY THERE, GANG. WE MISS ANYTHING?

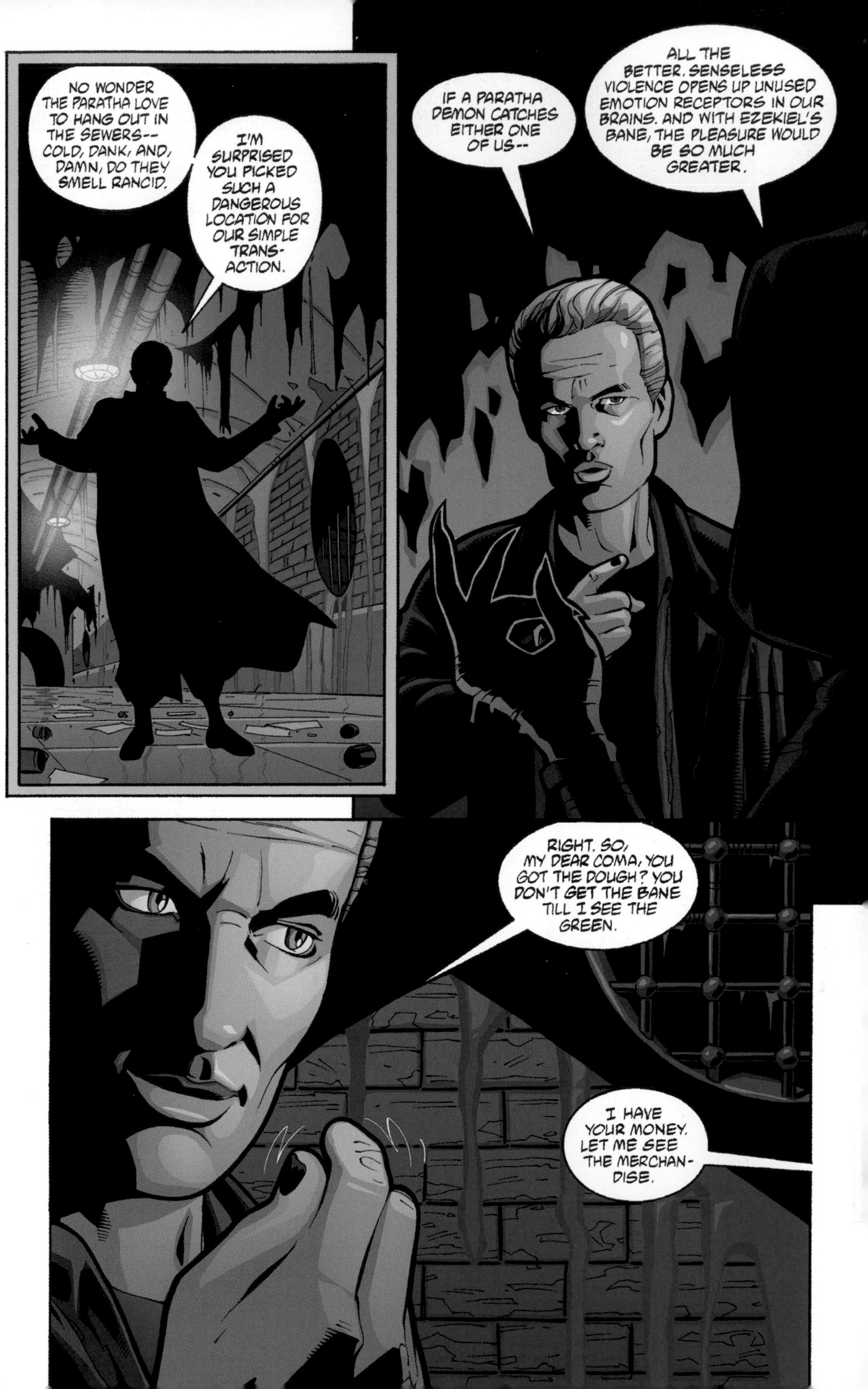
NO WONDER THE PARATHA LOVE TO HANG OUT IN THE SEWERS-- COLD, DANK, AND, DAMN, DO THEY SMELL RANCID.
I'M SURPRISED YOU PICKED SUCH A DANGEROUS LOCATION FOR OUR SIMPLE TRANS-ACTION.
IF A PARATHA DEMON CATCHES EITHER ONE OF US--
ALL THE BETTER. SENSELESS VIOLENCE OPENS UP UNUSED EMOTION RECEPTORS IN OUR BRAINS. AND WITH EZEKIEL'S BANE, THE PLEASURE WOULD BE SO MUCH GREATER.
RIGHT. SO, MY DEAR COMA, YOU GOT THE DOUGH? YOU DON'T GET THE BANE TILL I SEE THE GREEN.
I HAVE YOUR MONEY. LET ME SEE THE MERCHAN-DISE.

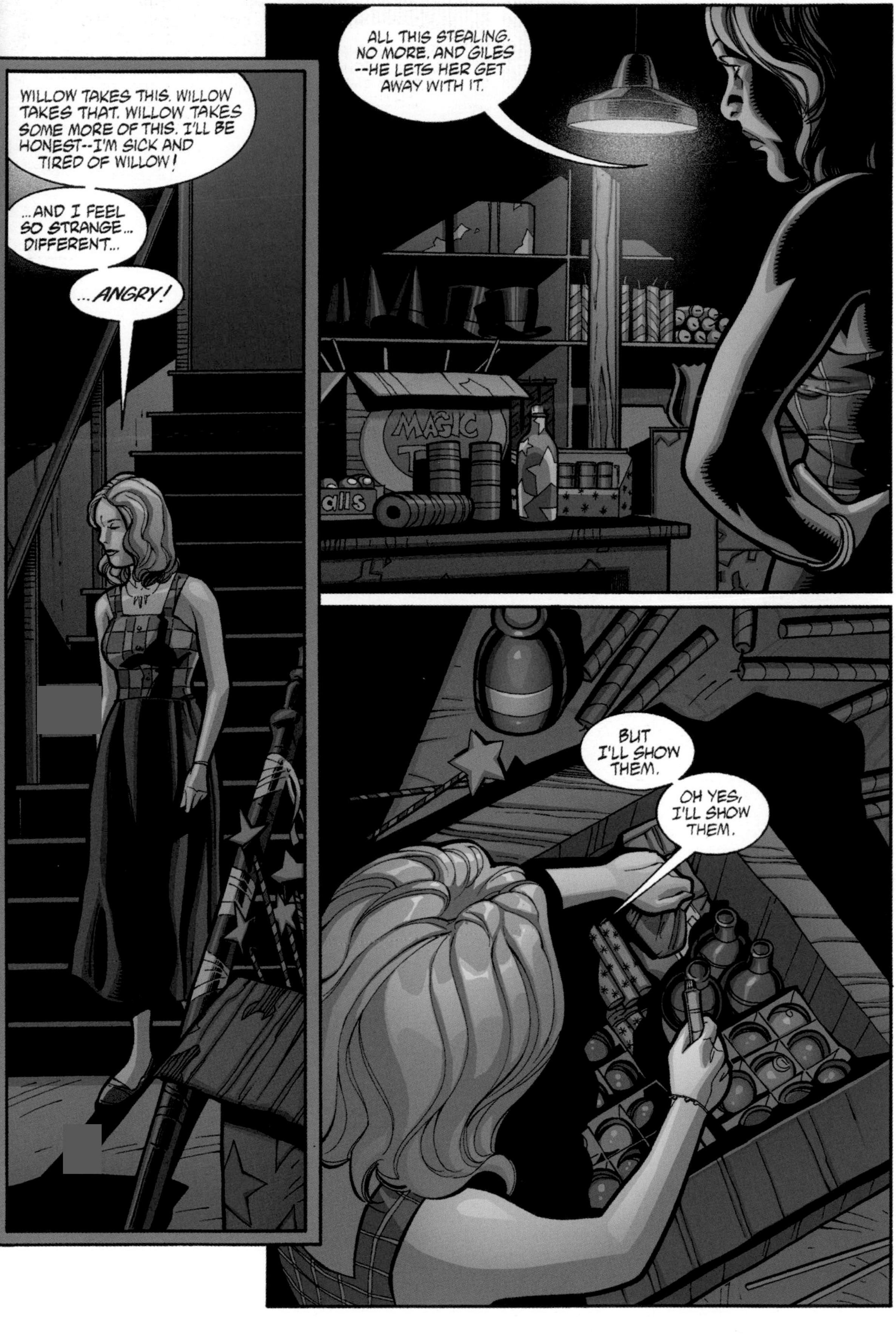
WILLOW TAKES THIS. WILLOW TAKES THAT. WILLOW TAKES SOME MORE OF THIS. I'LL BE HONEST--I'M SICK AND TIRED OF WILLOW!
...AND I FEEL SO STRANGE... DIFFERENT...
...ANGRY!
ALL THIS STEALING. NO MORE. AND GILES --HE LETS HER GET AWAY WITH IT.
MAGIC
alls
BUT I'LL SHOW THEM.
OH YES, I'LL SHOW THEM.

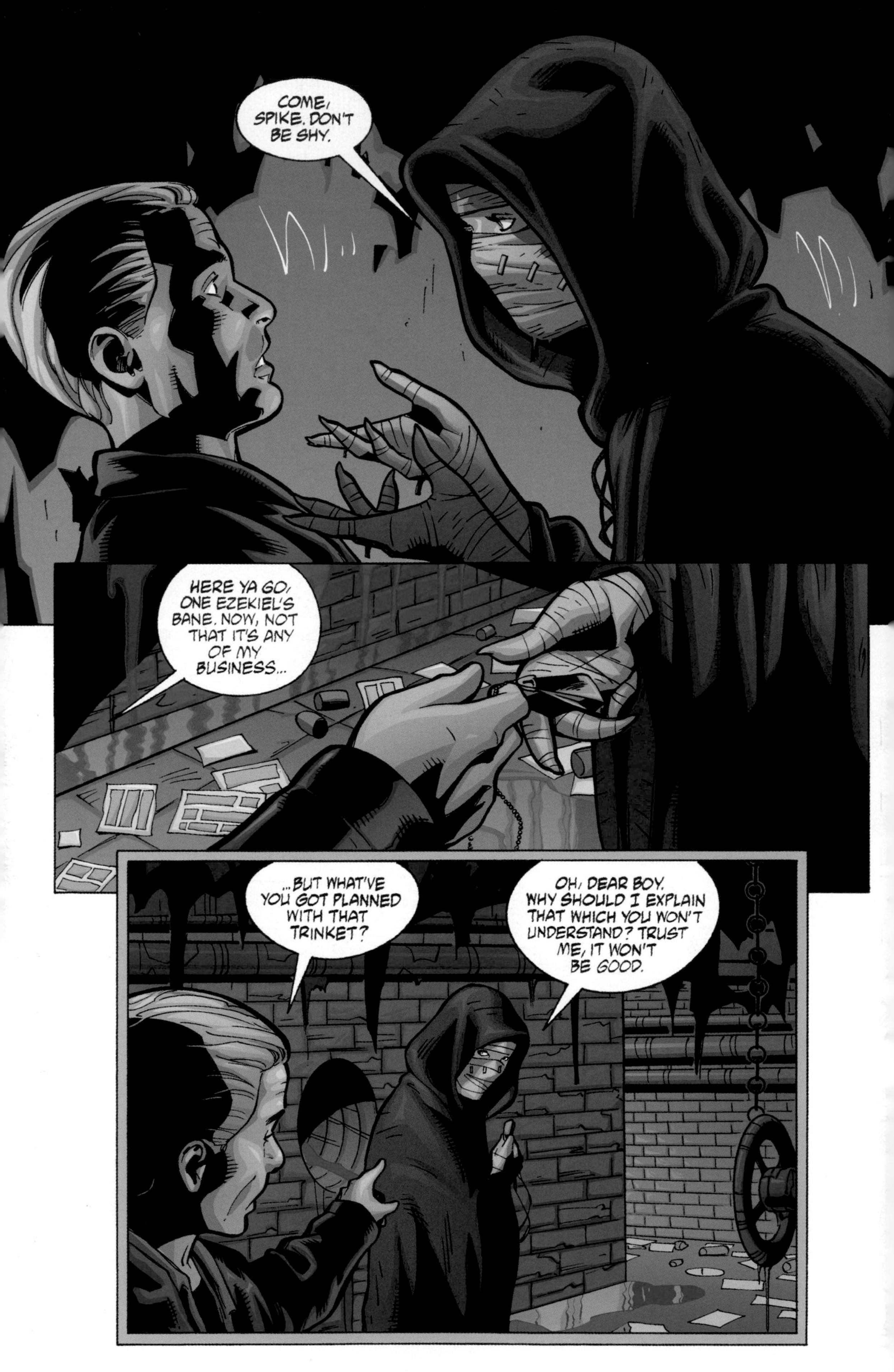
COME, SPIKE. DON'T BE SHY.
HERE YA GO, ONE EZEKIEL'S BANE. NOW, NOT THAT IT'S ANY OF MY BUSINESS...
...BUT WHAT'VE YOU GOT PLANNED WITH THAT TRINKET?
OH, DEAR BOY. WHY SHOULD I EXPLAIN THAT WHICH YOU WON'T UNDERSTAND? TRUST ME, IT WON'T BE GOOD.

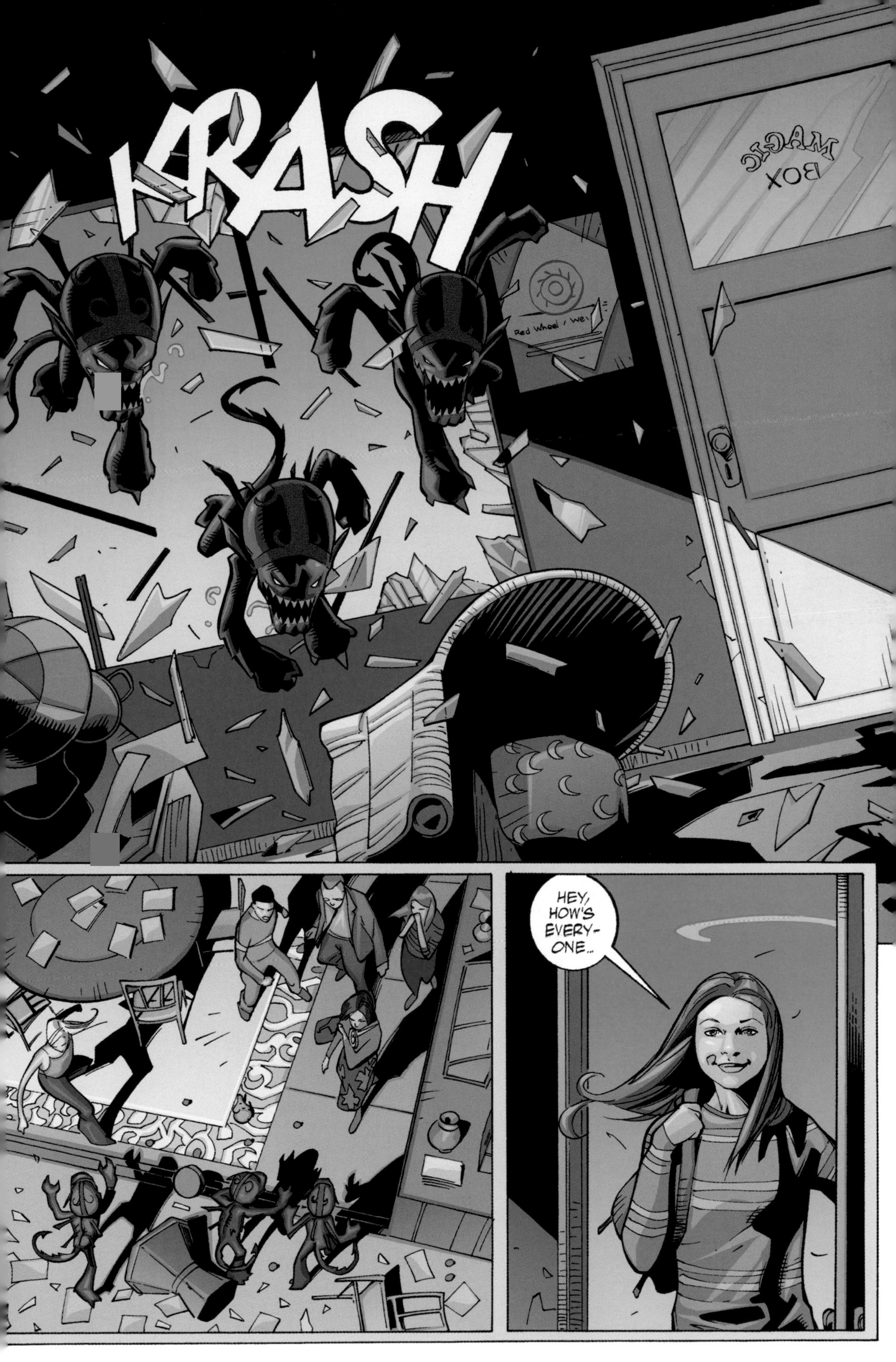
KRASH
HEY, HOW'S EVERY-ONE...

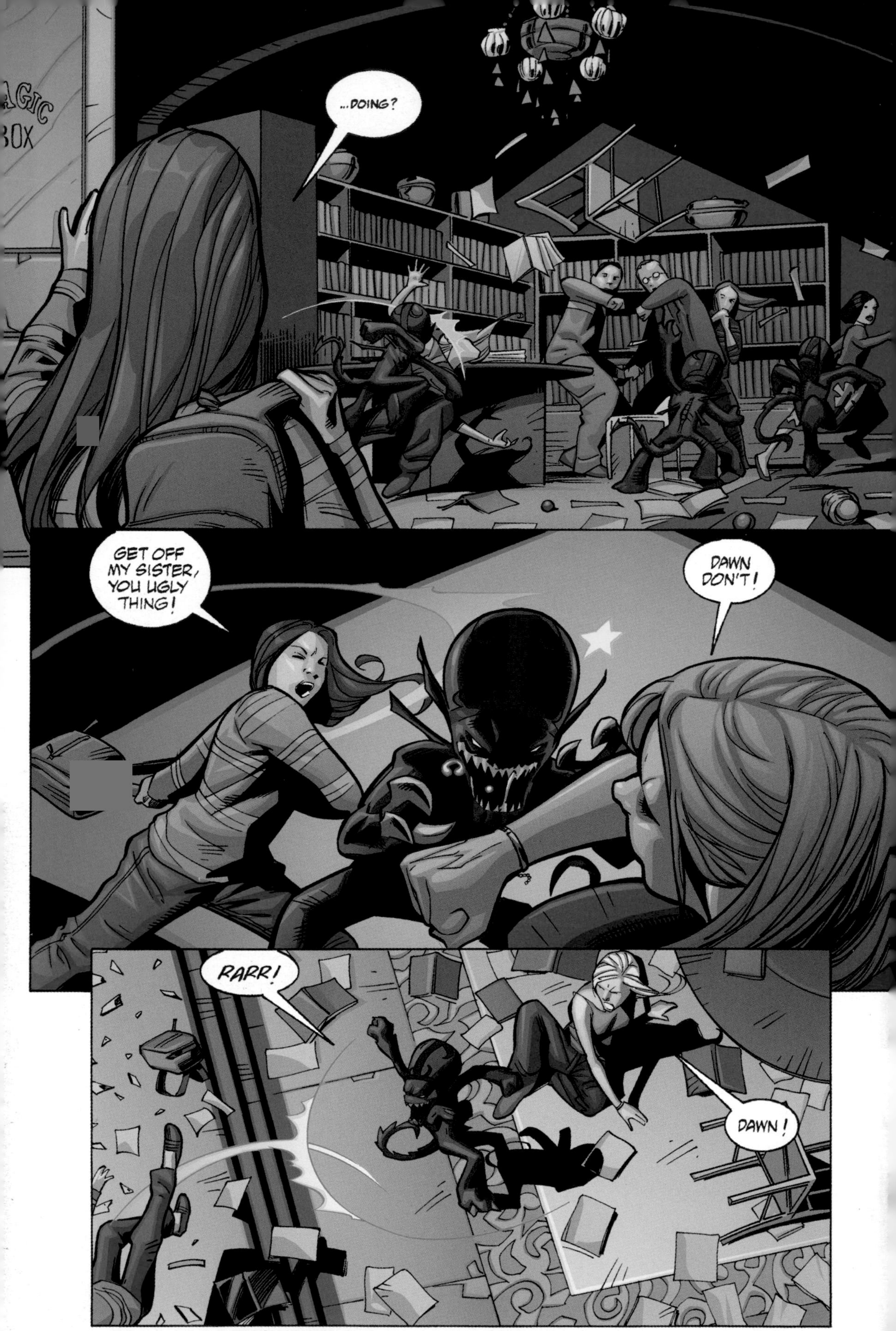
...DOING?
GET OFF MY SISTER, YOU UGLY THING!
DAWN DON'T!
RARR!
DAWN!

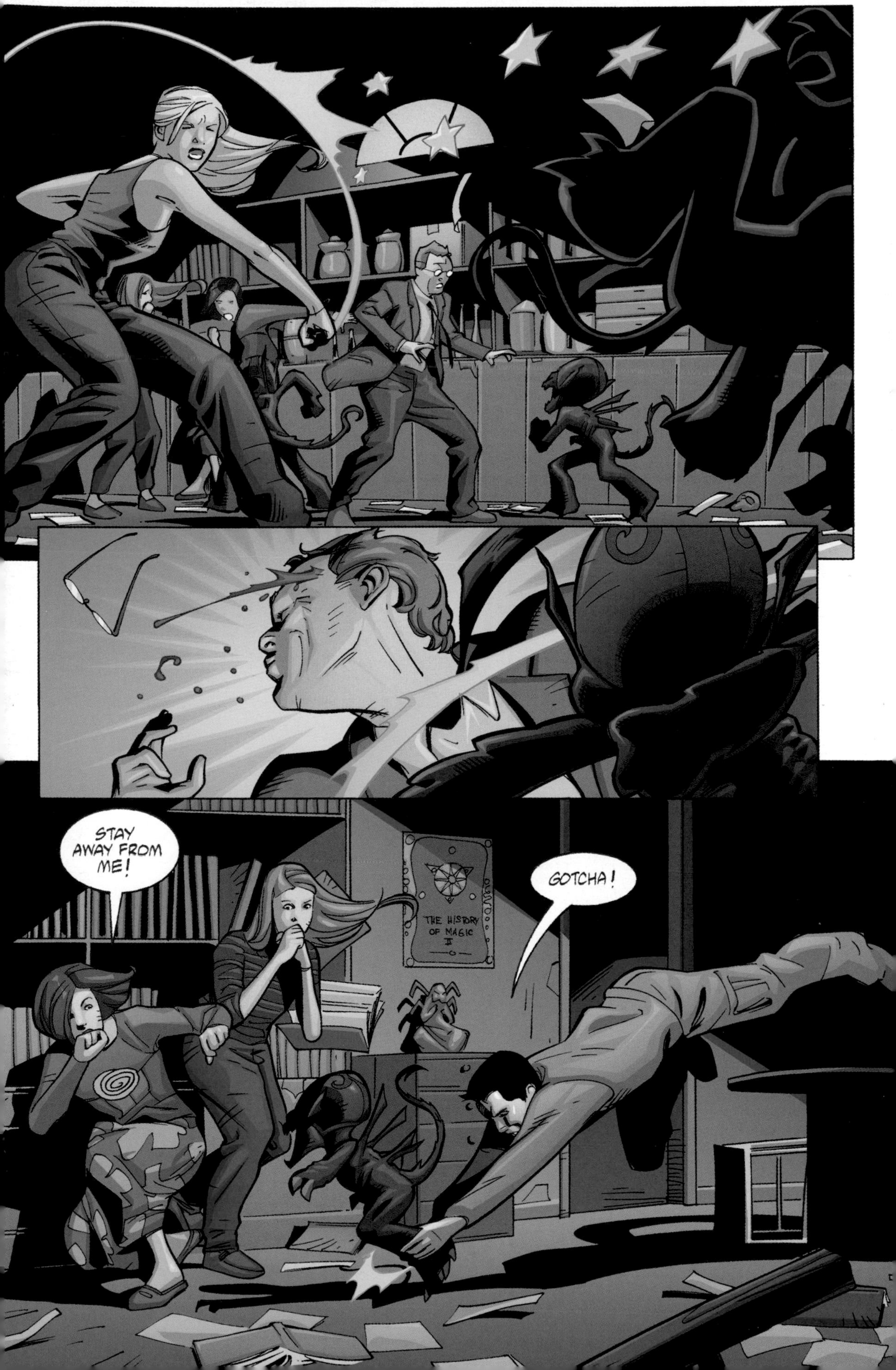
STAY AWAY FROM ME!
GOTCHA!
THE HISTORY OF MAGIC II

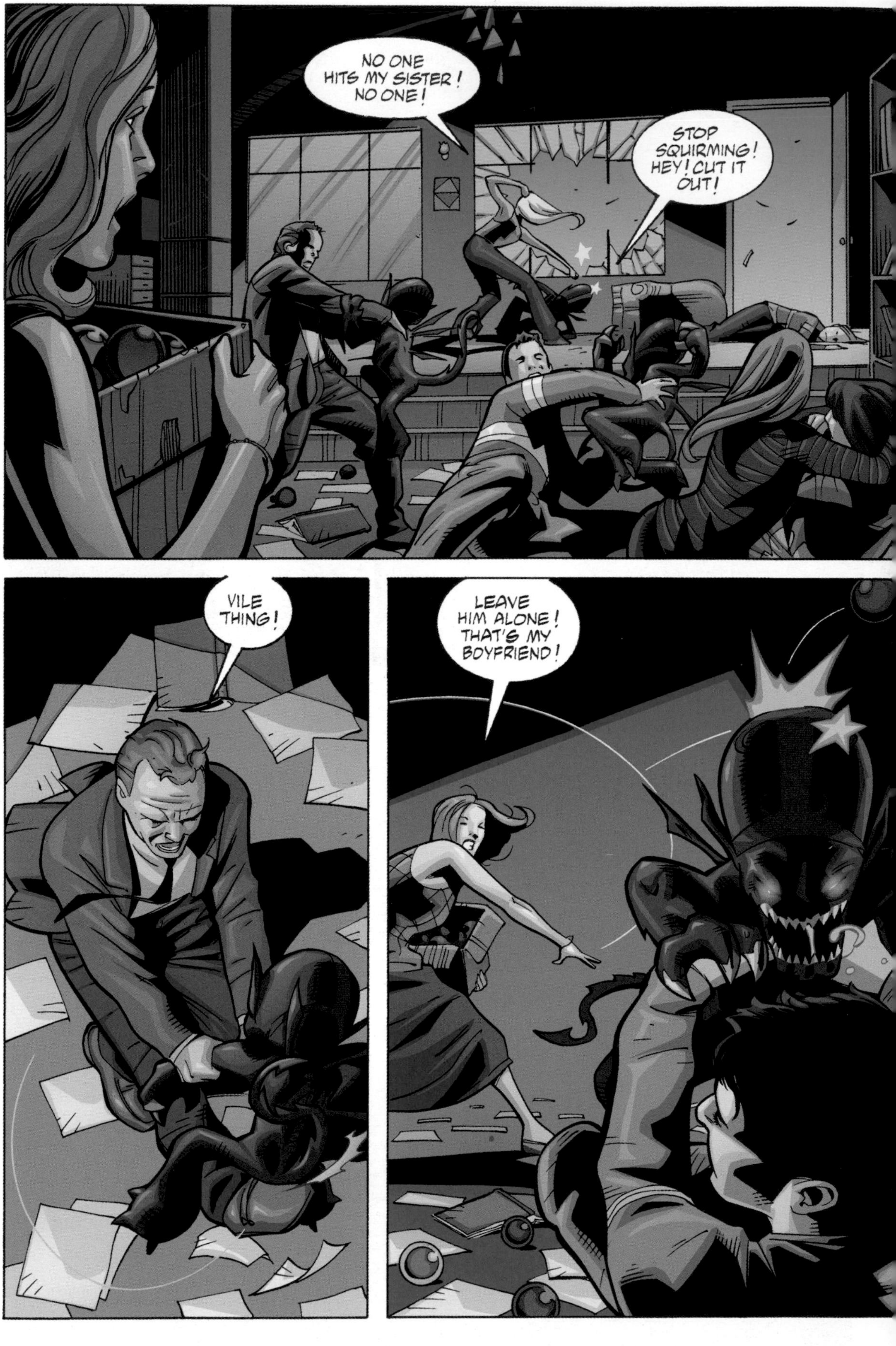
NO ONE HITS MY SISTER! NO ONE!
STOP SQUIRMING! HEY! CUT IT OUT!
VILE THING!
LEAVE HIM ALONE! THAT'S MY BOYFRIEND!

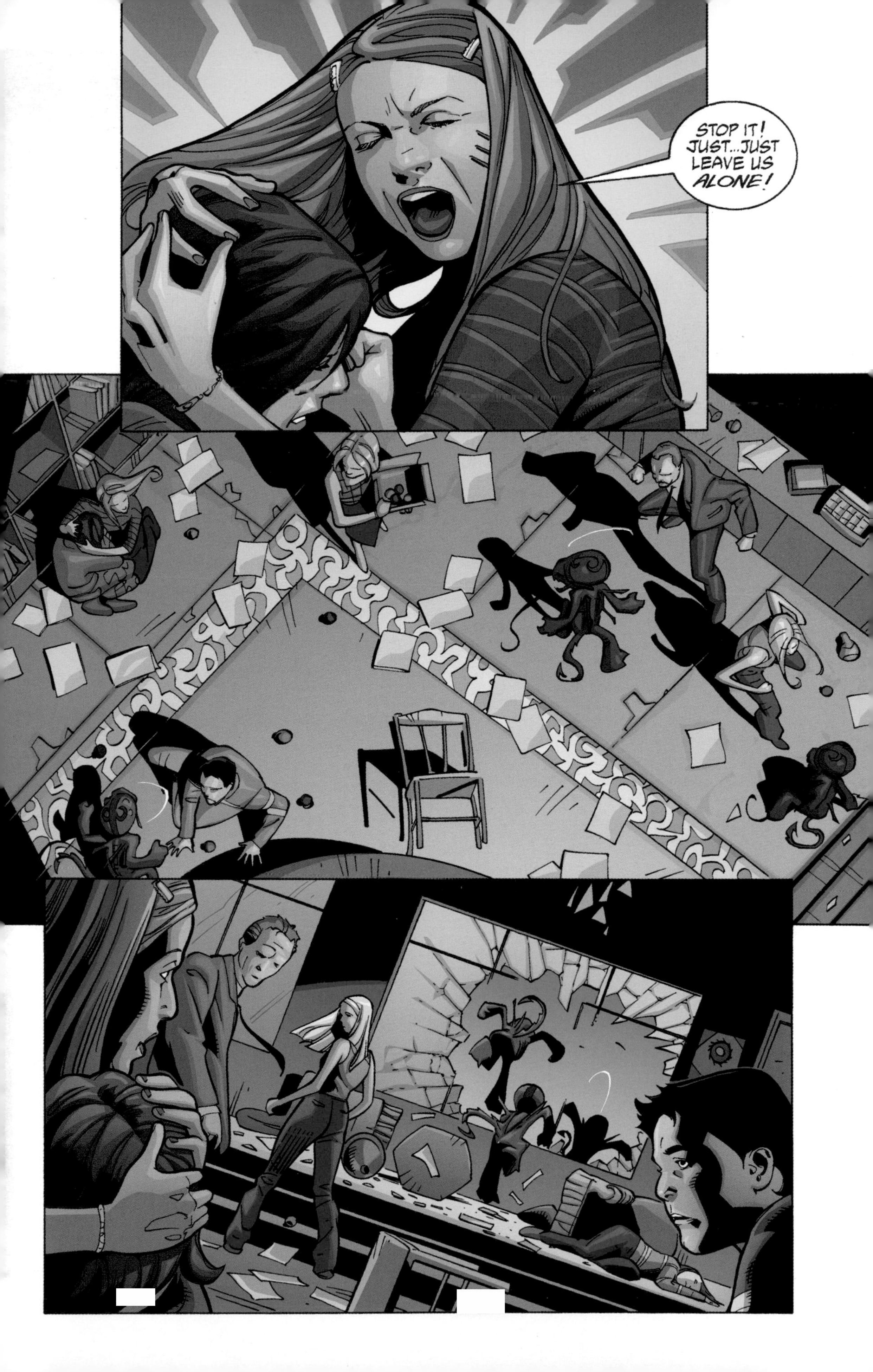
STOP IT! JUST...JUST LEAVE US ALONE!

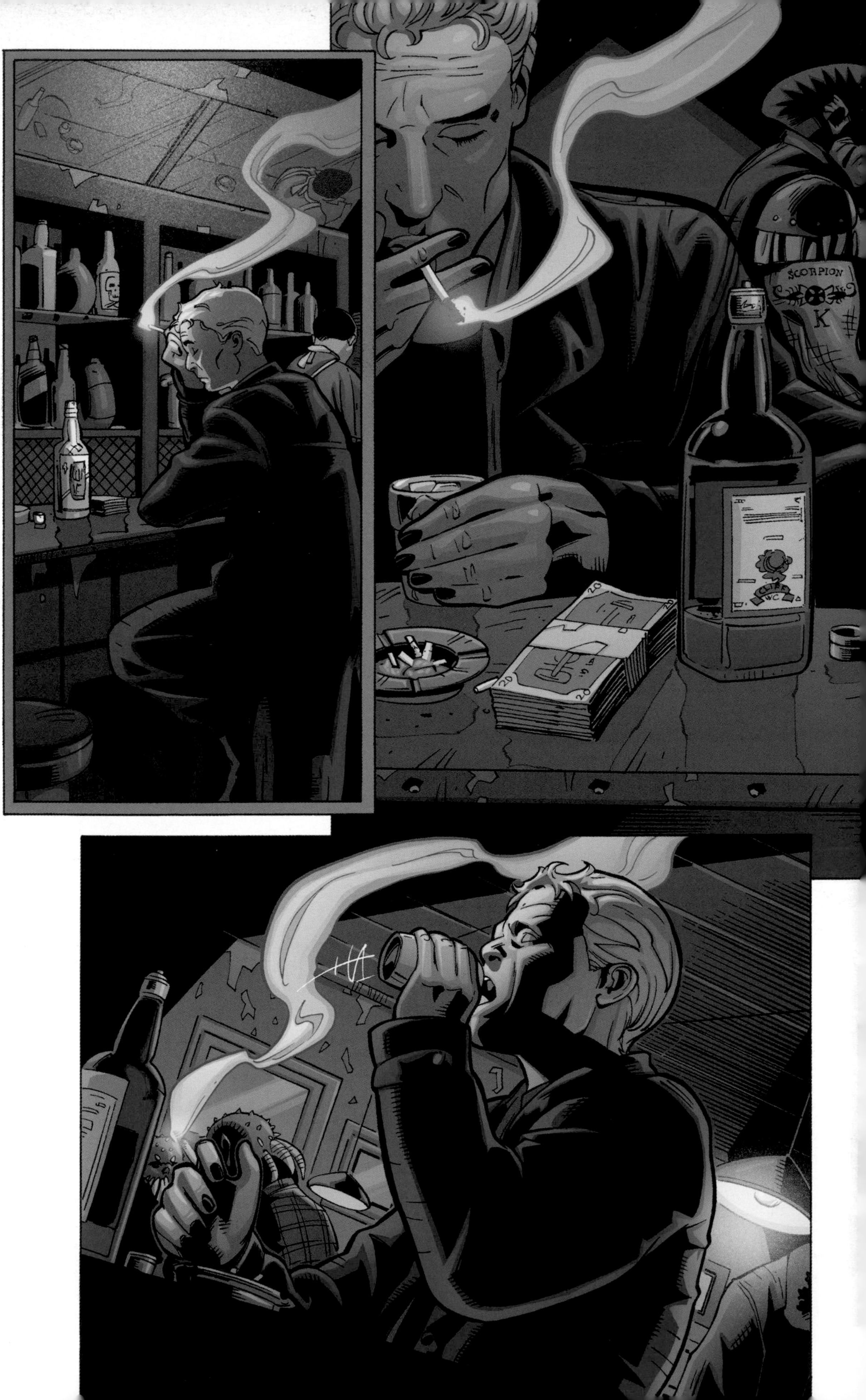
SCORPION
K

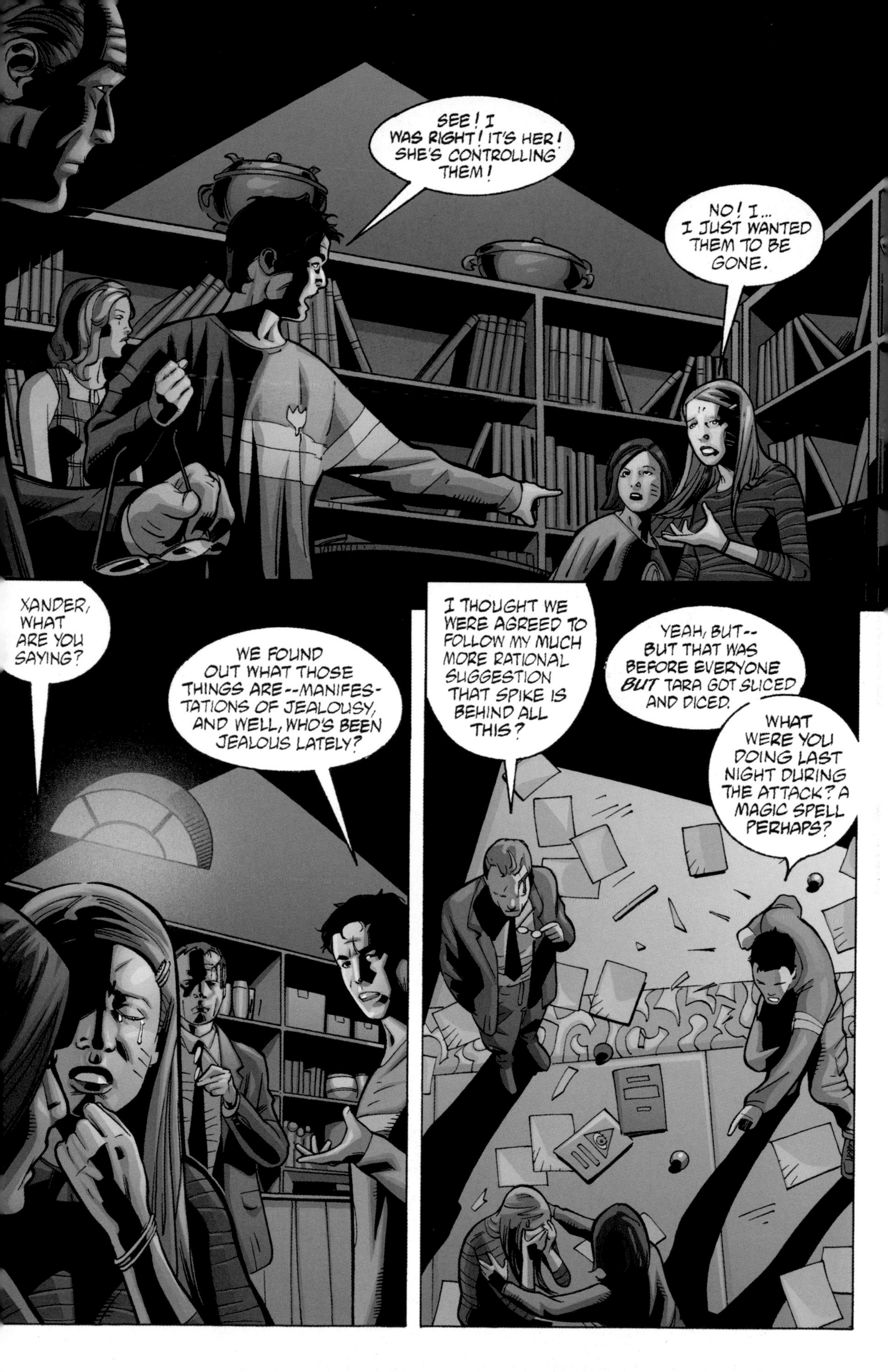
SEE! I WAS RIGHT! IT'S HER! SHE'S CONTROLLING THEM!
NO! I... I JUST WANTED THEM TO BE GONE.
XANDER, WHAT ARE YOU SAYING?
WE FOUND OUT WHAT THOSE THINGS ARE--MANIFESTATIONS OF JEALOUSY, AND WELL, WHO'S BEEN JEALOUS LATELY?
I THOUGHT WE WERE AGREED TO FOLLOW MY MUCH MORE RATIONAL SUGGESTION THAT SPIKE IS BEHIND ALL THIS?
YEAH, BUT-- BUT THAT WAS BEFORE EVERYONE BUT TARA GOT SLICED AND DICED.
WHAT WERE YOU DOING LAST NIGHT DURING THE ATTACK? A MAGIC SPELL PERHAPS?

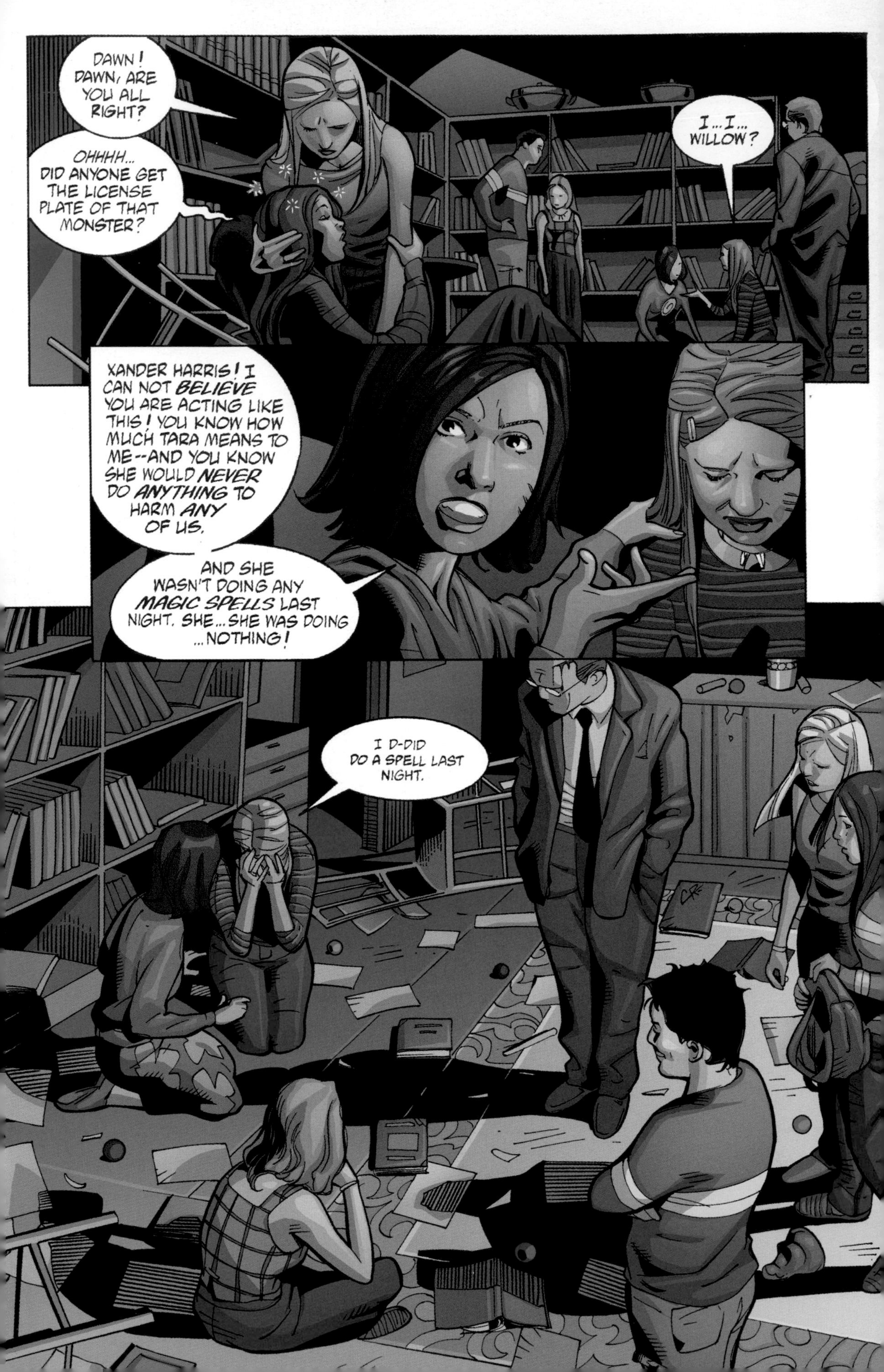
DAWN! DAWN, ARE YOU ALL RIGHT?
OHHHH... DID ANYONE GET THE LICENSE PLATE OF THAT MONSTER?
I... I... WILLOW?
XANDER HARRIS! I CAN NOT BELIEVE YOU ARE ACTING LIKE THIS! YOU KNOW HOW MUCH TARA MEANS TO ME--AND YOU KNOW SHE WOULD NEVER DO ANYTHING TO HARM ANY OF US.
AND SHE WASN'T DOING ANY MAGIC SPELLS LAST NIGHT. SHE... SHE WAS DOING ...NOTHING!
I D-DID DO A SPELL LAST NIGHT.

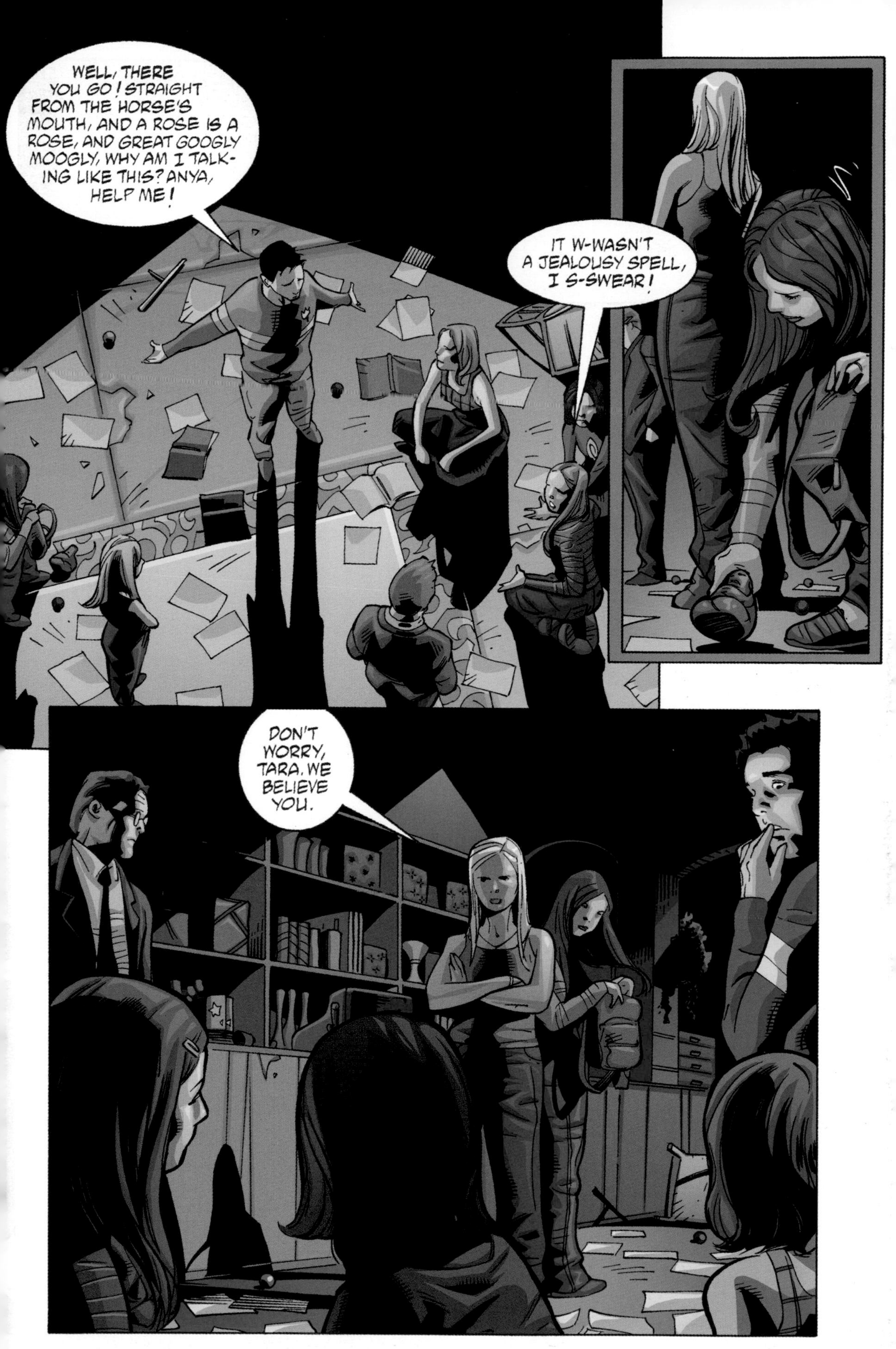
WELL, THERE YOU GO! STRAIGHT FROM THE HORSE'S MOUTH, AND A ROSE IS A ROSE, AND GREAT GOOGLY MOOGLY, WHY AM I TALKING LIKE THIS? ANYA, HELP ME!
IT W-WASN'T A JEALOUSY SPELL, I S-SWEAR!
DON'T WORRY, TARA. WE BELIEVE YOU.

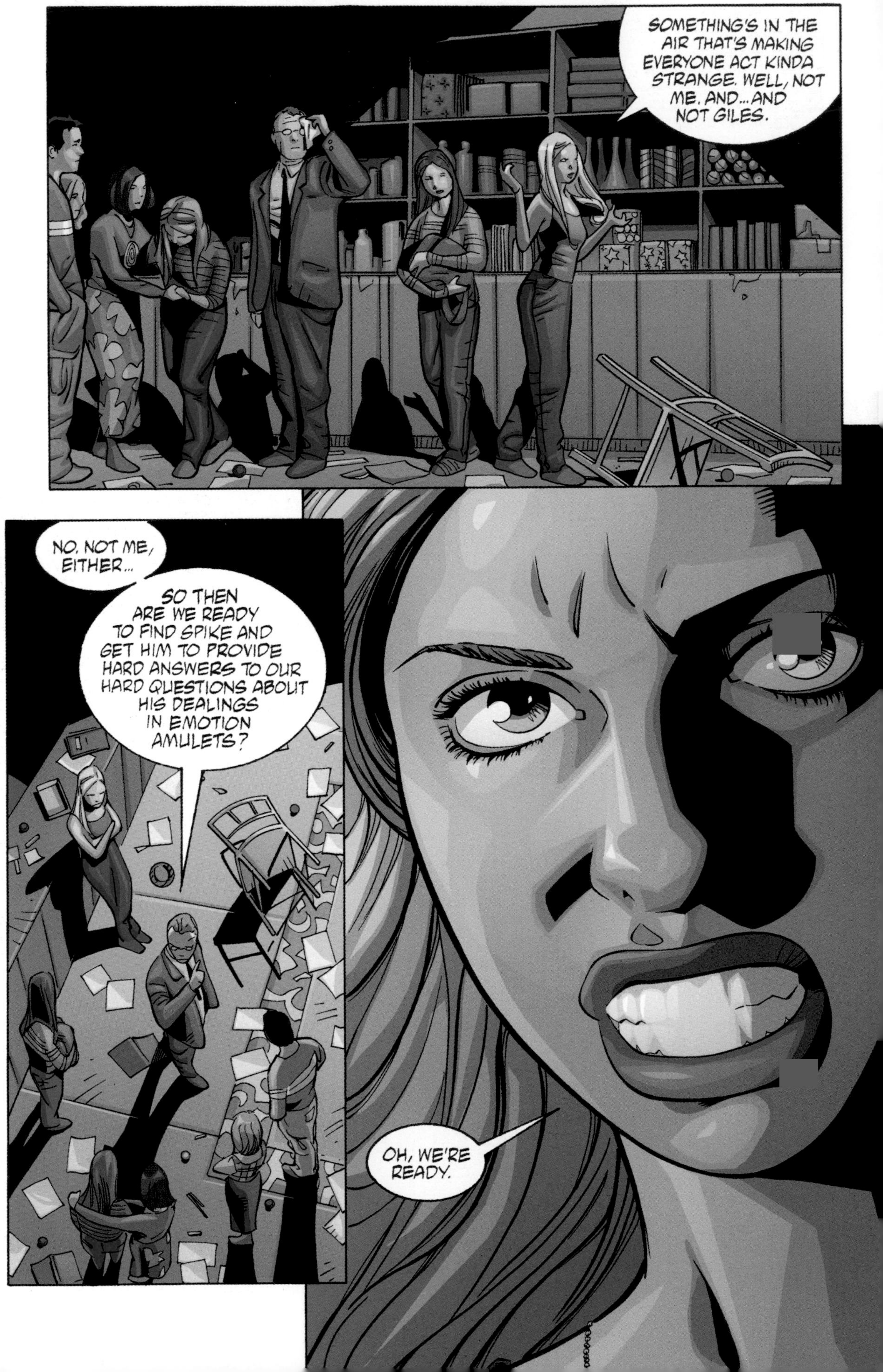
SOMETHING'S IN THE AIR THAT'S MAKING EVERYONE ACT KINDA STRANGE. WELL, NOT ME. AND... AND NOT GILES.
NO. NOT ME, EITHER...
SO THEN ARE WE READY TO FIND SPIKE AND GET HIM TO PROVIDE HARD ANSWERS TO OUR HARD QUESTIONS ABOUT HIS DEALINGS IN EMOTION AMULETS?
OH, WE'RE READY.

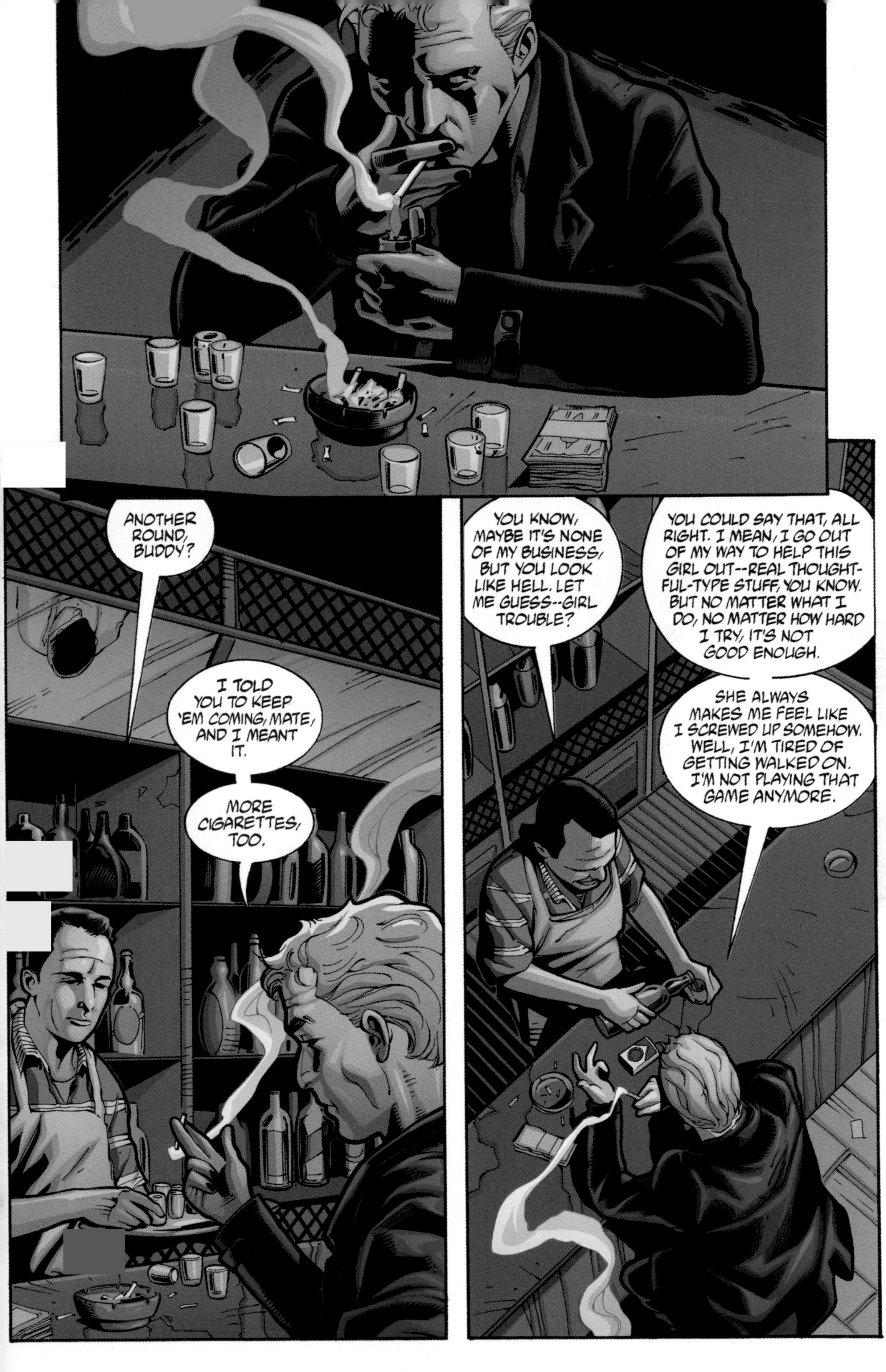
ANOTHER ROUND, BUDDY?
I TOLD YOU TO KEEP 'EM COMING, MATE, AND I MEANT IT.
MORE CIGARETTES, TOO.
YOU KNOW, MAYBE IT'S NONE OF MY BUSINESS, BUT YOU LOOK LIKE HELL. LET ME GUESS--GIRL TROUBLE?
YOU COULD SAY THAT, ALL RIGHT. I MEAN, I GO OUT OF MY WAY TO HELP THIS GIRL OUT--REAL THOUGHT-FUL-TYPE STUFF, YOU KNOW. BUT NO MATTER WHAT I DO, NO MATTER HOW HARD I TRY, IT'S NOT GOOD ENOUGH.
SHE ALWAYS MAKES ME FEEL LIKE I SCREWED UP SOMEHOW. WELL, I'M TIRED OF GETTING WALKED ON. I'M NOT PLAYING THAT GAME ANYMORE.

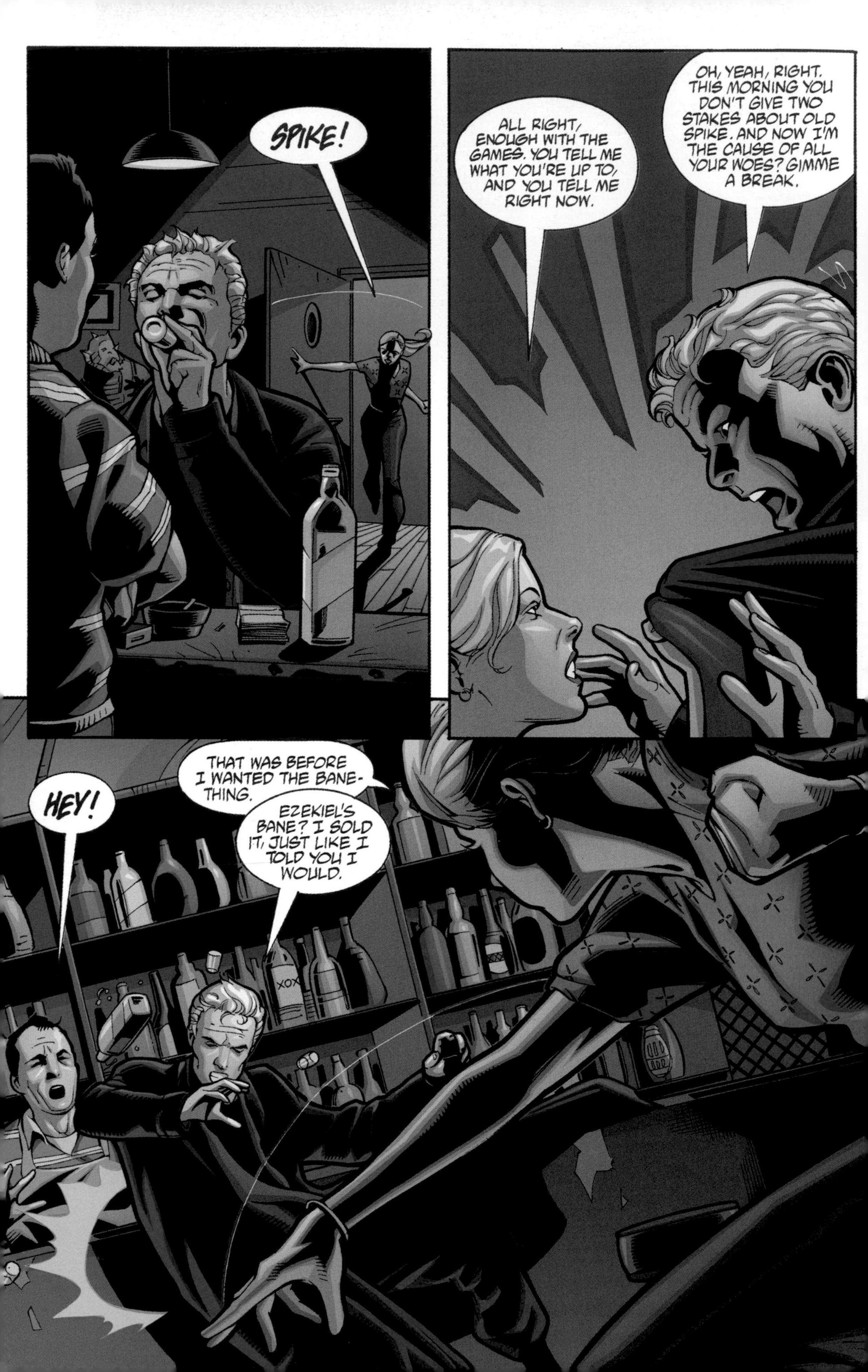
SPIKE!
ALL RIGHT, ENOUGH WITH THE GAMES. YOU TELL ME WHAT YOU'RE UP TO, AND YOU TELL ME RIGHT NOW.
OH, YEAH, RIGHT. THIS MORNING YOU DON'T GIVE TWO STAKES ABOUT OLD SPIKE. AND NOW I'M THE CAUSE OF ALL YOUR WOES? GIMME A BREAK.
HEY!
THAT WAS BEFORE I WANTED THE BANE-THING.
EZEKIEL'S BANE? I SOLD IT, JUST LIKE I TOLD YOU I WOULD.

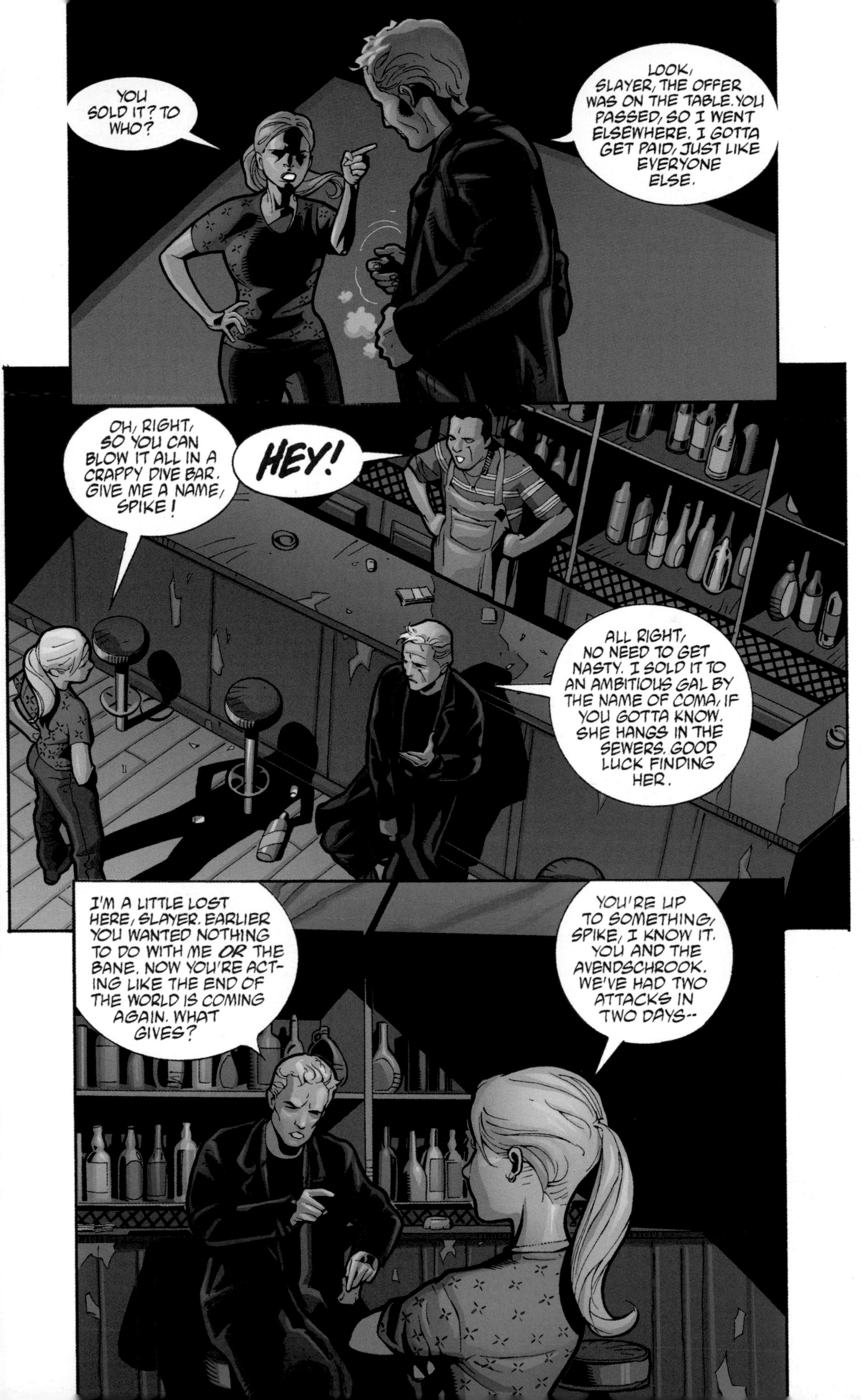

YOU SOLD IT? TO WHO?
LOOK, SLAYER, THE OFFER WAS ON THE TABLE. YOU PASSED, SO I WENT ELSEWHERE. I GOTTA GET PAID, JUST LIKE EVERYONE ELSE.
OH, RIGHT, SO YOU CAN BLOW IT ALL IN A CRAPPY DIVE BAR. GIVE ME A NAME, SPIKE!
HEY!
ALL RIGHT, NO NEED TO GET NASTY. I SOLD IT TO AN AMBITIOUS GAL BY THE NAME OF COMA, IF YOU GOTTA KNOW. SHE HANGS IN THE SEWERS. GOOD LUCK FINDING HER.
I'M A LITTLE LOST HERE, SLAYER. EARLIER YOU WANTED NOTHING TO DO WITH ME *OR* THE BANE. NOW YOU'RE ACTING LIKE THE END OF THE WORLD IS COMING AGAIN. WHAT GIVES?
YOU'RE UP TO SOMETHING, SPIKE, I KNOW IT. YOU AND THE AVENDSCHROOK. WE'VE HAD TWO ATTACKS IN TWO DAYS--

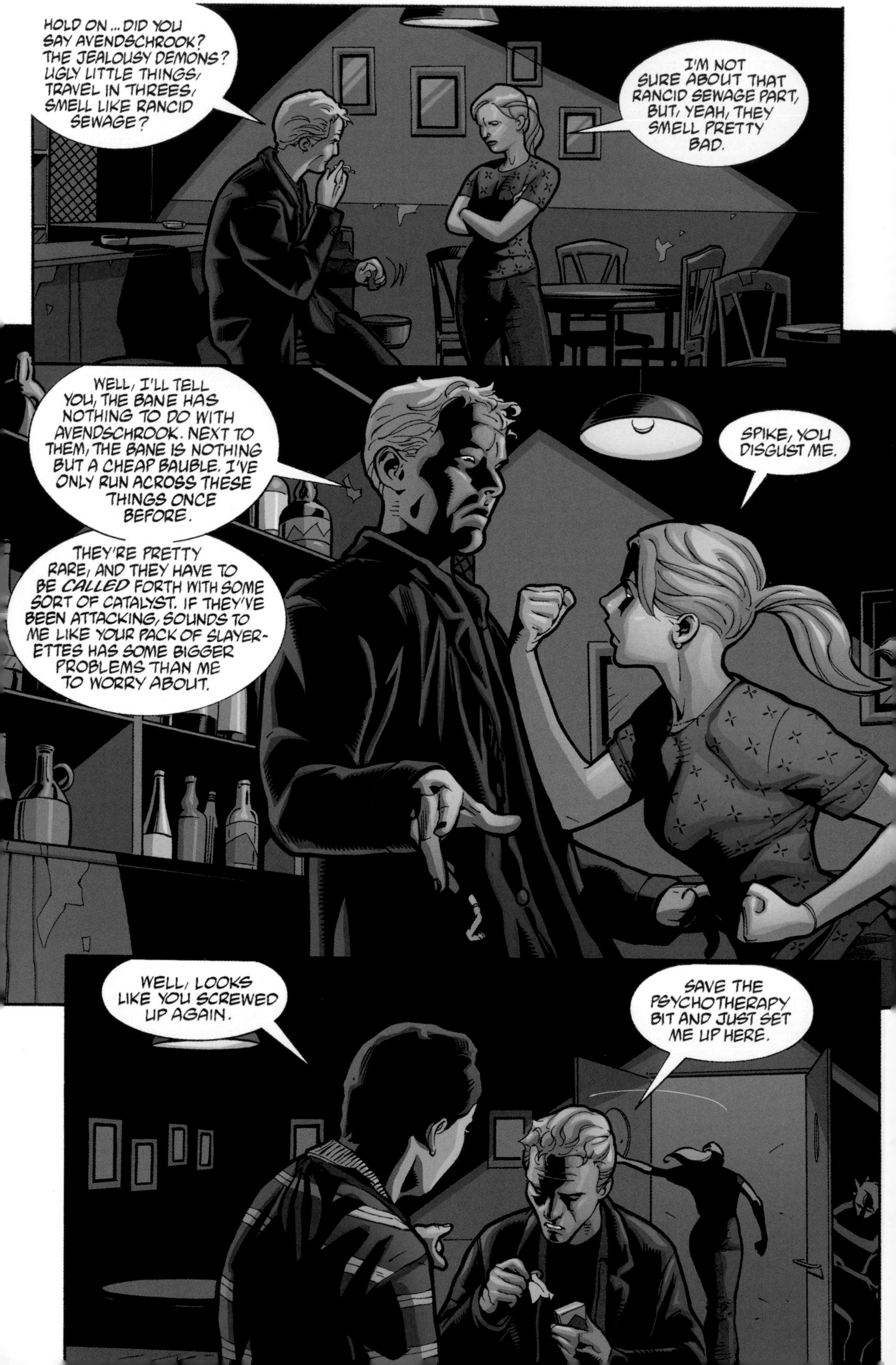
HOLD ON ... DID YOU SAY AVENDSCHROOK? THE JEALOUSY DEMONS? UGLY LITTLE THINGS, TRAVEL IN THREES, SMELL LIKE RANCID SEWAGE?
I'M NOT SURE ABOUT THAT RANCID SEWAGE PART, BUT, YEAH, THEY SMELL PRETTY BAD.
WELL, I'LL TELL YOU, THE BANE HAS NOTHING TO DO WITH AVENDSCHROOK. NEXT TO THEM, THE BANE IS NOTHING BUT A CHEAP BAUBLE. I'VE ONLY RUN ACROSS THESE THINGS ONCE BEFORE.
THEY'RE PRETTY RARE, AND THEY HAVE TO BE CALLED FORTH WITH SOME SORT OF CATALYST. IF THEY'VE BEEN ATTACKING, SOUNDS TO ME LIKE YOUR PACK OF SLAYER-ETTES HAS SOME BIGGER PROBLEMS THAN ME TO WORRY ABOUT.
SPIKE, YOU DISGUST ME.
WELL, LOOKS LIKE YOU SCREWED UP AGAIN.
SAVE THE PSYCHOTHERAPY BIT AND JUST SET ME UP HERE.

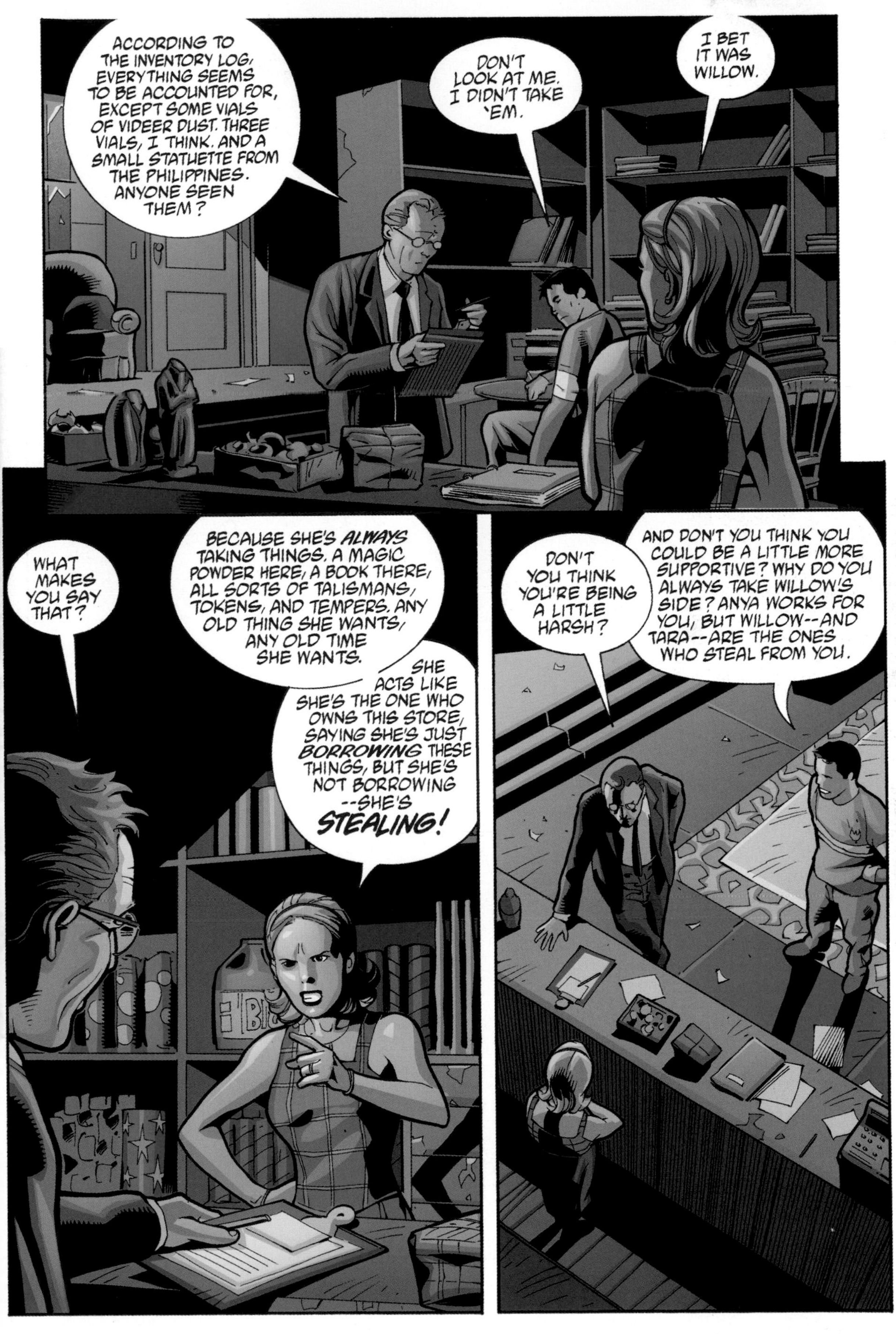
ACCORDING TO THE INVENTORY LOG, EVERYTHING SEEMS TO BE ACCOUNTED FOR, EXCEPT SOME VIALS OF VIDEER DUST. THREE VIALS, I THINK. AND A SMALL STATUETTE FROM THE PHILIPPINES. ANYONE SEEN THEM?
DON'T LOOK AT ME. I DIDN'T TAKE 'EM.
I BET IT WAS WILLOW.
WHAT MAKES YOU SAY THAT?
BECAUSE SHE'S ALWAYS TAKING THINGS. A MAGIC POWDER HERE, A BOOK THERE, ALL SORTS OF TALISMANS, TOKENS, AND TEMPERS. ANY OLD THING SHE WANTS, ANY OLD TIME SHE WANTS.
SHE ACTS LIKE SHE'S THE ONE WHO OWNS THIS STORE, SAYING SHE'S JUST BORROWING THESE THINGS, BUT SHE'S NOT BORROWING --SHE'S STEALING!
DON'T YOU THINK YOU'RE BEING A LITTLE HARSH?
AND DON'T YOU THINK YOU COULD BE A LITTLE MORE SUPPORTIVE? WHY DO YOU ALWAYS TAKE WILLOW'S SIDE? ANYA WORKS FOR YOU, BUT WILLOW--AND TARA--ARE THE ONES WHO STEAL FROM YOU.

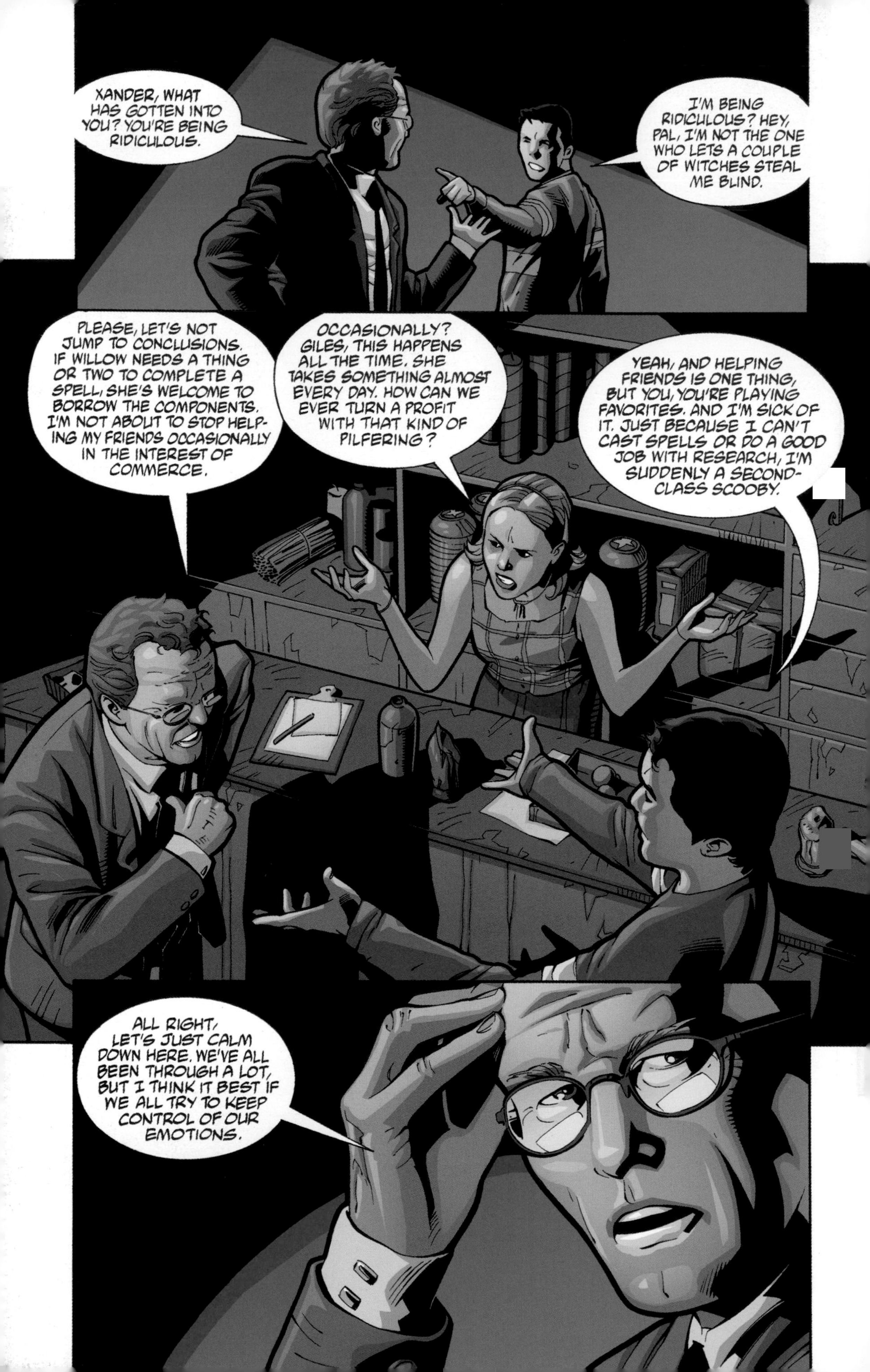
XANDER, WHAT HAS GOTTEN INTO YOU? YOU'RE BEING RIDICULOUS.
I'M BEING RIDICULOUS? HEY, PAL, I'M NOT THE ONE WHO LETS A COUPLE OF WITCHES STEAL ME BLIND.
PLEASE, LET'S NOT JUMP TO CONCLUSIONS. IF WILLOW NEEDS A THING OR TWO TO COMPLETE A SPELL, SHE'S WELCOME TO BORROW THE COMPONENTS. I'M NOT ABOUT TO STOP HELPING MY FRIENDS OCCASIONALLY IN THE INTEREST OF COMMERCE.
OCCASIONALLY? GILES, THIS HAPPENS ALL THE TIME. SHE TAKES SOMETHING ALMOST EVERY DAY. HOW CAN WE EVER TURN A PROFIT WITH THAT KIND OF PILFERING?
YEAH, AND HELPING FRIENDS IS ONE THING, BUT YOU, YOU'RE PLAYING FAVORITES. AND I'M SICK OF IT. JUST BECAUSE I CAN'T CAST SPELLS OR DO A GOOD JOB WITH RESEARCH, I'M SUDDENLY A SECOND-CLASS SCOOBY.
ALL RIGHT, LET'S JUST CALM DOWN HERE. WE'VE ALL BEEN THROUGH A LOT, BUT I THINK IT BEST IF WE ALL TRY TO KEEP CONTROL OF OUR EMOTIONS.

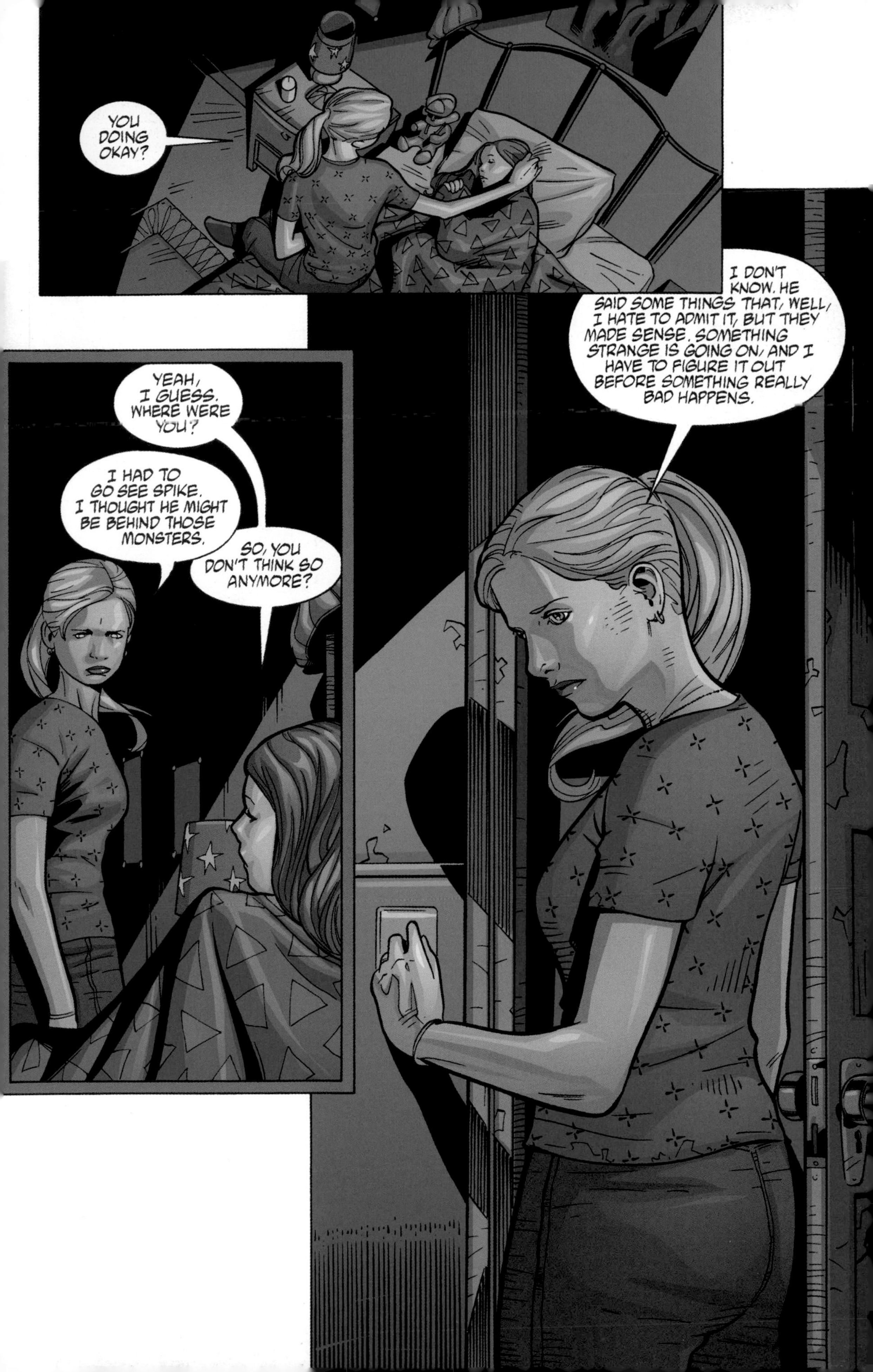
YOU DOING OKAY?
YEAH, I GUESS. WHERE WERE YOU?
I HAD TO GO SEE SPIKE. I THOUGHT HE MIGHT BE BEHIND THOSE MONSTERS.
SO, YOU DON'T THINK SO ANYMORE?
I DON'T KNOW. HE SAID SOME THINGS THAT, WELL, I HATE TO ADMIT IT, BUT THEY MADE SENSE. SOMETHING STRANGE IS GOING ON, AND I HAVE TO FIGURE IT OUT BEFORE SOMETHING REALLY BAD HAPPENS.

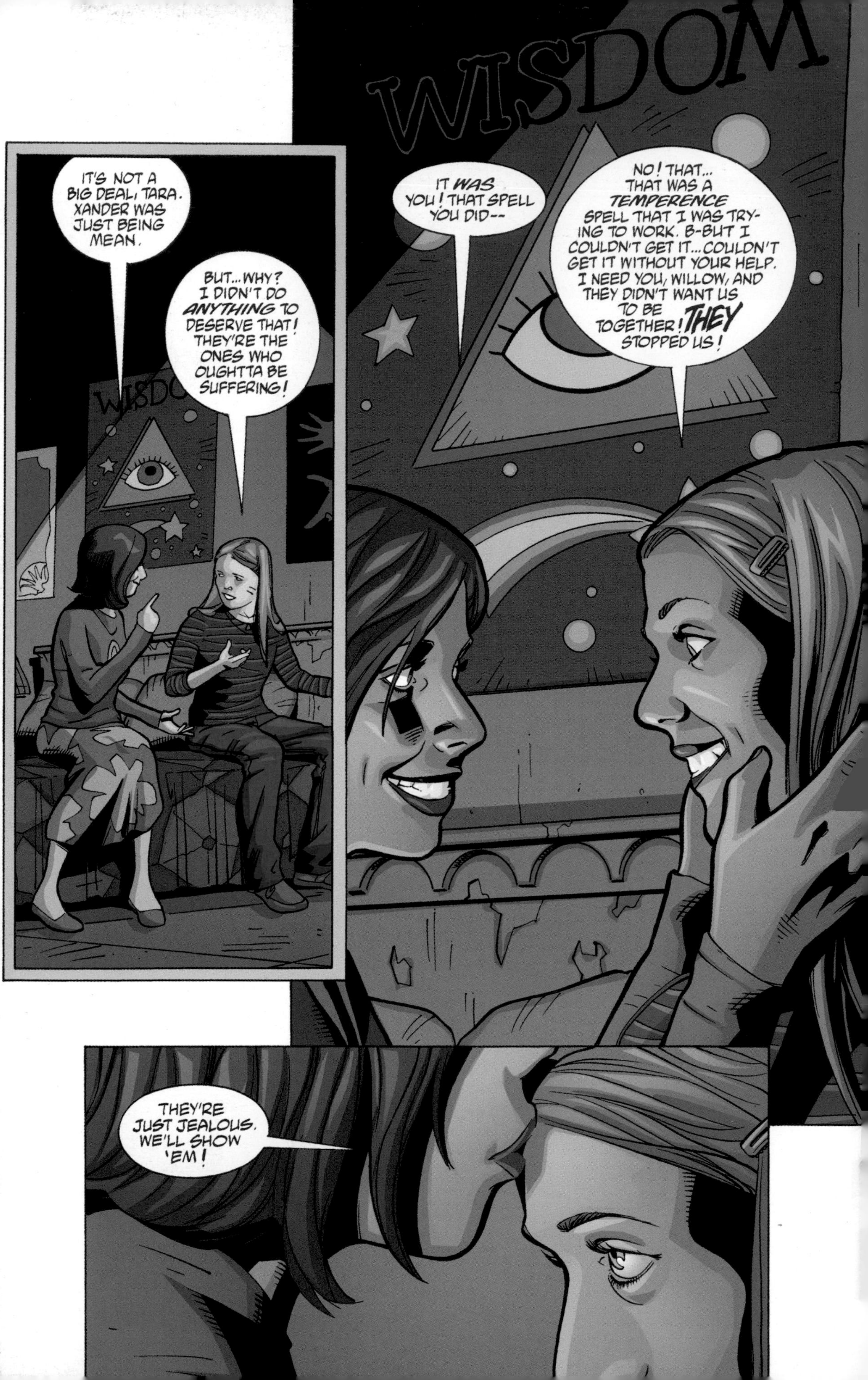
WISDOM
IT'S NOT A BIG DEAL, TARA. XANDER WAS JUST BEING MEAN.
BUT... WHY? I DIDN'T DO ANYTHING TO DESERVE THAT! THEY'RE THE ONES WHO OUGHTTA BE SUFFERING!
IT WAS YOU! THAT SPELL YOU DID--
NO! THAT... THAT WAS A TEMPERENCE SPELL THAT I WAS TRYING TO WORK. B-BUT I COULDN'T GET IT... COULDN'T GET IT WITHOUT YOUR HELP. I NEED YOU, WILLOW, AND THEY DIDN'T WANT US TO BE TOGETHER! THEY STOPPED US!
THEY'RE JUST JEALOUS. WE'LL SHOW 'EM!

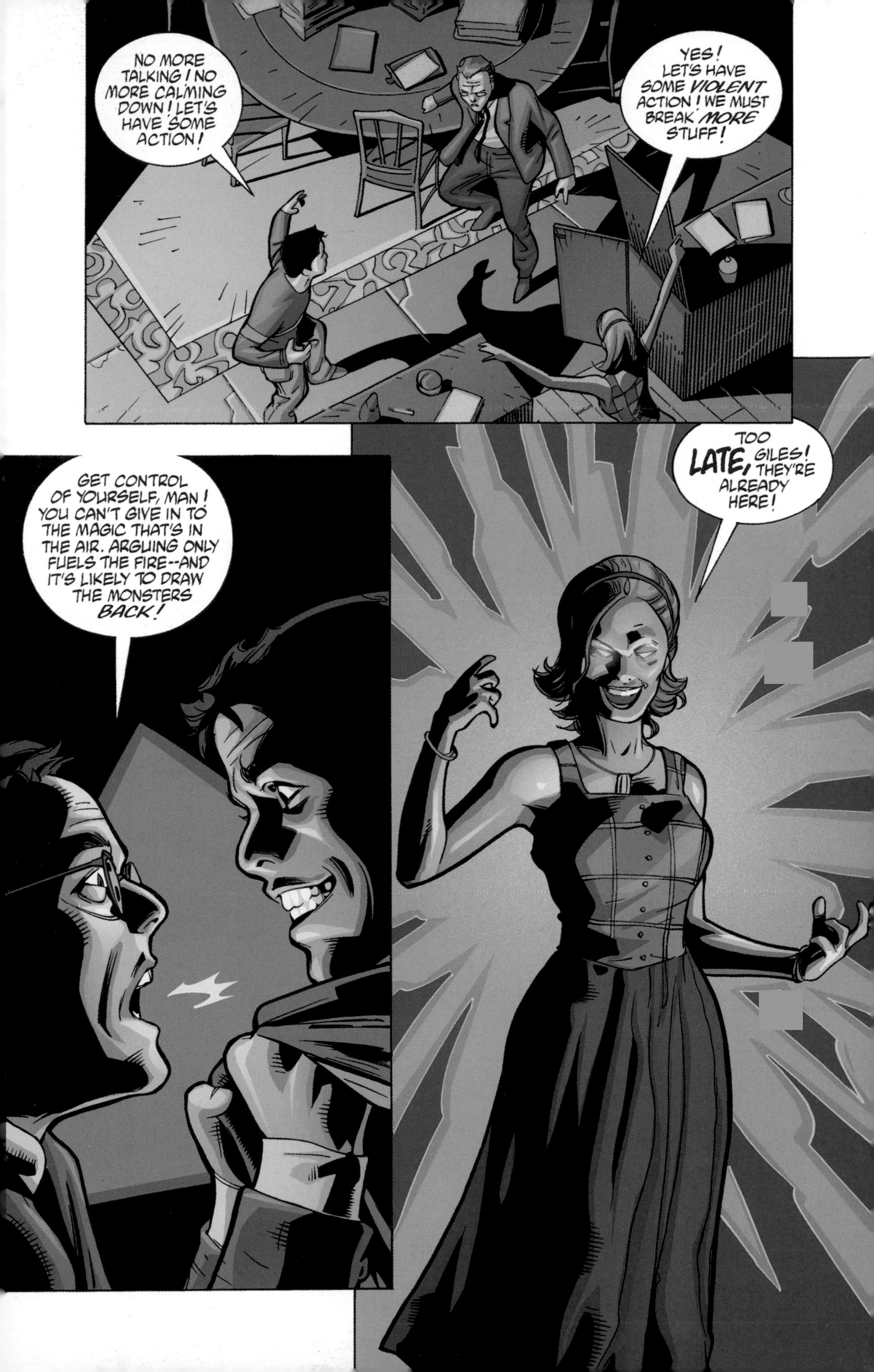
NO MORE TALKING! NO MORE CALMING DOWN! LET'S HAVE SOME ACTION!
YES! LET'S HAVE SOME VIOLENT ACTION! WE MUST BREAK MORE STUFF!
GET CONTROL OF YOURSELF, MAN! YOU CAN'T GIVE IN TO THE MAGIC THAT'S IN THE AIR. ARGUING ONLY FUELS THE FIRE--AND IT'S LIKELY TO DRAW THE MONSTERS BACK!
TOO LATE, GILES! THEY'RE ALREADY HERE!

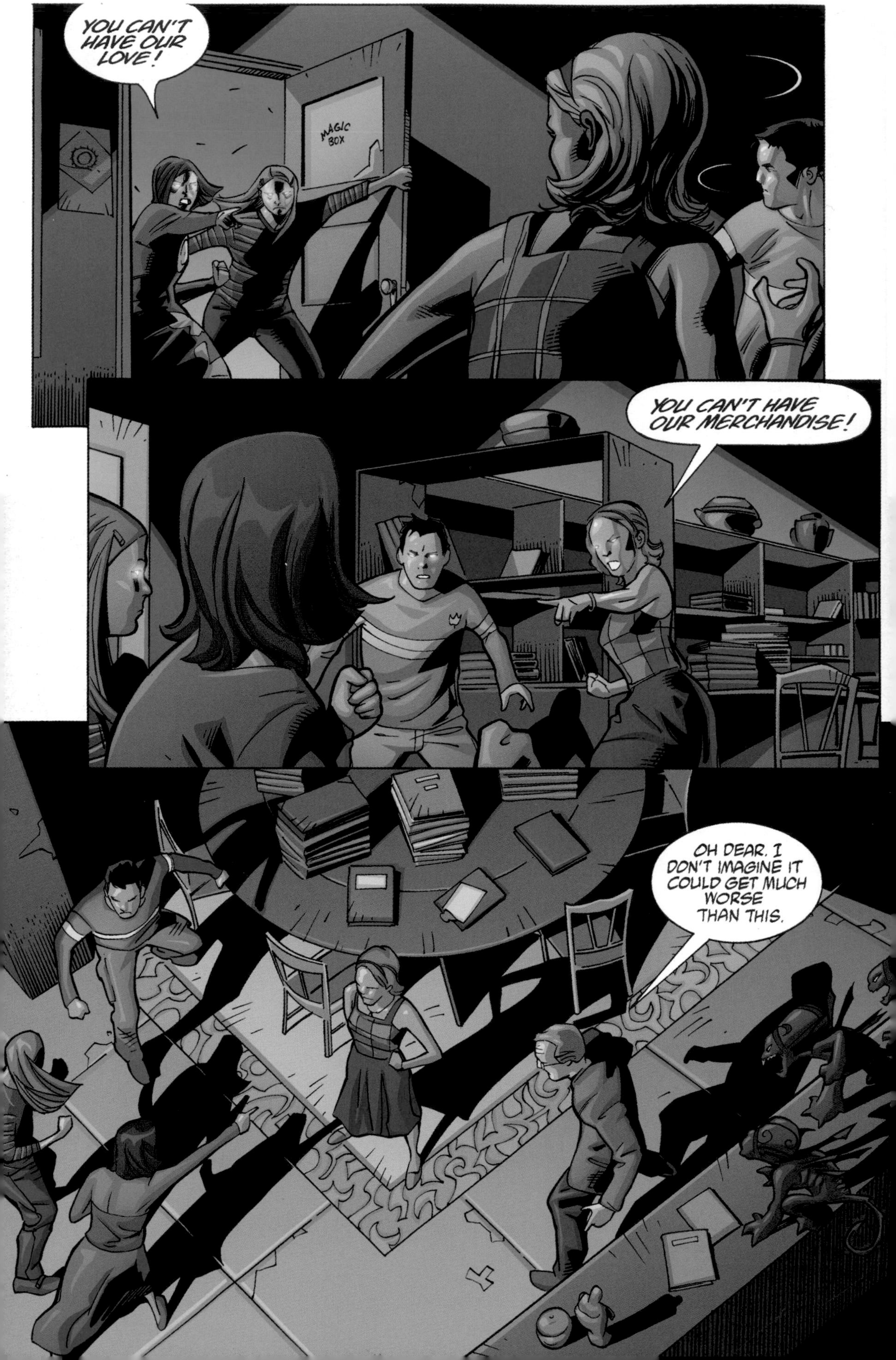
YOU CAN'T HAVE OUR LOVE!
MAGIC BOX
YOU CAN'T HAVE OUR MERCHANDISE!
OH DEAR. I DON'T IMAGINE IT COULD GET MUCH WORSE THAN THIS.

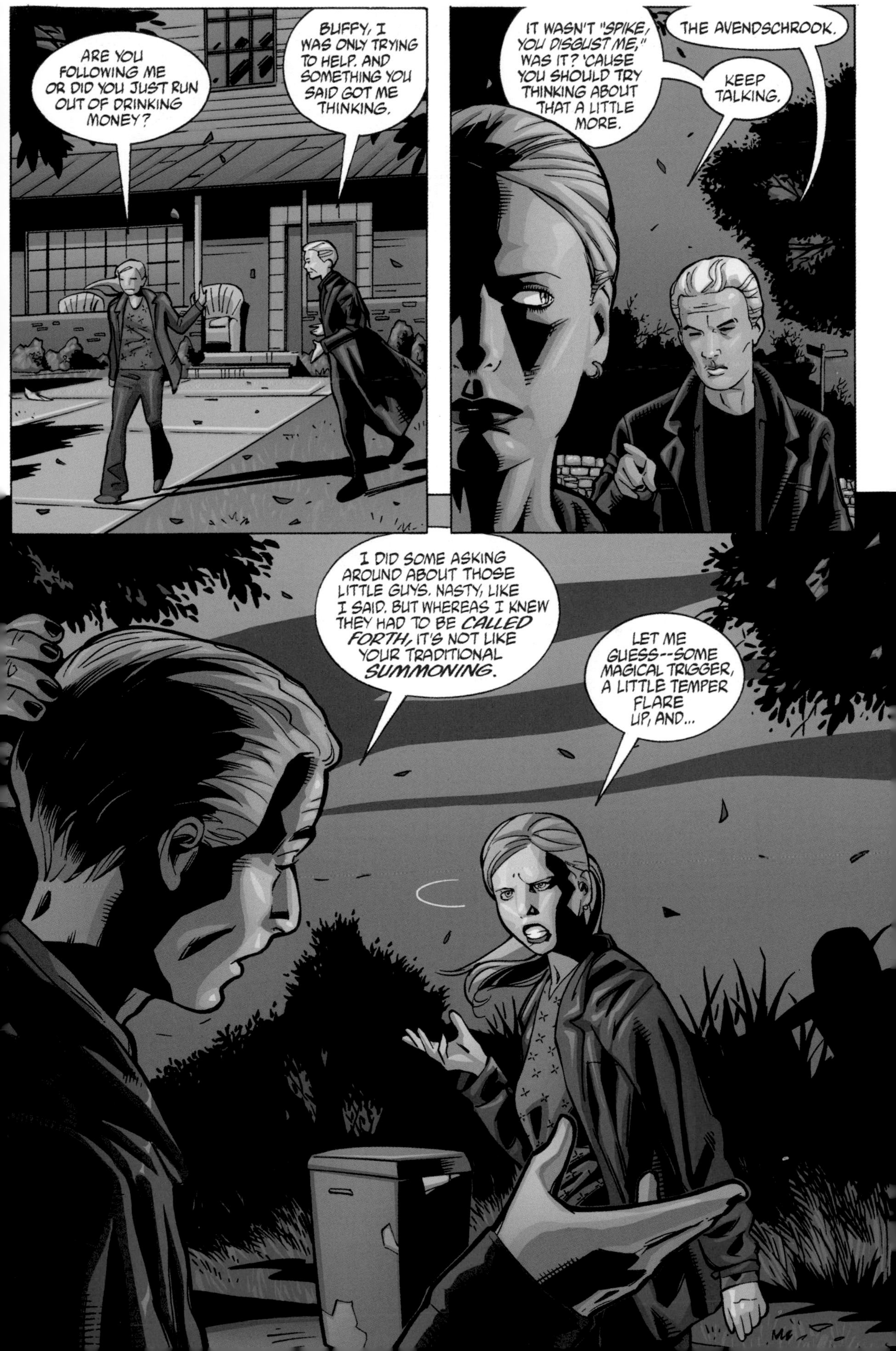
ARE YOU FOLLOWING ME OR DID YOU JUST RUN OUT OF DRINKING MONEY?
BUFFY, I WAS ONLY TRYING TO HELP. AND SOMETHING YOU SAID GOT ME THINKING.
IT WASN'T "SPIKE, YOU DISGUST ME," WAS IT? 'CAUSE YOU SHOULD TRY THINKING ABOUT THAT A LITTLE MORE.
KEEP TALKING.
THE AVENDSCHROOK.
I DID SOME ASKING AROUND ABOUT THOSE LITTLE GUYS. NASTY, LIKE I SAID. BUT WHEREAS I KNEW THEY HAD TO BE CALLED FORTH, IT'S NOT LIKE YOUR TRADITIONAL SUMMONING.
LET ME GUESS--SOME MAGICAL TRIGGER, A LITTLE TEMPER FLARE UP, AND...

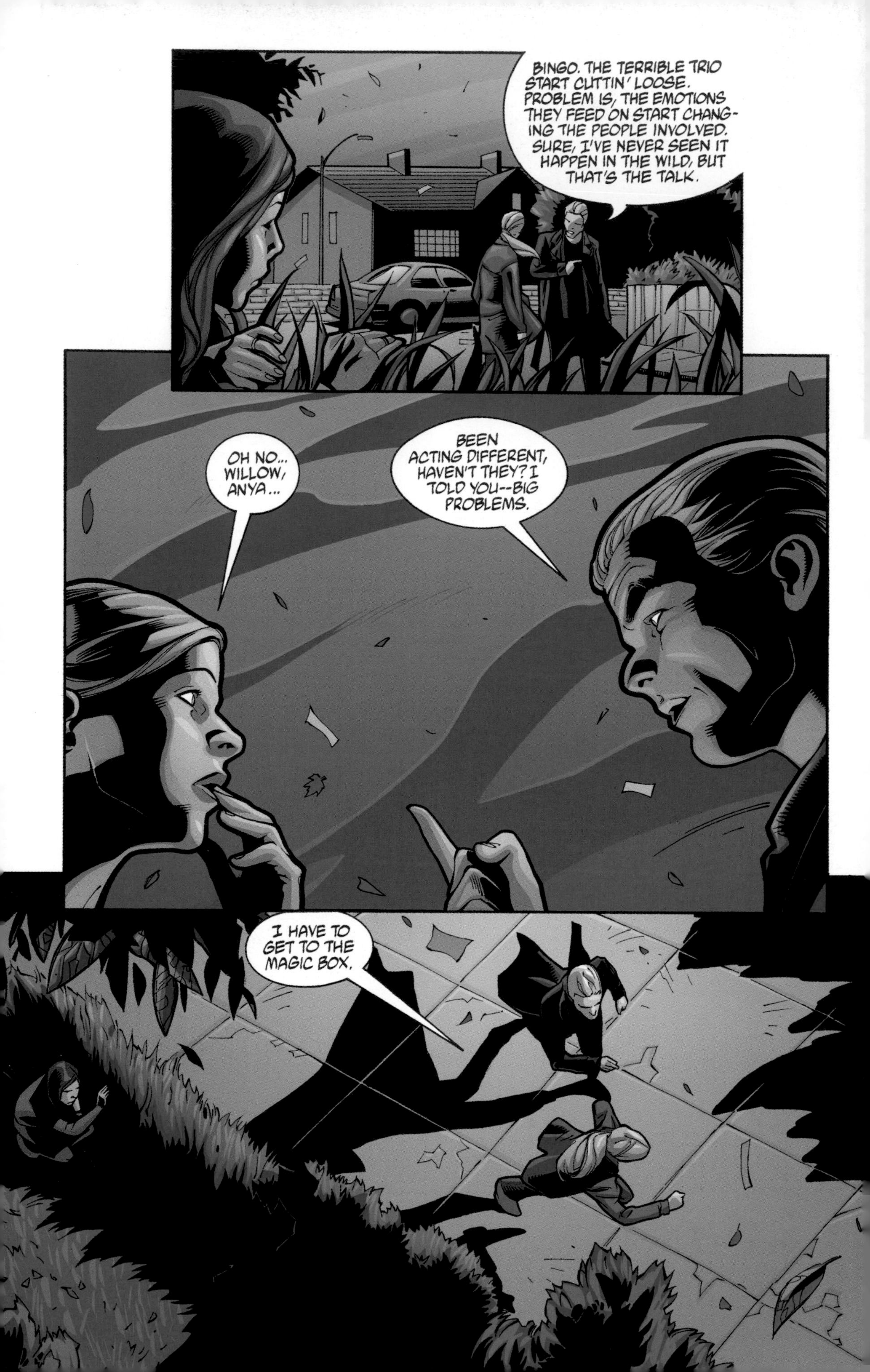
BINGO. THE TERRIBLE TRIO START CUTTIN' LOOSE. PROBLEM IS, THE EMOTIONS THEY FEED ON START CHANGING THE PEOPLE INVOLVED. SURE, I'VE NEVER SEEN IT HAPPEN IN THE WILD, BUT THAT'S THE TALK.
OH NO... WILLOW, ANYA...
BEEN ACTING DIFFERENT, HAVEN'T THEY? I TOLD YOU--BIG PROBLEMS.
I HAVE TO GET TO THE MAGIC BOX.

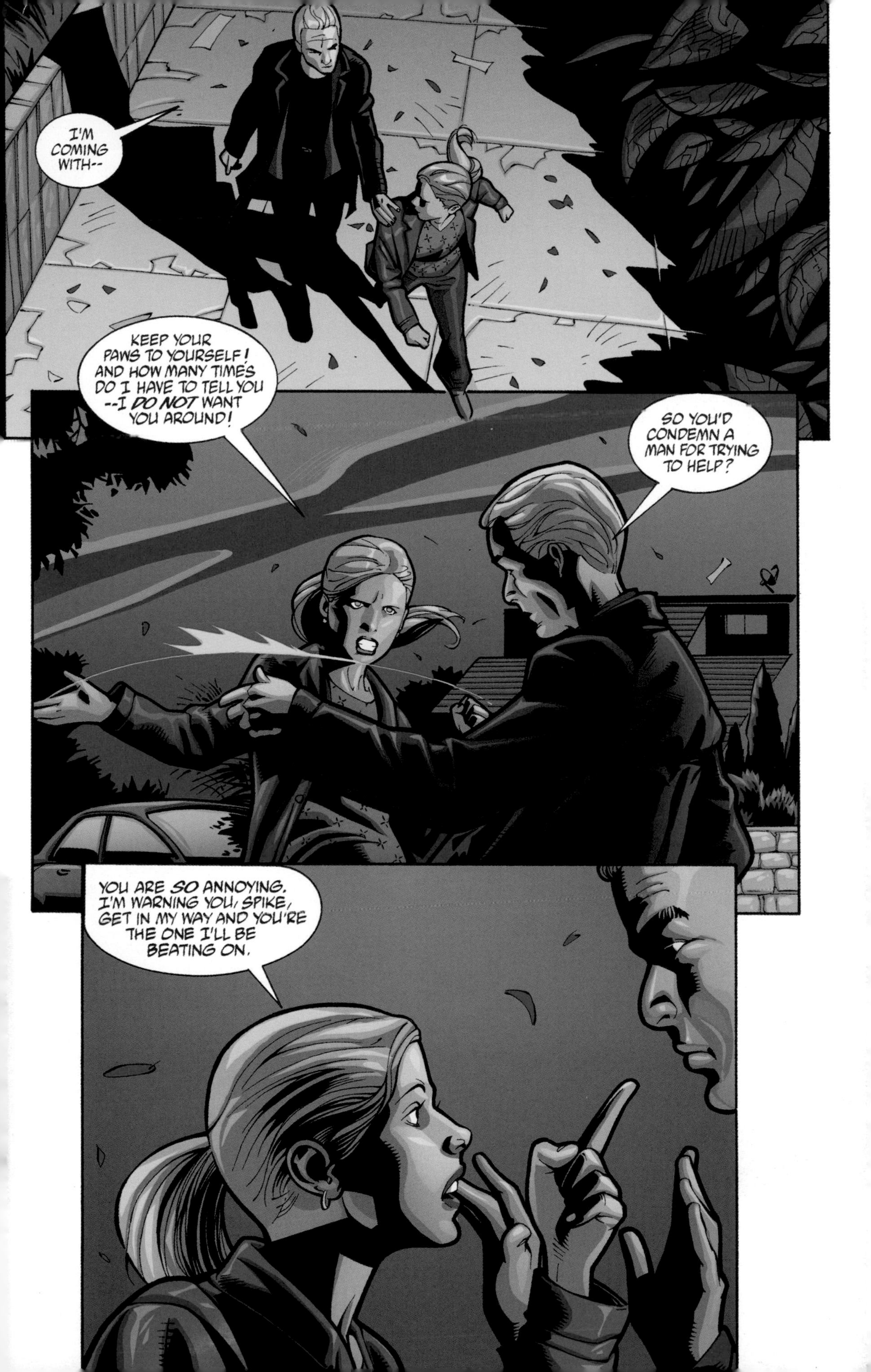
I'M COMING WITH--
KEEP YOUR PAWS TO YOURSELF! AND HOW MANY TIMES DO I HAVE TO TELL YOU --I DO NOT WANT YOU AROUND!
SO YOU'D CONDEMN A MAN FOR TRYING TO HELP?
YOU ARE SO ANNOYING. I'M WARNING YOU, SPIKE, GET IN MY WAY AND YOU'RE THE ONE I'LL BE BEATING ON.

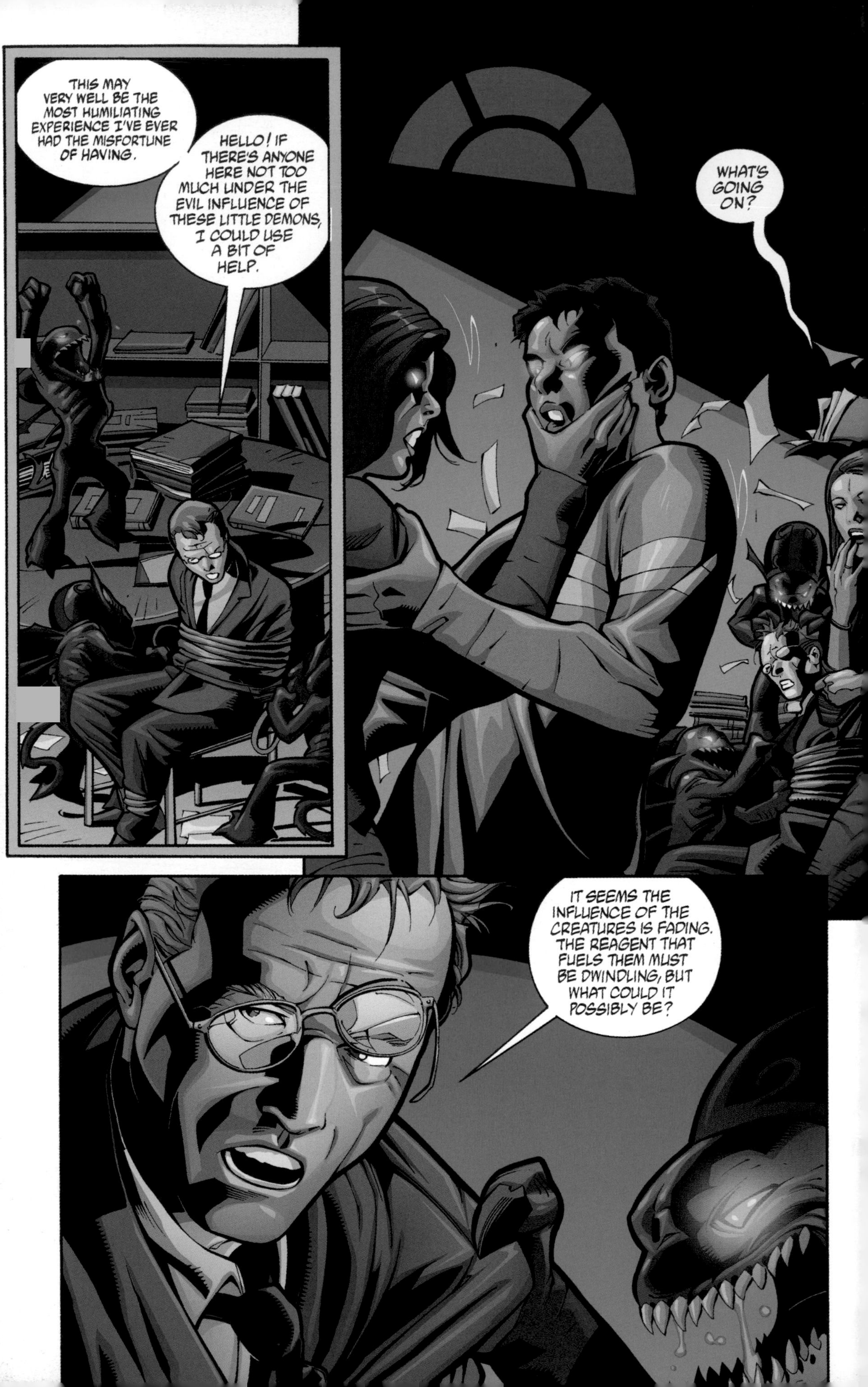
THIS MAY VERY WELL BE THE MOST HUMILIATING EXPERIENCE I'VE EVER HAD THE MISFORTUNE OF HAVING.
HELLO! IF THERE'S ANYONE HERE NOT TOO MUCH UNDER THE EVIL INFLUENCE OF THESE LITTLE DEMONS, I COULD USE A BIT OF HELP.
WHAT'S GOING ON?
IT SEEMS THE INFLUENCE OF THE CREATURES IS FADING. THE REAGENT THAT FUELS THEM MUST BE DWINDLING, BUT WHAT COULD IT POSSIBLY BE?

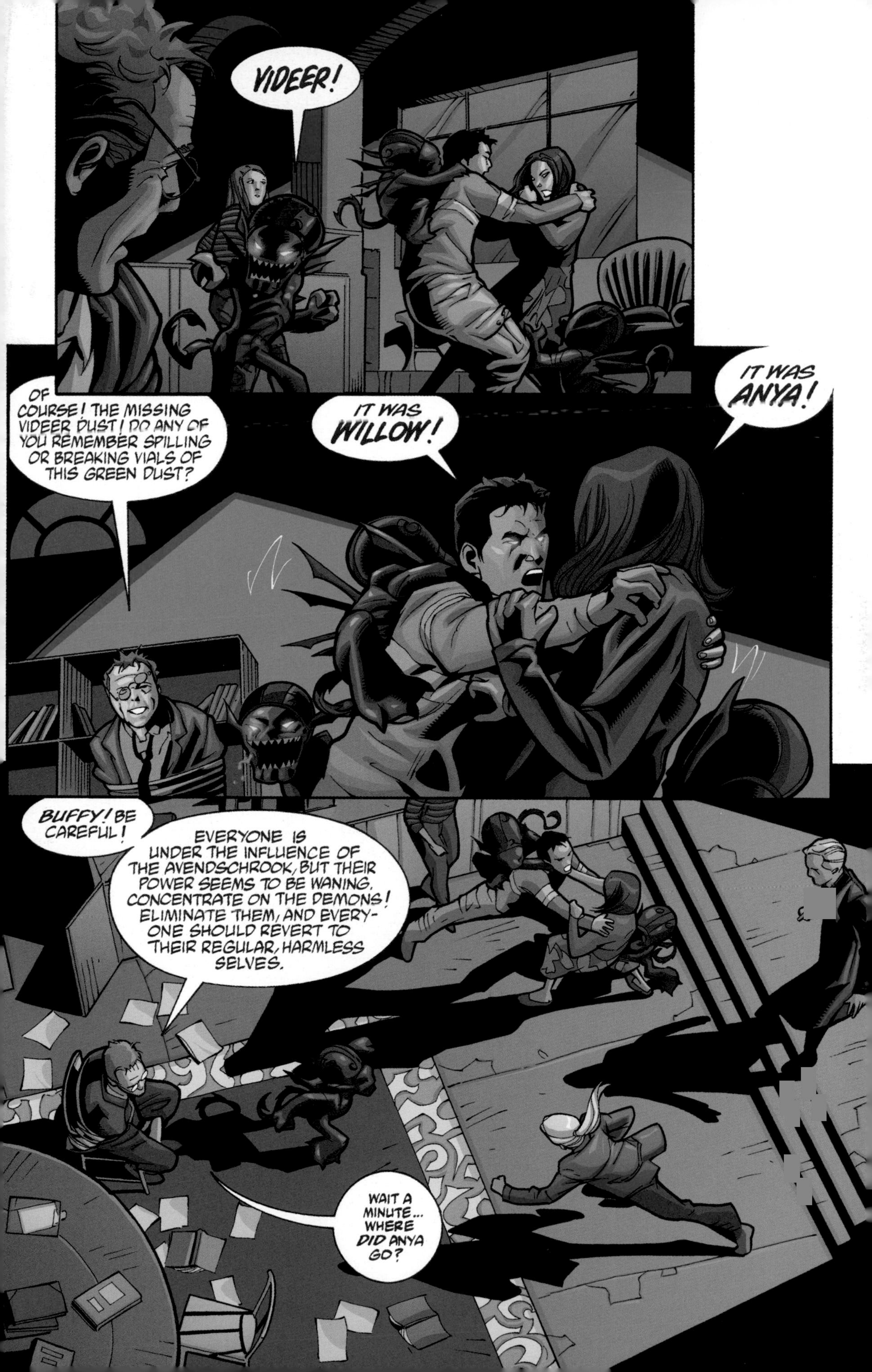
VIDEER!
OF COURSE! THE MISSING VIDEER DUST! DO ANY OF YOU REMEMBER SPILLING OR BREAKING VIALS OF THIS GREEN DUST?
IT WAS WILLOW!
IT WAS ANYA!
BUFFY! BE CAREFUL!
EVERYONE IS UNDER THE INFLUENCE OF THE AVENDSCHROOK, BUT THEIR POWER SEEMS TO BE WANING. CONCENTRATE ON THE DEMONS! ELIMINATE THEM, AND EVERY-ONE SHOULD REVERT TO THEIR REGULAR, HARMLESS SELVES.
WAIT A MINUTE... WHERE DID ANYA GO?

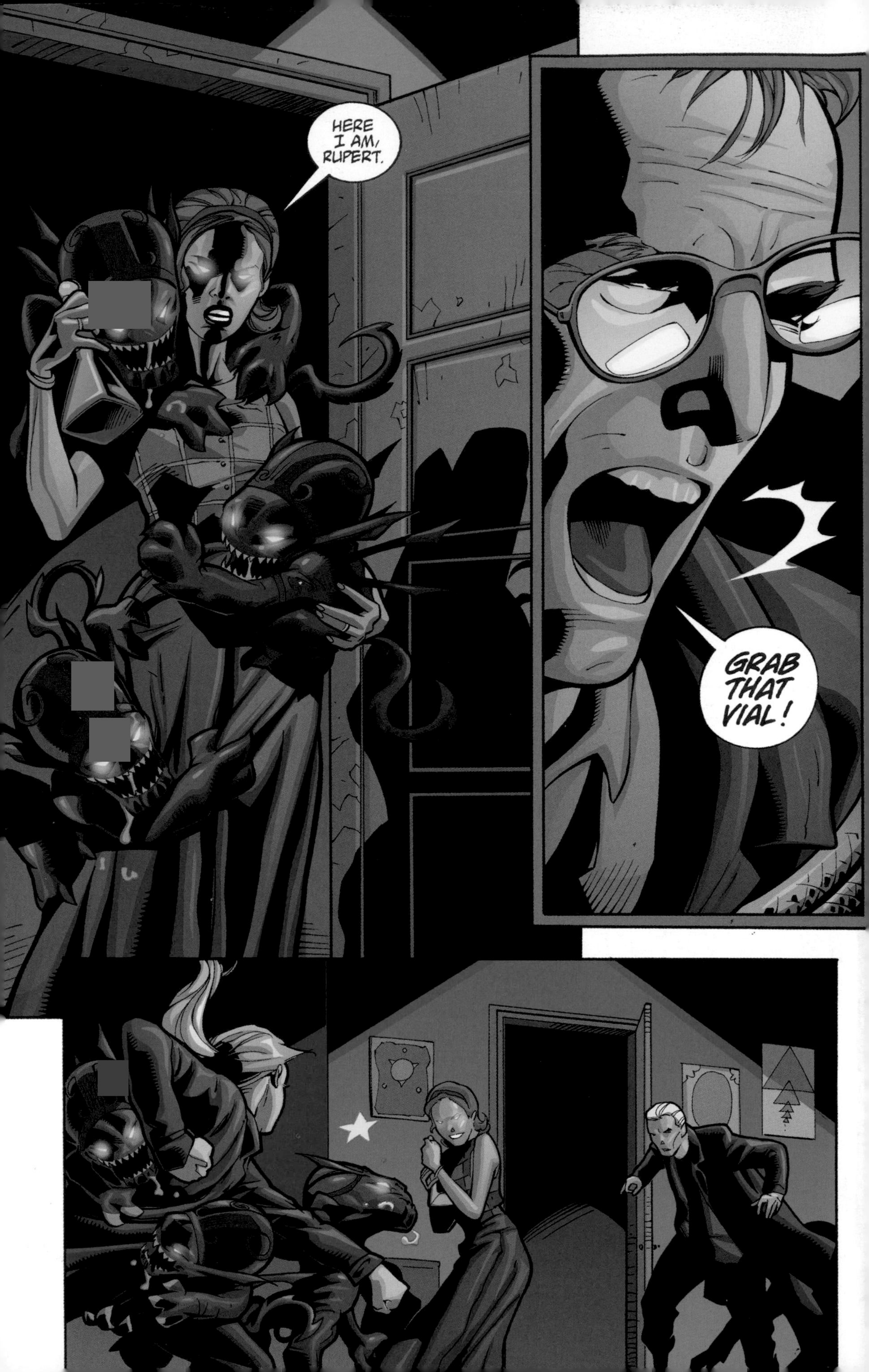
HERE I AM, RUPERT.
GRAB THAT VIAL!

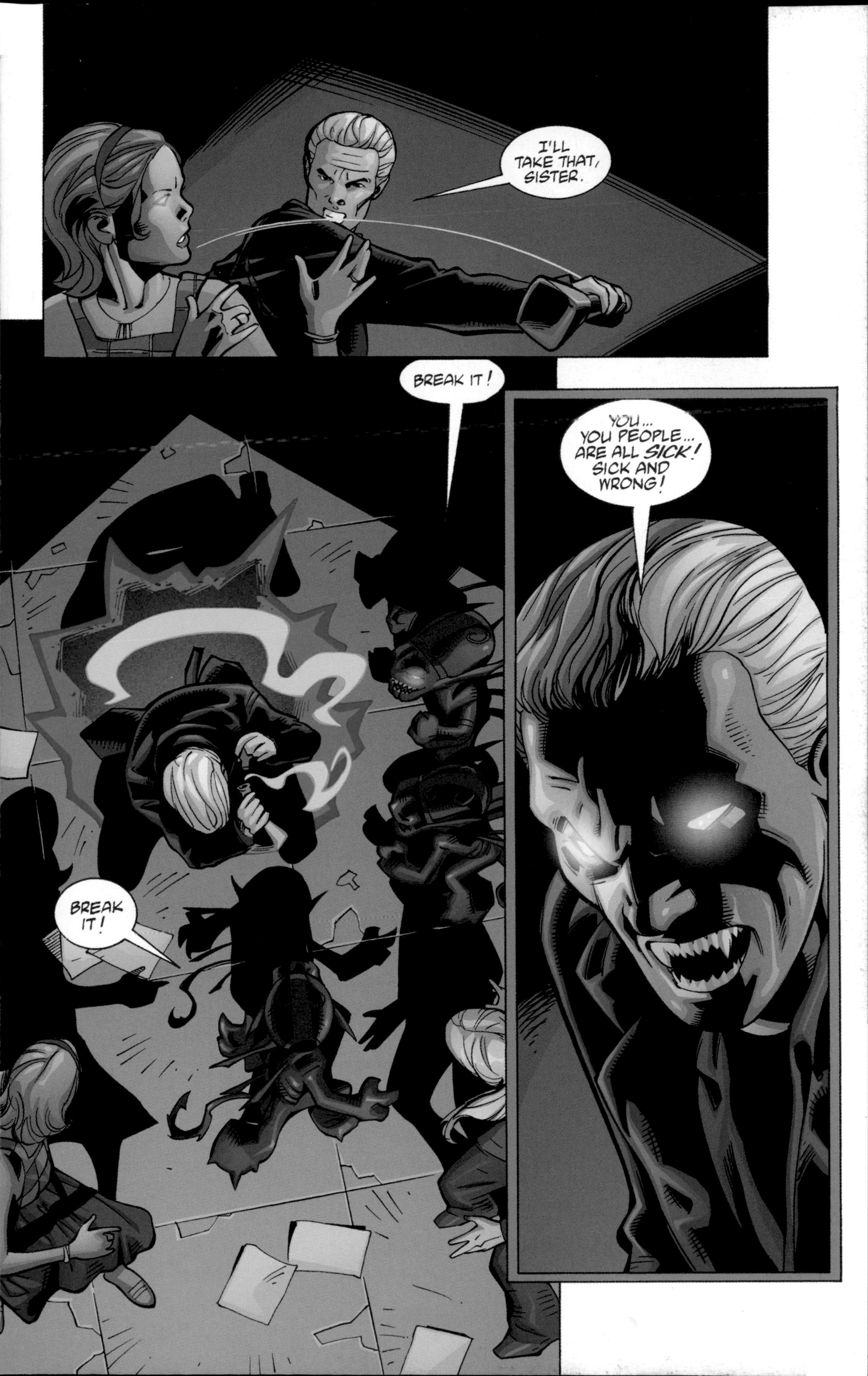
I'LL TAKE THAT, SISTER.
BREAK IT!
BREAK IT!
YOU... YOU PEOPLE... ARE ALL SICK! SICK AND WRONG!

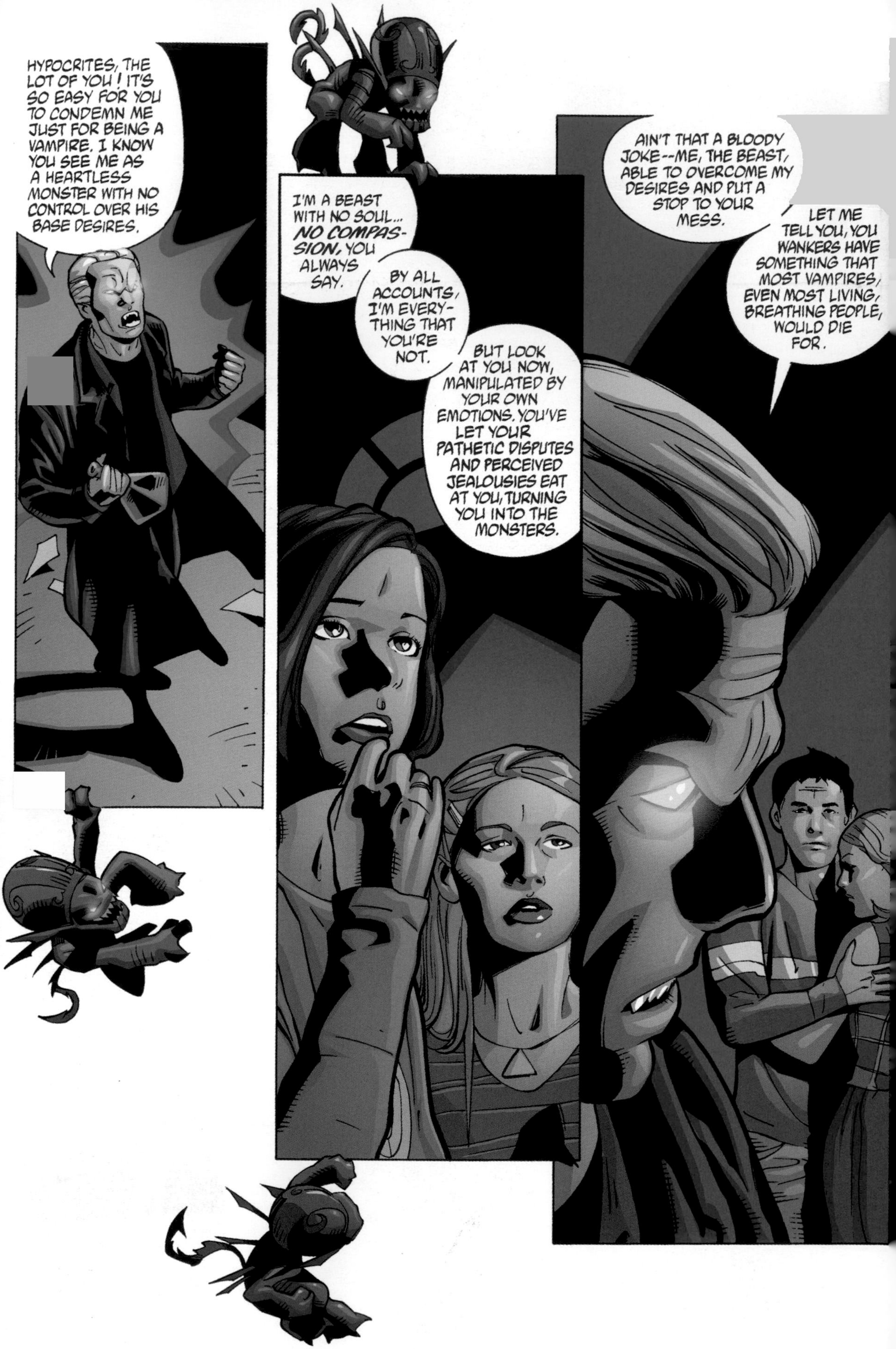

HYPOCRITES, THE LOT OF YOU! IT'S SO EASY FOR YOU TO CONDEMN ME JUST FOR BEING A VAMPIRE. I KNOW YOU SEE ME AS A HEARTLESS MONSTER WITH NO CONTROL OVER HIS BASE DESIRES.
I'M A BEAST WITH NO SOUL... NO COMPASSION, YOU ALWAYS SAY.
BY ALL ACCOUNTS, I'M EVERYTHING THAT YOU'RE NOT.
BUT LOOK AT YOU NOW, MANIPULATED BY YOUR OWN EMOTIONS. YOU'VE LET YOUR PATHETIC DISPUTES AND PERCEIVED JEALOUSIES EAT AT YOU, TURNING YOU INTO THE MONSTERS.
AIN'T THAT A BLOODY JOKE--ME, THE BEAST, ABLE TO OVERCOME MY DESIRES AND PUT A STOP TO YOUR MESS.
LET ME TELL YOU, YOU WANKERS HAVE SOMETHING THAT MOST VAMPIRES, EVEN MOST LIVING, BREATHING PEOPLE, WOULD DIE FOR.

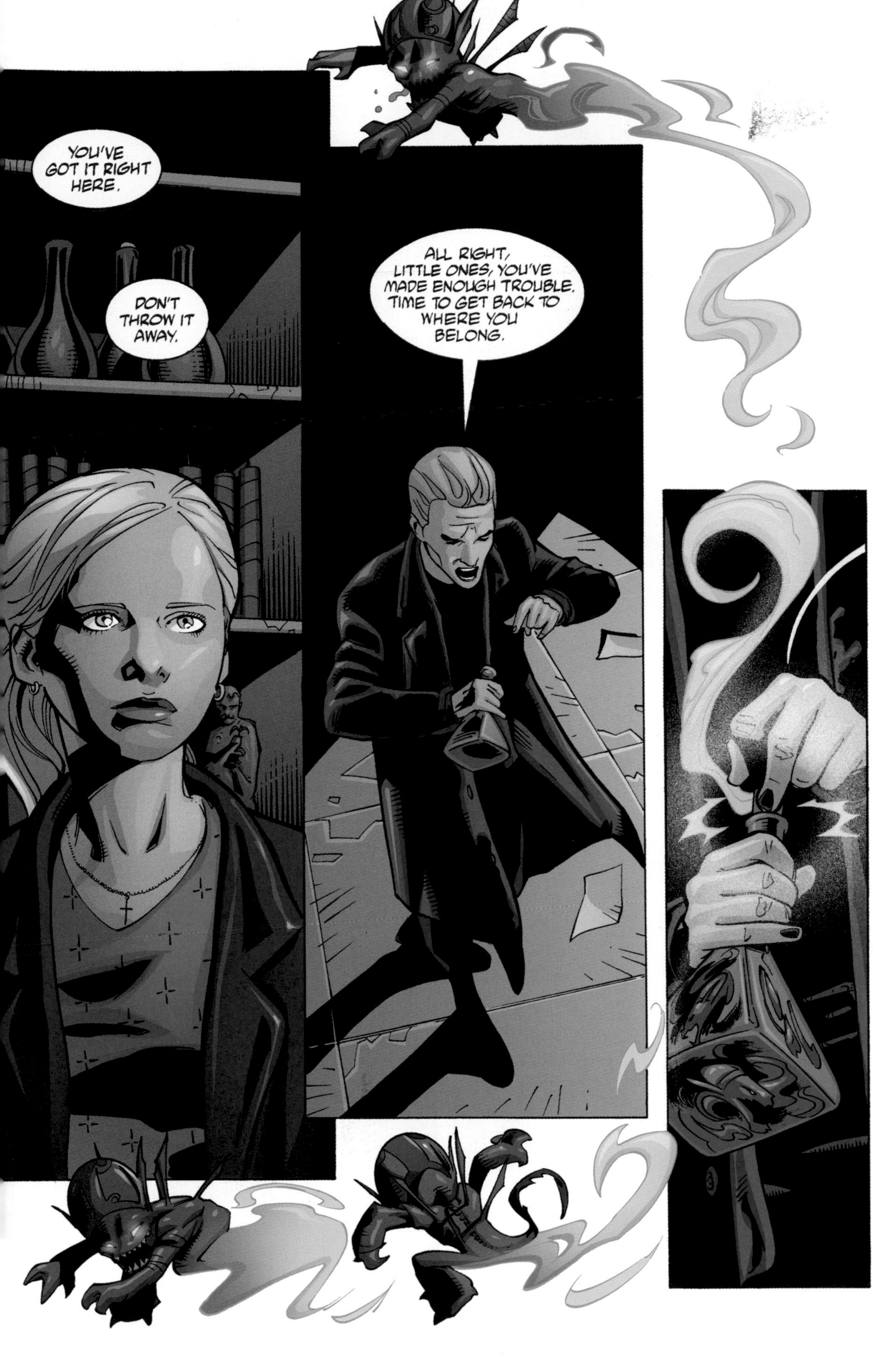
YOU'VE GOT IT RIGHT HERE.
DON'T THROW IT AWAY.
ALL RIGHT, LITTLE ONES, YOU'VE MADE ENOUGH TROUBLE. TIME TO GET BACK TO WHERE YOU BELONG.

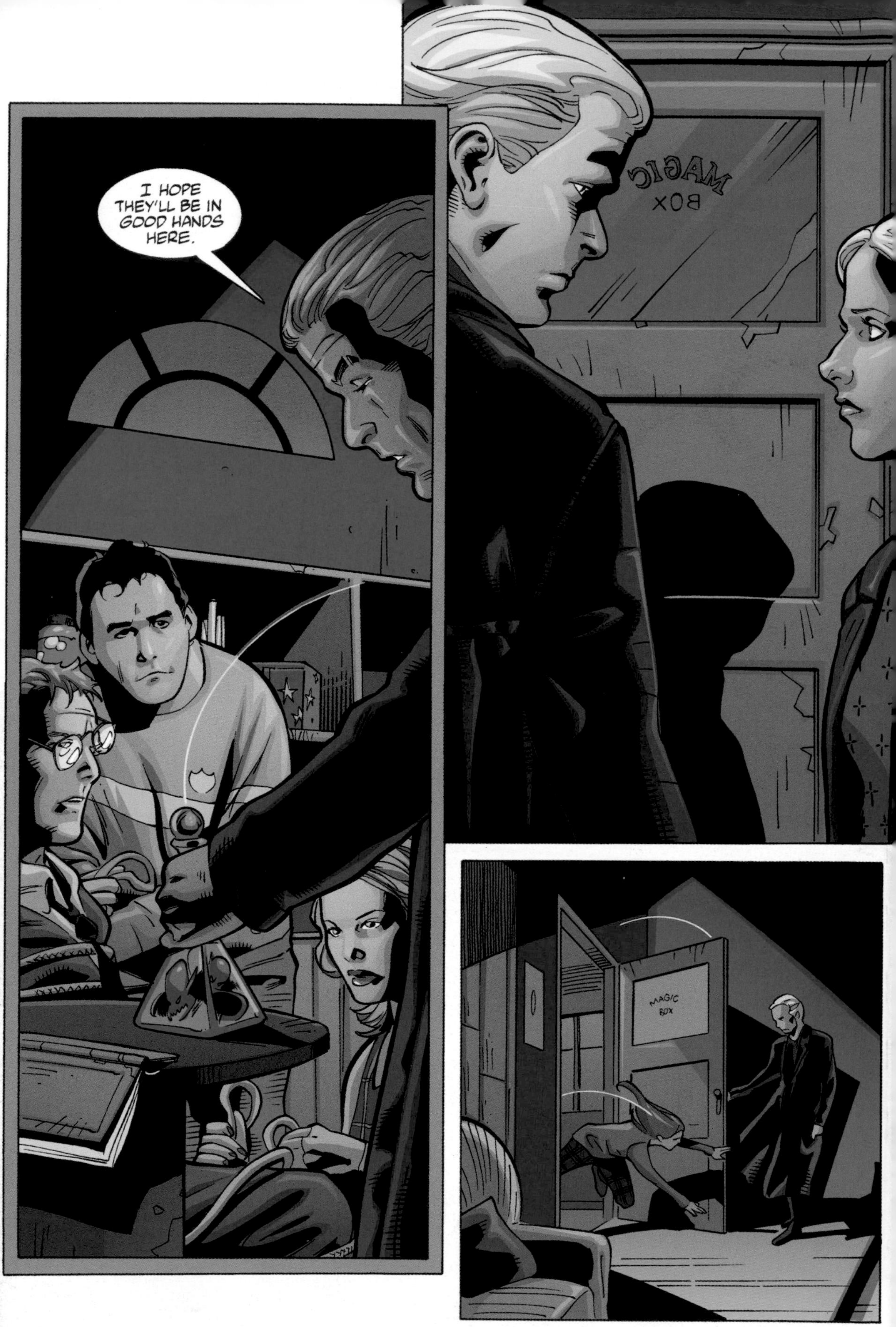
I HOPE THEY'LL BE IN GOOD HANDS HERE.
MAGIC BOX
MAGIC BOX

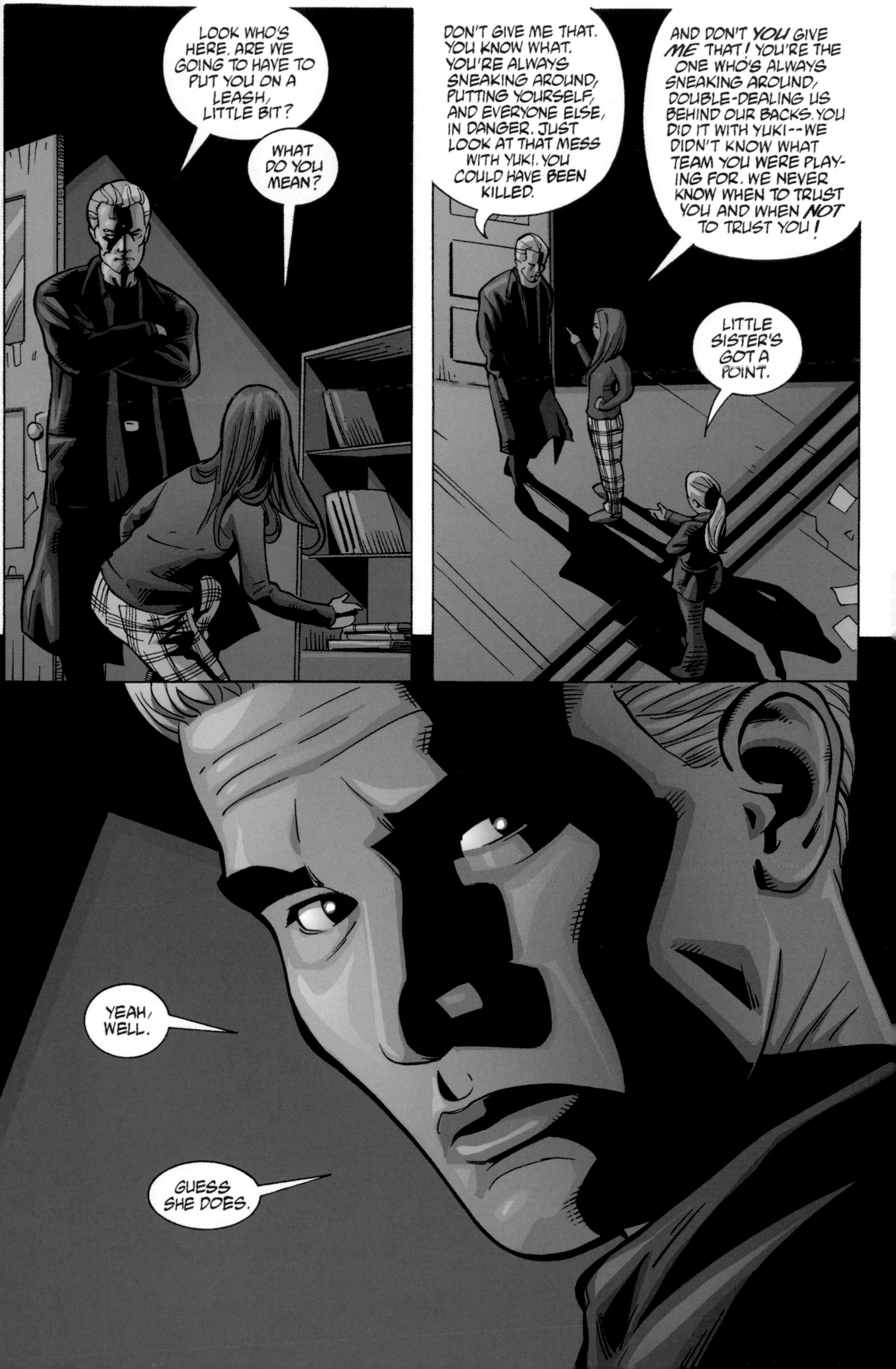
LOOK WHO'S HERE. ARE WE GOING TO HAVE TO PUT YOU ON A LEASH, LITTLE BIT?
WHAT DO YOU MEAN?
DON'T GIVE ME THAT. YOU KNOW WHAT. YOU'RE ALWAYS SNEAKING AROUND, PUTTING YOURSELF, AND EVERYONE ELSE, IN DANGER. JUST LOOK AT THAT MESS WITH YUKI. YOU COULD HAVE BEEN KILLED.
AND DON'T YOU GIVE ME THAT! YOU'RE THE ONE WHO'S ALWAYS SNEAKING AROUND, DOUBLE-DEALING US BEHIND OUR BACKS. YOU DID IT WITH YUKI--WE DIDN'T KNOW WHAT TEAM YOU WERE PLAYING FOR. WE NEVER KNOW WHEN TO TRUST YOU AND WHEN NOT TO TRUST YOU!
LITTLE SISTER'S GOT A POINT.
YEAH, WELL.
GUESS SHE DOES.

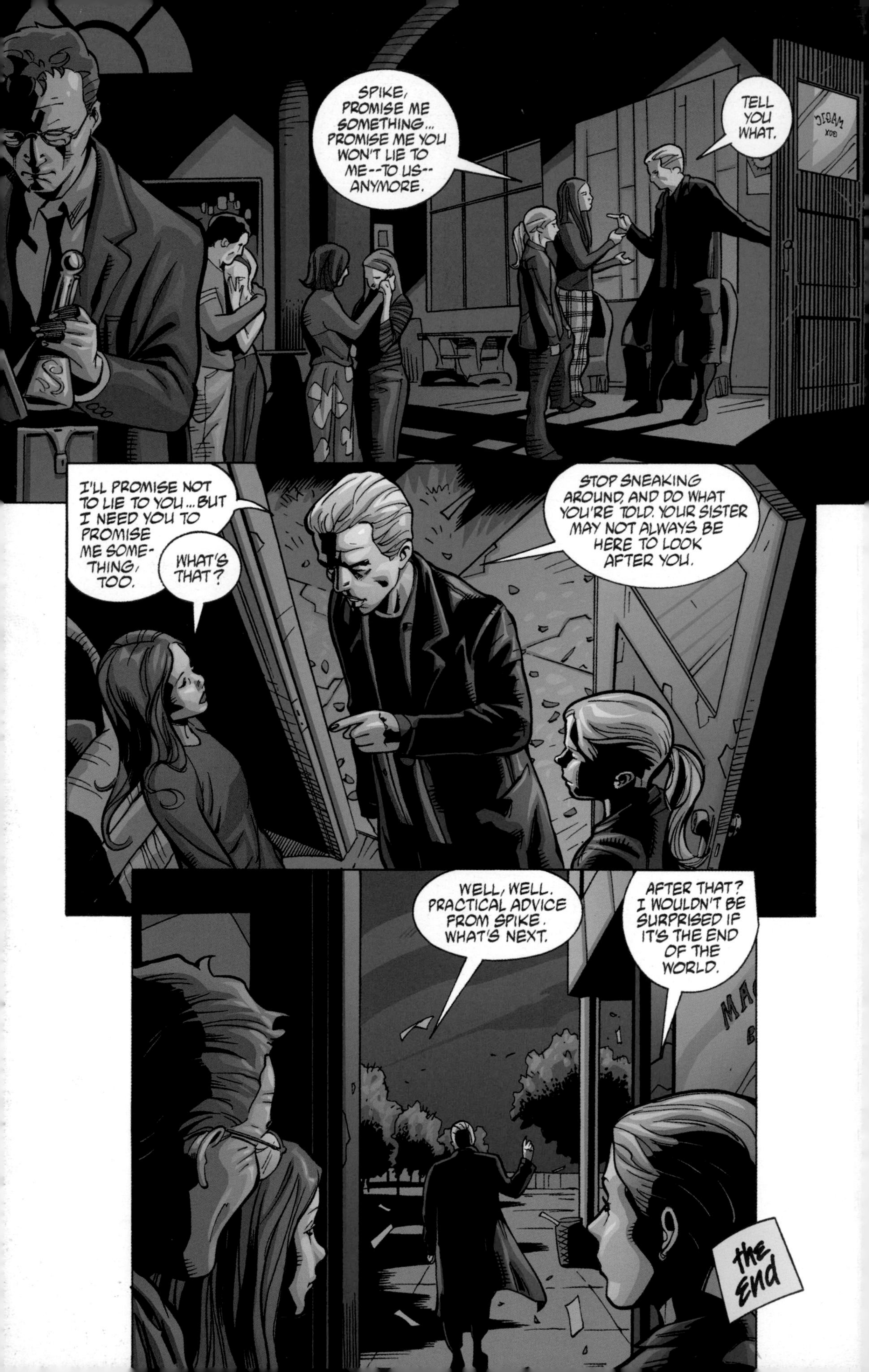
SPIKE, PROMISE ME SOMETHING... PROMISE ME YOU WON'T LIE TO ME--TO US--ANYMORE.
TELL YOU WHAT.
I'LL PROMISE NOT TO LIE TO YOU...BUT I NEED YOU TO PROMISE ME SOMETHING, TOO.
WHAT'S THAT?
STOP SNEAKING AROUND, AND DO WHAT YOU'RE TOLD. YOUR SISTER MAY NOT ALWAYS BE HERE TO LOOK AFTER YOU.
WELL, WELL. PRACTICAL ADVICE FROM SPIKE. WHAT'S NEXT.
AFTER THAT? I WOULDN'T BE SURPRISED IF IT'S THE END OF THE WORLD.
the End

Jeff Matsuda's
Ugly Little Monsters
sketchbook*

Jeff Matsuda was competing against Paul Lee and Brian Horton for cover gigs on the monthly comic. The big upcoming storyline was the *Death of Buffy*, tying into her Season Five death. Jeff had dibs on it. But when I got the final pitch for *Ugly Little Monsters*, it became obvious to me that Jeff would be far better suited to cover this series, and Paul and Brian's paintings would work better on the *Death* series.

The original cover to the first story in this collection, "Night of a Thousand Vampires," had been done by Jeff quite some time ago, as an inventory cover. Well, a couple years had gone by, and I decided that the only way we were going to use it was to base a story around it. So a copy went to writers Tom Fassbender and Jim Pascoe, providing the inspiration for that story. Specific characters from the cover were referred to in the script, so Cliff Richards also needed a copy to work from. Covers would provide yet more important reference on the following issues.

Buffy #39 cover: Inks by Jon Sibal.

*All colors by Dave McCaig.

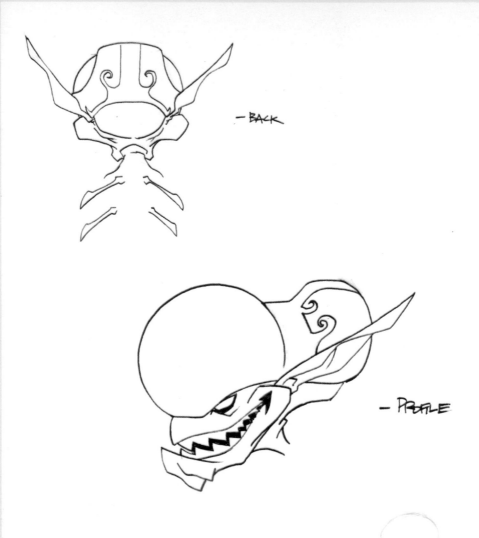

— BACK

— PROFILE

Jeff is currently a character designer on the *Jackie Chan* cartoon, and I wanted to put that skill to use here. Tom and Jim had certain ideas for very scary, creepy little monsters in the long story reprinted here, but I thought it made sense to let Jeff give them the manga look, which the writers referred to in dialogue in a later chapter, after seeing the first covers. Part of his job on the cartoon is creating design sheets for other artists to work from, so I had him do a set for Cliff.

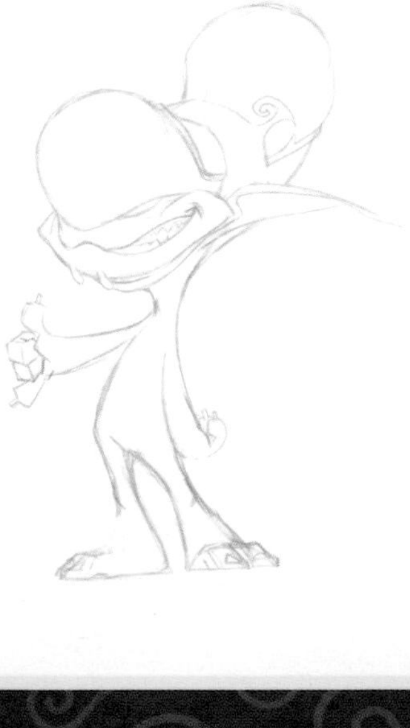

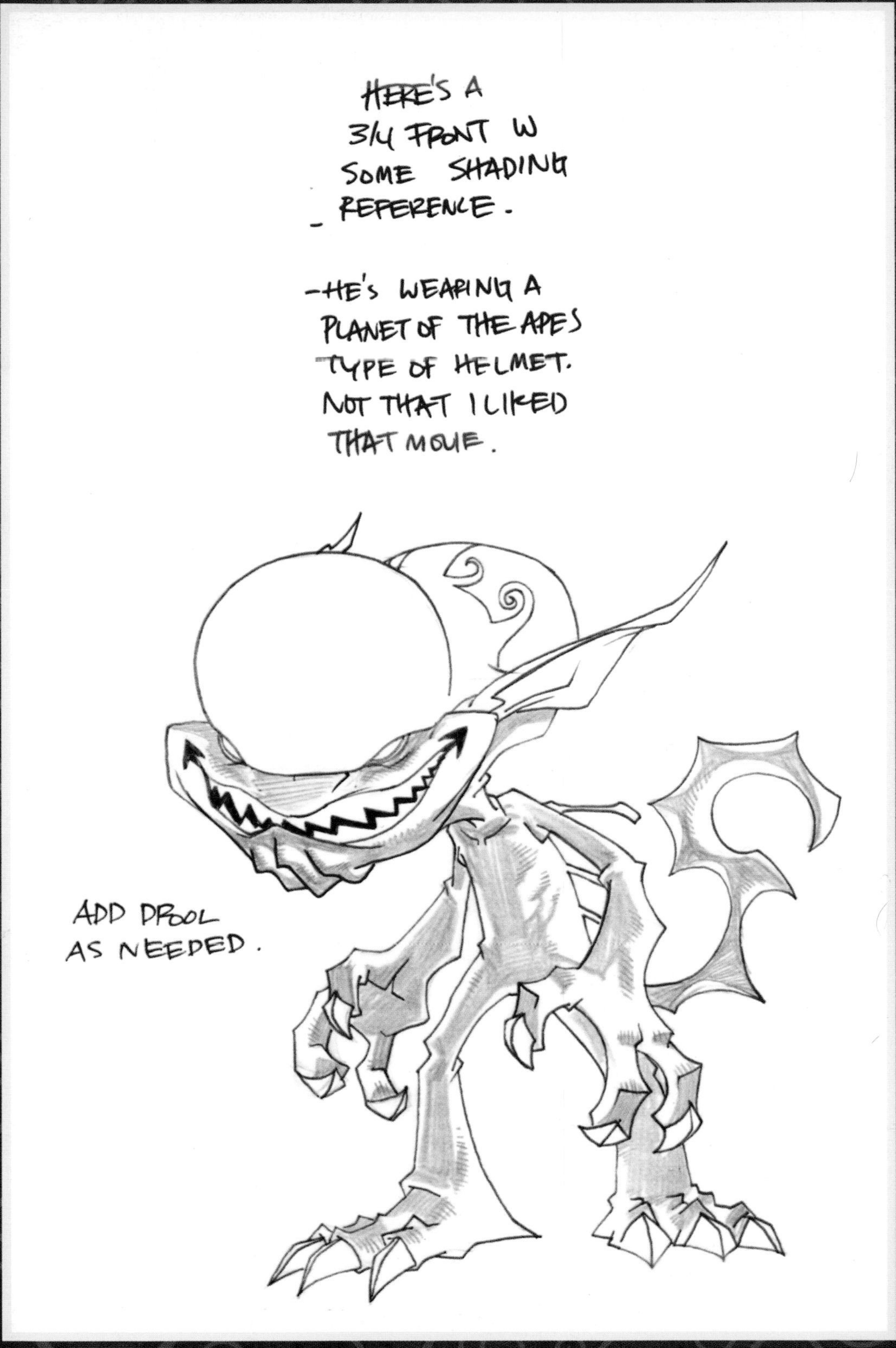
HERE'S A
3/4 FRONT W
SOME SHADING
- REFERENCE -
-HE'S WEARING A
PLANET OF THE APES
TYPE OF HELMET.
NOT THAT I LIKED
THAT MOVIE.
ADD DROOL
AS NEEDED.

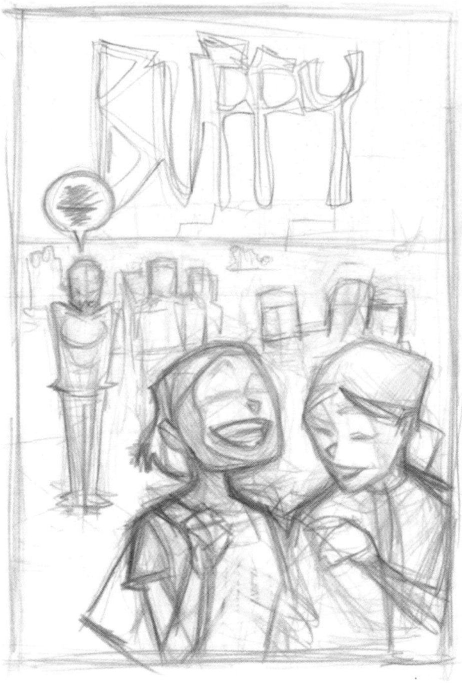

Buffy #40 cover sketch.

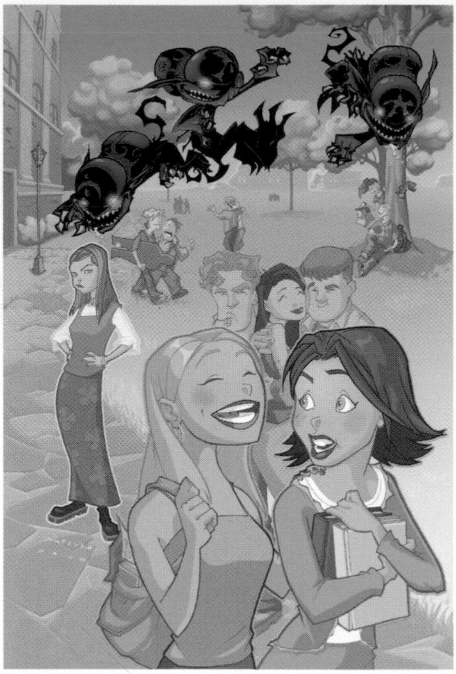

Final art.

Over the phone, we came up with the idea of having the characters wrap around the logo, hang from it, block significant portions of it. This mainly presented a nightmare for Dark Horse's production department, since Jeff is not the one to put the logo in place.

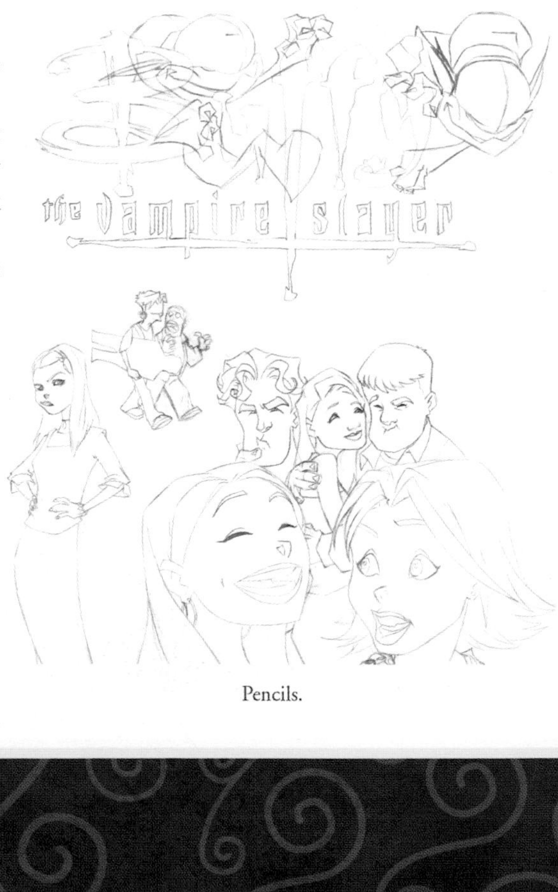
the vampire slayer

Pencils.

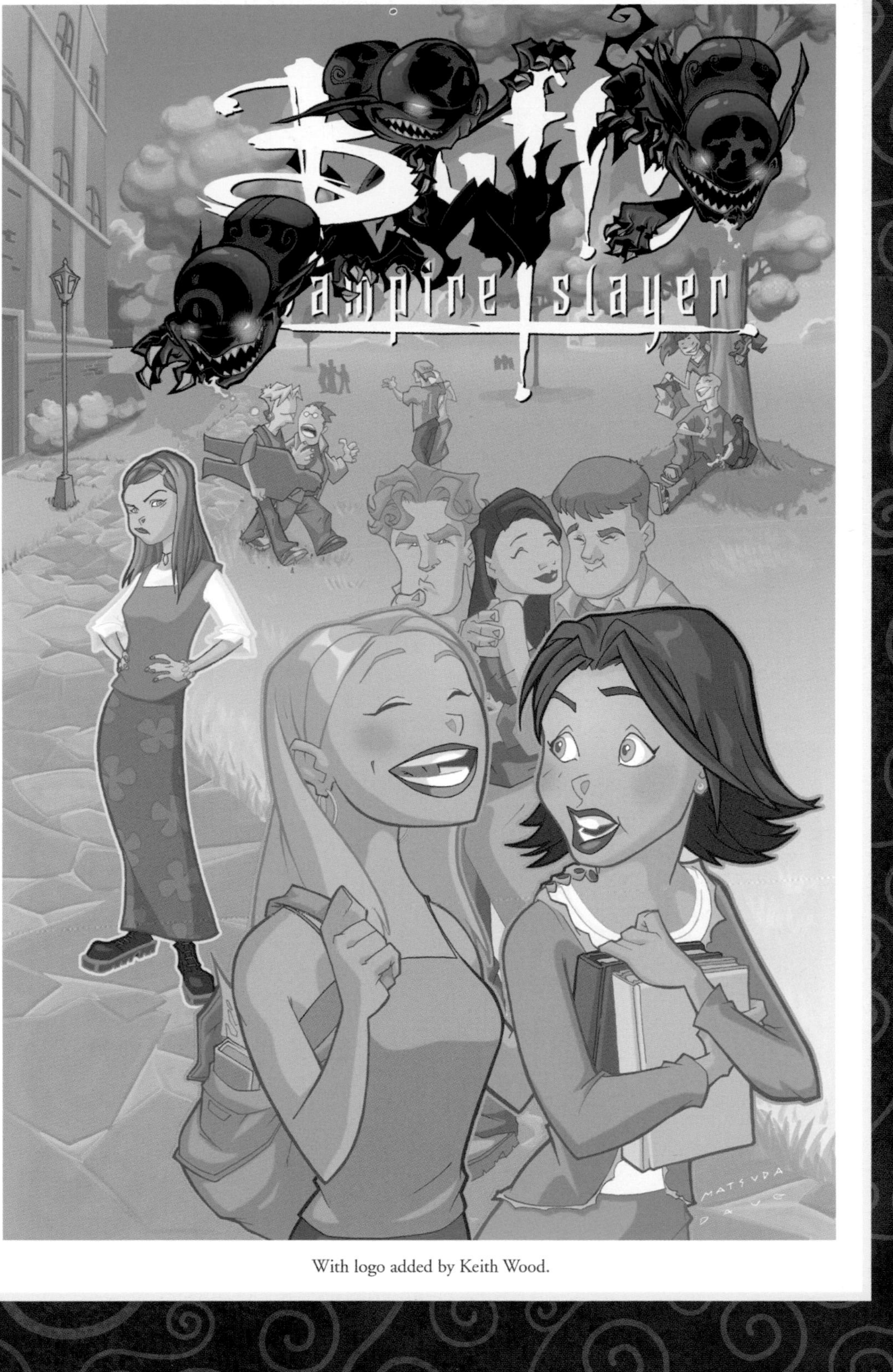
Buffy
the vampire slayer
MATSUDA
DAVE

With logo added by Keith Wood.

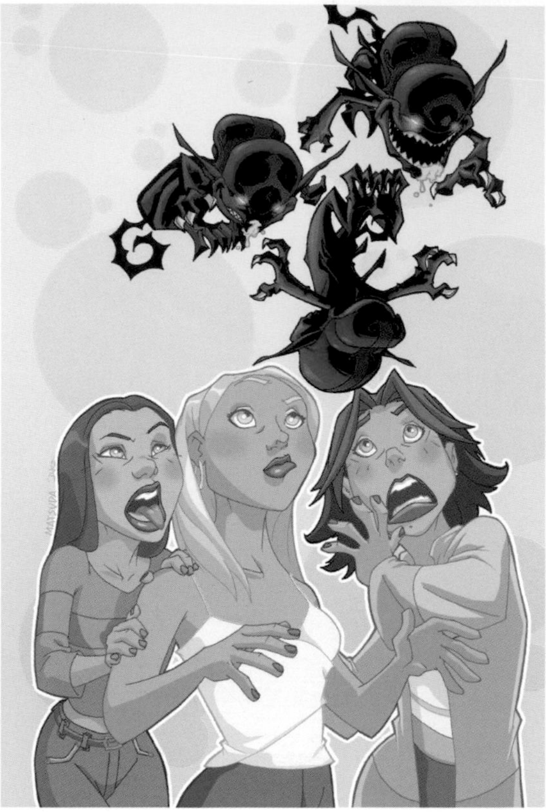

Buffy #41 cover: background was changed before logo was added. See p. 28 of this volume.

The covers to the series also gave Dave McCaig a chance to design the color look for the series, which included triadic color schemes to reflect the recurring motif of Threes.

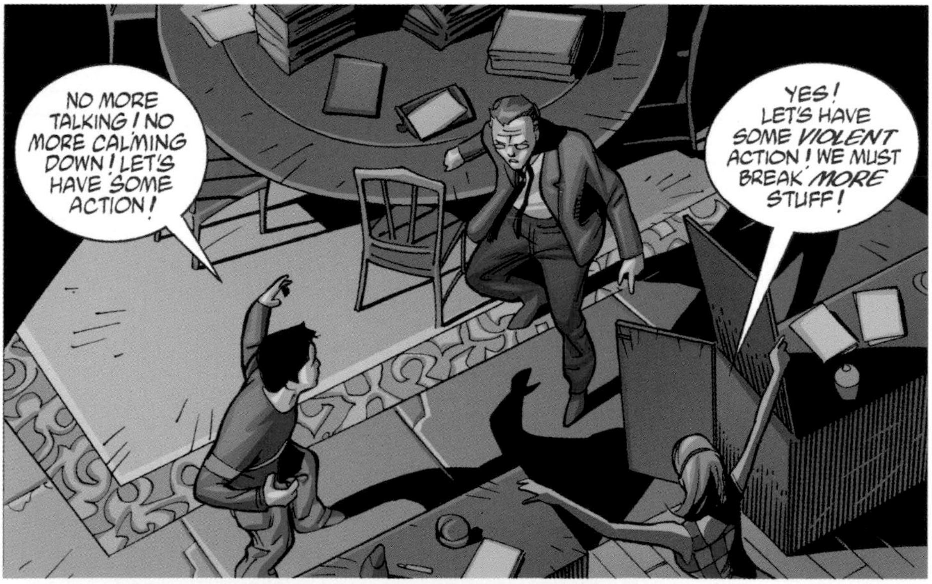
NO MORE TALKING! NO MORE CALMING DOWN! LET'S HAVE SOME ACTION!
YES! LET'S HAVE SOME *VIOLENT* ACTION! WE MUST BREAK *MORE* STUFF!

Triadic composition and color scheme. By Richards, Conrad, and McCaig.

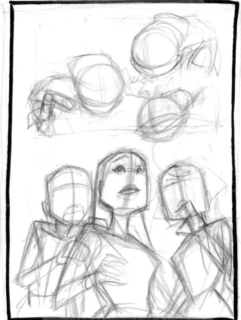

Buffy #41 cover sketch.

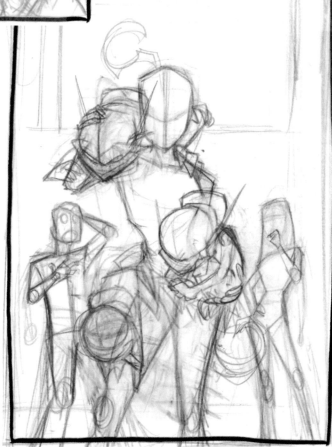

Buffy #42 cover sketch.

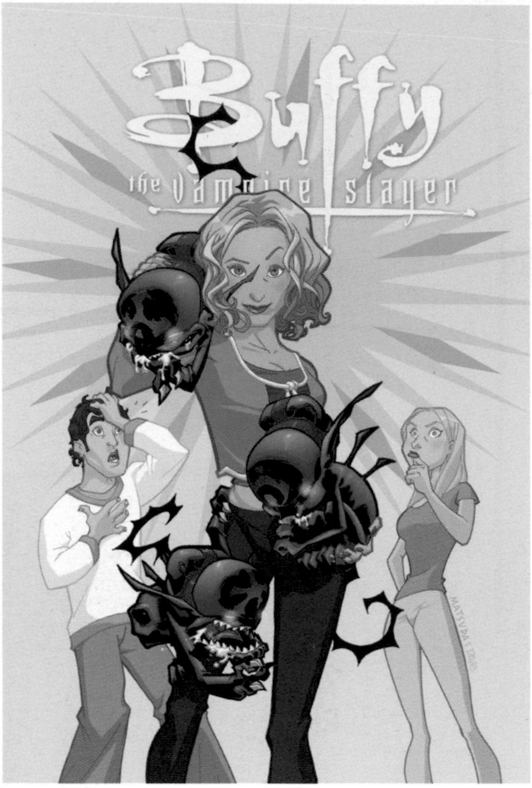
Buffy
the vampire slayer

Buffy #42 cover art.

In the end, the covers further influenced the story—a habit Tom and Jim had developed on *False Memories*, in which they borrowed background images from the covers and gave them important meaning in the story itself. Here, Tom and Jim asked Cliff to loosely base a panel in the third issue upon that cover.

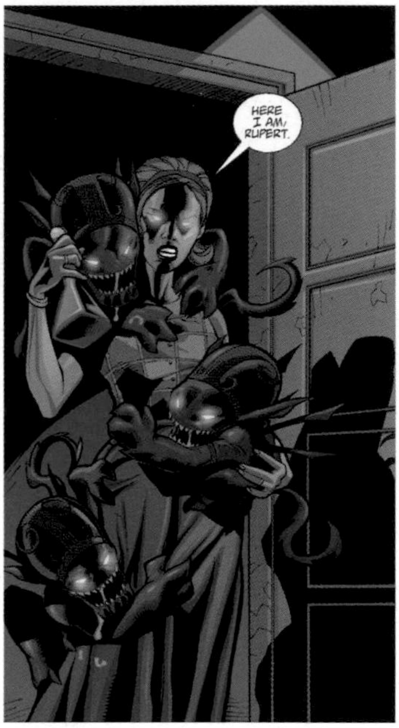
HERE I AM, RUPERT.

Panel from *Buffy* #42. By Richards, Pimentel, and McCaig.

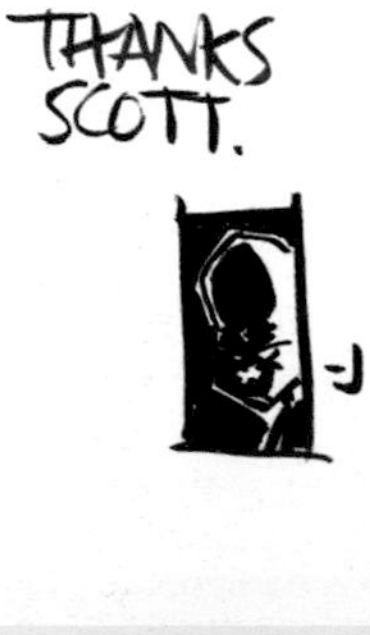
THANKS
SCOTT.
-J

Ugly Little Monsters stands as not one of the most in depth of Fassbender and Pascoe's *Buffy* tales, but definitely one of the most fun.

—Scott Allie

Stake out these Angel and Buffy the Vampire Slayer trade paperbacks

ANGEL
The Hollower
Buffy the vampire slayer
ANGEL
Surrogates
ANGEL
Earthly Possessions
ANGEL
Hunting Ground
Buffy the Vampire Slayer
The Blood of Carthage
Buffy the Vampire Slayer
Out of the Woodwork
Buffy the Vampire Slayer
the Origin
Buffy the Vampire Slayer
False Memories
Buffy the Vampire Slayer
Ring of Fire
Buffy the Vampire Slayer
Bad Blood
Buffy the Vampire Slayer
Crash Test
Demons
Buffy the Vampire Slayer
Pale Reflections
Buffy the Vampire Slayer
Spike and Dru
Buffy the Vampire Slayer
Food Chain
Buffy the Vampire Slayer
Autumnal
Buffy the vampire slayer
ANGEL
Past Lives

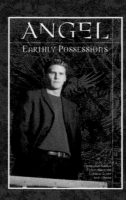

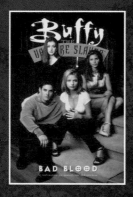

Into every generation
a Slayer is born.

Buffy
the vampire slayer™
roleplaying game

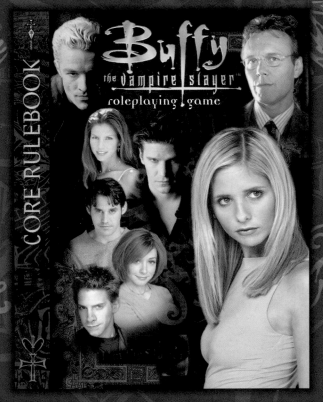

NOW YOU CAN JOIN
THE SLAYER'S WORLD

Want to know
more?

www.BTVSrpg.com

WWW.EDENSTUDIOS.NET